SO-CEZ-548

Run Your Own Corporation

How to Legally Operate and Properly Maintain Your Company into the Future

GARRETT SUTTON, ESQ.

Run Your Own Corporation

How to Legally Operate and Properly Maintain Your Company into the Future

GARRETT SUTTON, ESQ.

BZK PRESS

If you purchase this book without a cover you should be aware that this book may have been stolen property and reported as "unsold and destroyed" to the publisher. In such case neither the author nor the publisher has received any payment for this "stripped book."

This publication is designed to provide competent and reliable information regarding the subject matter covered. However, it is sold with the understanding that the author and publisher are not engaged in rendering legal, financial, or other professional advice. Laws and practices often vary from state to state and country to country and if legal or other expert assistance is required, the services of a professional should be sought. The author and publisher specifically disclaim any liability that is incurred from the use or application of the contents of this book.

Copyright © 2012 by Garrett Sutton, Esq. All rights reserved. Except as permitted under the U.S. Copyright Act of 1976, no part of this publication may be reproduced, distributed, or transmitted in any form or by any means or stored in a database or retrieval system, without the prior written permission of the publisher.

Published by BZK Press, LLC

Rich Dad Advisors, B-I Triangle, CASHFLOW Quadrant and other Rich Dad marks are registered trademarks of CASHFLOW Technologies, Inc.

BZK Press LLC
2248 Meridian Blvd.
Suite H
Minden, NV 89423
775-782-2201

Visit our Web sites: BZKPress.com and MyBestAdvisors.com

Printed in the United States of America

First Edition: September 2012

ISBN: 978-1-937832-10-0

Read The Book That Started It All

Robert Kiyosaki has challenged and changed the way tens of millions of people around the world think about money. With perspectives that often contradict conventional wisdom, Robert has earned a reputation for straight talk, irreverence and courage. He is regarded worldwide as a passionate advocate for financial education.

Rich Dad Poor Dad will...

- Explode the myth that you need to earn a high income to become rich
- Challenge the belief that your house is an asset
- Show parents why they can't rely on the school system to teach their kids about money
- Define once and for all an asset and a liability
- Teach you what to teach your kids about money for their future financial success

Rich Dad Poor Dad — The #1 Personal Finance Book of All Time!

Order your copy at
richdad.com today!

Acknowledgments

I would like to thank Robert Kiyosaki, Brandi MacLeod, Lyn Millard, Cindie Geddes, Mona Gambetta, Tom Wheelwright, Melvin Jackson and Gerri Detweiler for their assistance in shaping, critiquing, producing and getting this book out.

I would also like to thank my children, Teddy, Emily and Sarah, for their wonderful support and encouragement. Utterances such as "Dad, when are you going to finish the book!" and "Dad, you are way past the deadline on this one!" certainly in some way contributed to the enjoyment I experienced in writing this book.

Best-Selling Books
In the Rich Dad Advisors Series

by Blair Singer

SalesDogs
You Don't Have to Be an Attack Dog to Explode Your Income

Team Code of Honor
The Secrets of Champions in Business and in Life

by Garrett Sutton, Esq.

Start Your Own Corporation
Why the Rich Own Their Own Companies and Everyone Else Works for Them

Writing Winning Business Plans
*How to Prepare a Business Plan that Investors will Want to Read —
and Invest In*

Buying and Selling a Business
How You Can Win in the Business Quadrant

The ABCs of Getting Out of Debt
Turn Bad Debt into Good Debt and Bad Credit into Good Credit

Run Your Own Corporation
*How to Legally Operate and Properly Maintain Your Company
into the Future*

The Loopholes of Real Estate
Secrets of Successful Real Estate Investing

by Ken McElroy

The ABCs of Real Estate Investing
The Secrets of Finding Hidden Profits Most Investors Miss

The ABCs of Property Management
What You Need to Know to Maximize Your Money Now

The Advanced Guide to Real Estate Investing
How to Identify the Hottest Markets and Secure the Best Deals

by Tom Wheelwright

Tax-Free Wealth
How to Build Massive Wealth by Permanently Lowering Your Taxes

And Coming Soon:

by Josh and Lisa Lannon

The Social Capitalist
Entrepreneur's Journey from Passion to Profits

Contents

Foreword
by Robert Kiyosaki

This book, *Run Your Own Corporation,* is the perfect follow up to Garrett's *Start Your Own Corporation*.

I like this book because I am not an attorney. This book is written for a person like me, an entrepreneur who needs to know how to run my own corporation, legally.

I like this book because Garrett keeps things simple using simple real life stories and real life situations.

WHY THIS BOOK IS IMPORTANT

This book is important if you are planning on becoming rich...and especially so if you are not rich today.

As the economy changes and the gap between the rich and the rest of the world grows wider, more people will attempt to steal from the rich. This is why this book is important.

Over the years, as I grew wealthier, I was surprised to find out who my real friends were and were not. When the economy split, I was shocked to have a number of "friends" come after my wealth after they lost their wealth. This is why this book is important.

As I grew wealthier, I found that just having corporate entities was not enough for asset protection. As I grew wealthier, I had to get smarter at running my corporations as well as protecting my wealth. This is why this book is important.

As you grow wealthier, you will need to become better at maintaining your corporate veil, running your business and protecting your assets. Just having basic asset protection is not enough. The thieves of the world are getting smarter. So should you. Master how to keep your corporate veil strong, and a shield against thieves. This is why this book is important.

Robert Kiyosaki

Introduction

Congratulations. By reading *Run Your Own Corporation* you are going to learn the strategies the rich have used to maintain and run their corporations, limited liability companies and other limited liability entities to maximum benefit.

Perhaps you have read the first book in this set, *Start Your Own Corporation*. In that book we illustrated the advantages and strategies for setting up a corporation, limited liability company ("LLC") or limited partnership ("LP"). Now we are going to discuss and review the necessary steps to properly run your entity in order to achieve asset protection, tax benefits and peace of mind.

The book is set up chronologically according to the life of your entity. As we learned in *Start Your Own Corporation* an entity is a separate legal being chartered by a state government which provides protection for the individual. And so when we refer to 'entity' we mean a corporation, LLC or LP set up for limited liability protection. In some cases we use the term 'corporation' in a way that is applicable to all these entities. We will start with issues to consider before incorporating and then issues to deal with on your first day, first week and so on through the fifth year.

Of course, some of the issues apply from day one and throughout your entity's duration. For example, employee issues and writing contracts apply right along. But we have chosen to include them in the fourth day and first week chapters, respectively, to even out the book. So please don't view the chapter contents as rigid. Much of the information contained throughout the book applies throughout your entity's existence. Or, to put it another way, you will want to read what happens at year one before your first year is up.

In the B.C. (Before Corporation) section, we include a discussion on the always important topic on choosing the right entity. If you have previously read *Start Your Own Corporation* or already know which entity you will use, feel free to skip over this section. (But please read the three cases as they carry through the book. What happens at the start will affect their endings.)

Running your own corporation, LLC or LP in a manner that protects you on an ongoing basis is one of the smartest (and, as you will learn, easiest) things an entrepreneur can do.

With that, let's begin...

Chapter One

B.C. (Before Corporation)

Control

There are many things we cannot control. Economic cycles, accidents and natural disasters, among others, are all beyond our individual grasp and control.

We also can't control our customers and clients. Some may be dissatisfied over one matter while others will never be satisfied with anything. We must appreciate this fact as we run our business and manage our real estate.

In the face of this lack of control, we must be ever more vigilant to properly control our own entity. Choosing the right entity is a start—a foundation for growth and protection. But as Robert Kiyosaki mentioned in the Foreword, basic asset protection isn't enough anymore. You need to take the next steps for better protection. Forming an entity is your foundation. Then you must follow the corporate formalities and tax laws. These are your building materials. You want to do it right using brick and not straw, and thus be protected. Your entity is a structure, and the more solid the foundation and building materials are, the more protection and control you will have.

Corporate Veil

You will be reading a great deal about the "corporate veil" and the piercing of a corporate veil in this book. Your corporate veil is the shield that protects your personal assets from creditor attacks. The strength of your corporate veil is determined by how well you follow the laws, regulations and requirements of your corporation. Piercing the corporate veil sounds painful, and it is! When the corporate veil is pierced, the entity's veil of limited liability is lifted and your personal assets are exposed to a creditor's claims.

So you want to focus on the separation between your entity and the owners of that entity, which we shall discuss throughout the book.

Know that one of the reasons to incorporate is to create that veil, so that you are not liable for the actions of the business—the debts, the mistakes and the liabilities of the corporation. The moment your corporate veil is breached, you are personally at risk.

Of course, the reason that anyone would attempt to pierce a corporate veil is because the corporation itself does not have enough assets to satisfy the claim. The creditor sees that the shareholders do have money, and seeks to get beyond the corporation to reach the individual's personal assets. A recent study found that piercing the veil was successful 48% of the time. That is a huge success rate, and it points out that far too few entrepreneurs and investors are taking the necessary steps to protect themselves.

The advice in this book is designed so that you may set up your business (or hold your real estate or other assets) in its own entity, separate from you and avoid a piercing of the veil. Understand that we are dealing with a veil. Not a wall, not a mirror, not a net. It's a veil—a sheer division where you can see the effect of what is happening, but you can't actually touch it, and it can't touch you. Unless it is pierced. Your corporation as a distinct entity is responsible for corporate duties and liabilities, and is entitled to credit and profit. If you set it up correctly, it will be a separate, compartmentalized entity, with limits and boundaries, all of which will benefit you. If not, all you have is a legal fiction. And obviously a fiction isn't going to help you in a courtroom reality.

Taxes

Although it may not be pleasant (and certainly not riveting) you will also be reading about taxes. One of the surest ways to protect your assets and to keep your corporate veil intact is to keep abreast of the taxes and obligations facing your entity. As well, if you let deadlines pass and your taxes (especially payroll taxes) go unpaid, penalties and interest will accrue and you will run afoul of IRS and state taxation authorities. You may face civil and even criminal penalties. There is no need to pierce any veil in these cases. The IRS can hold you personally responsible straight away. So you will follow the tax rules. With a good bookkeeper and accountant on your team you can certainly legally minimize your taxes. And you can certainly use the tax rules to your advantage (as the rich do every day). That said, from day one and then on, you will follow the tax rules and timely file your taxes. Did we mention that you will follow the tax rules?

Good. Let's start...

One of the reasons for writing this book is that scores of clients have said to me, "I've set up my corporation, now what do I do?" It's hoped that this universal question will be satisfied by the contents of this book, and that you will be able to more confidently run your own corporation, LLC and LP. As mentioned, we have three cases, or stories, to help explain it all. So let's start with our first one...

Case 1: Tom and Nancy

Tom and Nancy Green were professional engineers. Tom was Nordic, from the Pacific Northwest and had headed east for college. Nancy was half Irish and half Latina, from Texas and had headed north for college. They had met in graduate engineering school and married after just two months of dating. They were quite a couple, outgoing, athletic and hardworking. Tom was a good public speaker and was active in Toastmasters. Nancy was popular and tied into several networking and charitable groups. When they were out around town, jogging, biking or walking, they were always seen with their big, lovable Great Dane. The dog was named

'Dooger' and as many people in town seemed to know Dooger as they did Tom and Nancy.

After working for other engineering firms in the area Tom and Nancy had just recently gone out on their own. Nothing was set up or formalized, they hadn't obtained any insurance, and they planned to set up an entity when they had time.

One of their clients was the Righteous Rock Quarry on the outskirts of town. The owner of Righteous Rock, Steve, operated as a sole proprietor. In thirty years of business, he had never been sued. Despite the advice of his attorney and accountant to operate through a limited liability entity (i.e. a corporation or LLC) for asset protection purposes, Steve rejected all such suggestions. He argued that he had plenty of insurance to cover any claim. He argued that he did not want the extra costs of an entity tax return and the extra fees to maintain an entity. And because Steve was the sole owner, and very set in his ways, Righteous Rock continued to operate as a sole proprietor.

One day late in September, out of the blue as earthquakes do, a 7.2 tremor struck the region. The quaking was prolonged and devastating. A weakened section of the quarry wall cascaded down on top of the employee locker room. Two employees died instantly.

Tom and Nancy happened to be at Righteous Rock that day, consulting with Steve. Luckily, all three survived the disaster.

Unfortunately, a great deal of expensive equipment was destroyed in the massive earthquake. Even worse, the families of the two workers told Steve they would be suing Righteous Rock as the responsible party for the loss of life.

Steve immediately contacted his insurance agent. He needed help with getting his operations up and going again as well as with the upcoming wrongful death lawsuit. Steve was stunned to learn he was not covered. He did not have an earthquake insurance policy. On his regular coverage, the quake was considered an Act of God, which specifically excluded the insurance company from responsibility for any and all claims.

Steve was livid and lashed out at anyone and everyone. He blamed Tom and Nancy for not alerting him to the weakened section of the quarry.

They had a duty to warn him about it and thus were guilty of malpractice. Within weeks, Steve sued the couple to cover all his mounting damages, including the wrongful death suits.

Tom and Nancy were blindsided by this lawsuit. They had not yet set up an entity and so were considered general partners. There was no asset protection with a general partnership. They had not yet purchased professional liability insurance. There was no insurance company to cover the claim or defend them in court. All of their assets, the main one being their one real estate investment, a fourplex in their individual names, were now exposed to Steve's wrath.

So Tom and Nancy had to use all of their savings to hire an attorney to defend them in court. After a lengthy and very expensive trial a jury found Tom and Nancy not guilty. One email from Tom to Steve suggesting that the employee locker room be moved away from the quarry wall was a huge help. And their overall defense strategy worked: The jury agreed that a massive earthquake was at fault, not Tom and Nancy.

When all the lawsuits were concluded, the earthquake's continuing aftershocks left Steve destitute. As a sole proprietor, all of his assets were exposed. Not only did he lose the quarry but he also lost his free and clear house, his bank account and his boat. Steve would never recover.

As it was, Tom and Nancy were left drained, both financially and emotionally, from the experience.

It would take some time before they were back on their feet...

Choice of Success

Businesses come with decisions to be made, lots and lots of decisions. A primary decision is: What service or product will you sell? In other words: How will you make money?

Hopefully you will spend a good amount of time reaching the answer to this one. Consider what you are good at, what makes you happy, and whether you can succeed at it in business. Think about what it will take to finance a business, where you will get supplies, and where you will find customers. If you are considering opening an art gallery, you may imagine days spent buying and selling quality artwork. If you are thinking of becoming a life coach, you may fantasize about the people you will listen to and help. If you are planning to buy and sell real estate, you may study the ins and outs of making deals and anticipate your first closing. Let your mind wander on it all. Envision your success. But then be sure to come back to the reality of running a business. The paperwork and the details. The licenses and legal requirements. The business of running a business. Because to pursue your dream you have to be grounded in reality. And that's why you are reading this book. To be ready for what lies ahead.

Choice of Entity

One of the first major decisions you will need to make is: What entity will you use to run your business and hold your real estate? Most people will be choosing between the following:

- Sole Proprietorship
- General Partnership
- C Corporation
- S Corporation
- Limited Liability Company (or LLC)
- Limited Liability Partnership (or LP)

We went through these extensively in *Start Your Own Corporation*. And we will touch upon them here. They are all choices you can make (although two of them aren't very good choices).

But before we get into it, let's consider our next team:

Case 2: Alana and Sherri

Alana and Sherri were two very attractive sisters who wanted out of the rat race. They had each worked for demanding and intolerant bosses. It was time for a change.

Alana and Sherri had each obtained the training to cut hair and perform beautician services early in their careers. Back then, it seemed like everyone was getting into the business. There were salons springing up everywhere. In the face of such competition they had each gone on to other pursuits.

Sherri found a job at the mall selling jewelry from a kiosk. She was personable and a good salesperson. But her boss, an older woman who put absolutely zero time into the business, wanted her to sell more. Sherri knew she was the best salesperson in the mall. She was operating at her highest level already, without any incentive on sales. And yet her boss wanted more.

Alana had left the beauty business to work in a title company. While she had never been detail oriented in school or as a beautician, her new job as a closing assistant for all types of real estate transactions got her head into the minutia, the small details that mattered. Her closing documents had to be letter perfect, and they were.

But her boss had over expanded during the real estate boom. With so much real estate being sold, there was a lot of money to be made providing title insurance and closing documents. When the crash came, he had four offices and enough work for just one. As he retrenched to survive he demanded more and more work out of the remaining few employees. As well, several payroll checks had bounced, which had created a cascade of bounced checks for all of the employees. Their complaints to the boss only made him more defensively intolerant. Alana had stopped enjoying going to work.

Alana and Sherri discussed their situation and decided it was time to get back into the beauty business. On their own. The competition had subsided, and they knew many people around town from their current careers who could become customers.

A significant impediment for Alana and Sherri moving forward was their husbands. Neither Will nor Clint wanted their wives to leave a steady paycheck behind. Starting a business involved huge risks, they argued. Who was going to sign a personal guarantee on a commercial lease?

The discussions lasted for weeks. There were raised voices and tears. Sherri and Clint had a young daughter, Ellie, who was scared by all the commotion. The arguments nearly tore the family apart. Finally, Alana and Sherri's father, Big Jim, stepped forward. He could not allow this controversy to continue. For the sake of his family, Big Jim agreed to be the personal guarantor on the lease of a commercial space in a shopping center yet to be located. If his daughters didn't make it in business he would be the one personally responsible for any lease payments until the end of the term. But he wanted to negotiate the lease. His daughters were ecstatic and grateful.

With the personal guarantee issue out of the way, Will and Clint grudgingly assented to their wives' plans. They also knew not to mess with Big Jim. But if they were going to do it, they were going to do it right. Both husbands knew their personal assets would still be exposed if their wives did it the wrong way.

Alana knew from her real estate title company days that choice of entity was important. She scheduled an appointment with an attorney she knew so they could review their options.

What entity will they choose?...

Choice of Entity

Choosing the correct entity is one of the most important decisions you can make. This one decision will dictate how you prepare your taxes, how you keep your books, how much of your business' income you keep and how much you don't. It will dictate your profits and losses, the financial security (and safety) of your family, maybe even your health and happiness.

Do not take the decision of which corporate entity you choose lightly. There is no part of your business that will not be affected by it. Let's review some of your choices:

Sole Proprietorship

Each entity choice has its pros and cons. There is no one-size-fits-all corporate entity that will be the best for every situation. (And beware of the advisor who tells you there is.) However, there is one entity that we call the bad entity. It is the Sole Proprietorship. One lawsuit and (as in the case of Righteous Rock) you can lose all of your assets, meaning both your business and personal assets. The sole proprietorship offers no asset protection. It is not an entity in the true sense of the word because there is no separateness. You don't file for a charter with your state, and thus there is no separate corporate legal identity. It is just you, doing business without any protection.

Why anyone would use it is simple: Because they do not bother to make a true decision about corporate structure. If you never choose a corporate entity but start up a business anyway, you are a sole proprietor. You are your business and your business is you. Making a bad decision or, in some cases, no decision can end up costing you not only your business assets but your personal assets as well.

There is no entity easier to set up than a sole proprietorship. You can easily set it up on your own because there is not that much to do. Once you start operating you will mostly forget about it. (Until you get sued and realize they can get everything you own.) You can run the business under your own name, if you choose, or apply for a fictitious name or a DBA (Doing Business As) at your county clerk's office. With a sole proprietorship, there are really no prerequisites for starting up, no amount of startup cash to be accumulated, no filings with the state, no bylaws or articles of incorporation. However, again, it is also the entity that exposes you and your business to the most risk.

The only official steps you have to take to start a sole proprietorship is obtain a business license with your municipal and state agencies, obtain an occupancy permit for your place of business (if you're not running e-commerce or working out of your home), and/or apply for a franchise certificate if you're opening a franchise. And that's it. You're not even required to open a separate bank account for the business.

At the end of the year, your business activities are included on your personal tax return. There can only be one owner in a sole proprietorship. If you are going to have partners you can't operate as a sole proprietorship (which removed it from Alana and Sherri's list of choices).

A sole proprietorship can be set up almost instantly. It can also get you into trouble almost instantly. With a sole proprietorship, you are your business, which means that if a creditor sues your business, that creditor sues you, and you're liable. When you set up your business as a sole proprietor, you put your house, your bank account, your car and all your assets on the line.

Quick and easy isn't always the best way.

General Partnership

A general partnership is the ugly entity. Unlike a sole proprietorship, a general partnership requires two or more owners, or partners, which means it could work for Sherri and Alana. Unfortunately, like a sole proprietorship, a general partnership, as Tom and Nancy learned, offers no asset protection. Again, there is no charter from the state, no legal separateness and, accordingly, no protection.

In a general partnership not only are you personally responsible for your own mistakes as in a sole proprietorship, but you are also personally responsible for your partner's mistakes. It is liability times two.

A partnership can be formed with a simple handshake between two or more people who agree to work together. You don't need a partnership agreement or any sort of written document. Such a loose agreement also leaves no paper trail for the partners to go back to when things go south.

When partners become adversaries and there's no written partnership agreement in place, the laws of the state in which the partnership was formed take precedence, and the partners are left without any choice in the matter. Similarly, if one partner leaves, dies or goes bankrupt, the partnership is terminated and the partners are liable for the company's debts and obligations.

I will not set up a general partnership, ever. Not only is there too much liability but it requires a great deal of document drafting. A general partnership agreement includes, at a minimum:

- Type of business.

- Finance requirements (the amount each partner is expected to contribute to finance the company up front).

- Rights and duties (what is expected of each partner).

- Dispute resolution procedures.

- Compensation (the method of sharing profits and losses).

- System authorizing cash withdrawals and salaries.

- Termination procedures (how the partnership will be dissolved if it becomes necessary).

For all the time and energy it takes to set up an ugly entity, you might as well set up a good one.

Corporations

Now let's get into the good entities, the ones that limit your liability and offer asset protection. Corporations, first chartered by the English Crown in the 1500's, are the oldest good entities, so we will start with them.

When you set up a corporation, you are creating a new legal person. Upon being chartered by the state, a corporation establishes its own legal identity. No matter how passionate you feel about your business, no matter how personal it is to you, you are not your corporation. This separation offers a big benefit. Because a corporation has its own legal presence and its own tax identity with the IRS, the corporation acts as a shield for the owners, whose liability is limited to the money they invested to start the corporation. If the corporation is sued, it is the corporation itself, as a separate legal entity, that is sued, not the owners, whose personal assets are not part of the company and are protected by the corporate veil. (That is, unless you sign a separate Personal Guarantee agreeing to be personally responsible for the debt if your entity doesn't pay it.) And because the corporation is its own separate legal entity the death of a shareholder doesn't mean death of the corporation. In a corporation, ownership comes in the form of shares, and those shares can be transferred.

Starting a corporation (whether taxed as an S or a C corporation) requires some paperwork preparation, including:

- Organizational documents filed with the Secretary of State's office in the state in which you wish to incorporate. For a corporation these are called Articles of Incorporation, which set out the company name, initial Board of Directors and authorized shares of the company.

- Because Articles of Incorporation become a public record, nothing proprietary or confidential should be included.

- In some states, a list of corporate officers (which may just be you) are filed with the Secretary of State.

- Bylaws of the corporation are the rules of the corporation and are not filed with the state. (They really don't want all that much paperwork.)

C Corporations

Incorporating offers protection of your business and personal assets. However, a regular C corporation does feature double taxation. (Both the C and the S refer to the IRS code sections on corporate taxation.) In fact, the main drawback of a C corporation is that earnings are taxed twice. When the corporation makes a profit the corporation pays tax on the gain;

when dividends are paid to shareholders (owners) they're taxed as well. As such, you are taxed twice on the same dollar of income.

One way around this is to choose a corporate structure that allows for flow-through taxation, as illustrated here:

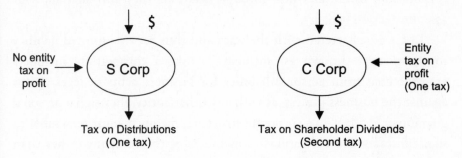

S Corp | No entity tax on profit | Tax on Distributions (One tax)

C Corp | Entity tax on profit (One tax) | Tax on Shareholder Dividends (Second tax)

S Corporations

By filing IRS Form 2553, Election by a Small Business Corporation, right after setting up your corporation, you can become an S corporation. The advantage to the S corporation is that it's a flow-through taxation entity. Essentially, when profits are made by the corporation, they are not taxed at the corporate level but rather flow through to the shareholder's personal tax return, meaning they are only taxed once.

There are a few drawbacks to an S corporation. If you're interested in taking your company public and publicly trading shares, you'll have to be a C corporation, but you can always elect to switch from S corporation to C corporation status once you're ready to go public. Another drawback is that once a corporation has elected to convert to a C corporation, there's no way to revert back to an S corporation again for five years. An S corporation can't have more than 100 shareholders or any nonresident shareholders. As well, an S corporation can't be owned by a traditional C corporation, a multimember LLC or many types of trusts.

But for minimizing payroll taxes, as discussed ahead, S corporation taxation is superior. And know that you can have an LLC taxed as an S corporation.

Limited Liability Companies (LLCs)

The LLC is a newer entity that combines the flow-through taxation of a partnership with the limited liability aspects of a corporation. Like an S corporation, LLCs offer flow-through taxation. They also offer superior asset protection benefits.

LLCs are chartered with the state and thus provide limited liability to the owners (known as "members"). Like a corporation, members are protected from personal liability for business debts or legal claims against the business (unless, as with any other entity, they sign a personal guarantee). And, as in a corporate structure, members must remember to sign contracts and obligations as members of the company rather than putting themselves at risk by signing individually.

LLCs allow for flexible management. Either the members (owners) or the managers (the president, etc.) can run the company. They also offer flexibility in division of profits and losses. In a corporation, dividends are allocated according to percentage ownership. In an LLC, members can utilize special allocations to divide profits between members. So, for example, profits in an LLC owned 50/50 can be allocated on a 70/30 basis.

With an LLC, Articles of Organization are filed with the Secretary of State. Instead of bylaws, an operating agreement is created. As with a corporation, to avoid personal liability in an LLC you must:

- Maintain timely filings with the state.
- Prepare entity tax returns.
- Maintain a separate bank account for the business.
- Separate personal and business matters.
- Have adequate capitalization (funding) of the business.
- Hold annual meetings of managers and members.

From being brand new in the 1980's, LLCs are now one of the most popular ways to do business and hold real estate.

Limited Partnerships (LP's)

A limited partnership is akin to a general partnership, but offers more protection. Instead of just general partners in a general partnership, in a limited partnership there are general and limited partners. General partners (as in a general partnership) are personally exposed. A creditor can go after each and every general partner and all of their personal assets. As well, general partners face personal liability for partnership debt. Limited partners are only liable to the point of their contribution of capital to the partnership. To deal with the risk of being a general partner, an LLC or corporation can be set up to serve as the general partner in a limited partnership, thus encapsulating unlimited liability in another limited liability entity.

But, as the chart below indicates, you will need to set up two entities to be completely protected in an LP arrangement. With an LLC, everyone is protected in one entity.

The Difference Between LLCs and LPs

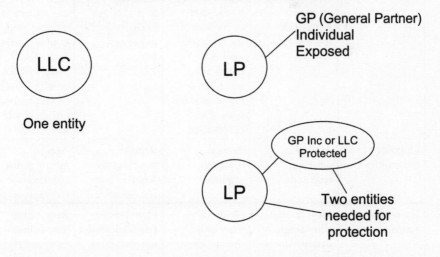

When you elect to form as an LP, you'll file a certificate of limited partnership with the Secretary of State's office, and a limited partnership agreement will serve as the operational road map for the entity.

A chart of the good entities helps to explain the differences and similarities:

	C Corporation	S Corporation	Limited Liability Co	Limited Partnership
Description of Entity	An entity of its own right, able to enter into contracts	A corporation that has elected flow-through tax status so taxes apply to individual shareholders	May be treated like a traditional corporation or as a flow-through tax entity like an S corporation	A limited liability partnership with flow-through taxation
Organizational Requirements	Articles of Incorporation filed with Secretary of State; bylaws required	Articles of Incorporation filed with Secretary of State; form 2553 filed with IRS; bylaws required	Articles filed with the Secretary of State; operating agreement not required but recommended	LP-1 filed with state; partnership agreement not required but recommended
Length of Entity	Can exist in perpetuity unless limited by state or Articles of Incorporation	Can exist in perpetuity unless limited by the state or Articles of Incorporation. Losing S corporation status does not change life span of an S corporation	Same as a C Corporation. Electing flow-through taxation does not affect length of an LLCs life	Can be limited by Partnership Agreement, or can operate in perpetuity as long as partners agree. Death, incapacitation or withdrawal of a partner can terminate the LP
Ongoing Formalities	Annual meetings required	Annual meetings required	Annual meetings not required but recommended	Annual meetings not required but recommended
Ownership Restrictions	Most states allow single shareholder corporations; some require two shareholders	No more than 100 shareholders; no domestic or foreign entities as shareholders; no nonresident aliens allowed	One-member LLCs allowed in most states	Required to have at least one general partner and one limited partner

	C Corporation	S Corporation	Limited Liability Co	Limited Partnership
Taxation of business profits	Corporate profits taxed at corporate rates at corporate level; shareholders taxed at individual level for dividends	Individual tax rates at individual level	Individual tax rates of members unless LLC elects corporate taxation	Individual tax rates of general and limited partners

Where to Incorporate

Many people incorporate in the state where they do most of their business. And sometimes this is the best choice—but not always.

Where your business is located does not have to dictate where the business is incorporated. In fact, you might be better off choosing to incorporate in a state thousands of miles from your home office. Choosing where to incorporate is not a matter of ease of distance but, rather, ease of business.

Corporations do not receive equal treatment across the country. Every state sets its own business laws and regulations. Some states are considered business-friendly. Others, like California, are almost anti-business. A decision as simple as where your business is incorporated can make a big difference to your bottom line and your peace of mind.

Nevada, Wyoming and Delaware are states which offer a favorable corporate law and low taxes. Nevada and Wyoming have no corporate or personal income tax. Delaware taxes entities doing business inside their state. But by setting up in those states you have the benefit of a favorable corporate law without the need to pay extra taxes.

Conversely, suppose you set up a California corporation to do business in Oregon. Not only would you have to pay Oregon taxes (because you are doing business there) but you would also have to pay California's notorious $800 per year franchise fee because you incorporated there. You won't set up in a high tax state to do business in another state.

What if you set up a Nevada corporation for your plumbing business in Ohio? Because you are doing business in Ohio you will submit the Nevada paperwork to the Ohio Secretary of State's office and 'qualify' to do business in Ohio. You will pay Ohio state taxes on your business profits. But because Nevada has no corporate tax you won't pay any extra money in taxes by setting up in Nevada. (You will, however, have to pay Nevada's annual fee and a registered agent fee in Nevada.)

Choosing which state to incorporate in is an important decision and may turn on what type of business you have, what your financial goals are and what the laws of your home state are compared to those of a favorable state. Be sure to consult with your professional team so that you understand all the pros and cons before you commit. As well, there is more information on these issues in *Start Your Own Corporation*.

Now let's review our third case...

Case 3: Bobo and Morton

Bobo and Morton had attended prep schools from kindergarten through high school together. Morton's full name was Morton Winthrop Trentham III. Bobo's full name was Anstergard VanDyke McGill, but because as a very young child he made quite a scene on the Bobo the Clown local afternoon TV show, everyone called him Bobo.

The two boys came from very wealthy families. Their great-great-whatever-grandfathers had been tycoons during the Gilded Age of the 1880's. The Trenthams and McGills had also been the original founders of The Thracian Club, a very posh country club offering golf, equestrian and yachting activities. Many well-heeled and accomplished people were members, most prominently a number of sophisticated Wall Street money managers, including financial wizard Frank Fodom. Many people wanted to get into The Thracian Club, or 'The Club' as members called it. Not everyone did. The list was long and the criteria rigid or, as some would say, snooty.

Bobo and Morton had no such acceptance worries. Because the two were direct descendants of the founders, they were automatic members of

The Club. Yet their family members knew that Bobo and Morton would never get in on their own merits.

Morton was short and spindly while Bobo was barrel chested and hefty. Together they resembled the famous comedy team of Laurel and Hardy. The comparison did not end there.

Unlike virtually all of their prep school friends, Bobo and Morton did not go on to expensive colleges. Neither of them did well in school nor did they have any interest in prolonging the pain. While their parents were well-connected and well-funded, that was not enough to guarantee a career for the two boys. And so as their other children moved on, both sets of parents knew they would have to come up with something for the boys to do.

The Trentham family had a large dog kennel on their very large property. The boys both liked dogs. The idea arose that Bobo and Morton should run a dog breeding business. Both families liked the whippet breed, which the American Kennel Club describes as "a medium size sight hound giving the appearance of elegance and fitness, denoting great speed, power and balance without coarseness." It was the perfect breed for the Trenthams and McGills. All Bobo and Morton knew was that these slightly built canines were miniature greyhounds that could run up to 35 miles per hour.

The Trenthams and McGills put together a business and funded a bank account. The boys received a small salary. They acquired six whippets for breeding and started to pay for feed, equipment, veterinarians and the like.

The breeding business was not lucrative. In fact, it brought in just one sale, and plenty of annual losses. The whippets did not respond to Bobo and Morton's unfocused, unscientific breeding attempts. When a friend said he used the soulful music of Barry White to set the mood, the boys tried that with the whippets. When Barry White didn't work they went on to the next half-hearted attempt at breeding.

Whenever they got the chance, the dogs would run away. While there was no way chunky Bobo could ever catch them, neither could spry Morton. The whippets were born to run, and run they did.

As dogs disappeared, their parents, somewhat strangely, and without question, approved the purchase of more whippets. This went on for over two years until two very dramatic things happened.

First, the County Sheriff, John Law, showed up at the kennel with a complaint. The runaway whippets were doing something they never did for Bobo and Morton—they were breeding. There was now a large pack of wild whippets roaming the county. They were knocking over garbage cans and cruelly taunting the authorities with their speed. Sheriff Law made it clear, in a very loud and angry voice, that he did not like to be cruelly taunted. He inquired where their dog breeding, health permit and city business licenses were located. When Bobo said he didn't know if they had any of that, Sheriff Law handed him an order to shut down the kennel. He departed in an official huff leaving the main gate ajar. Before Sheriff Law took five steps to his black and white patrol car, six whippets were out the gate and sprinting off into the countryside.

That same day, the boys' parents received a certified letter from the IRS. They were being audited on the dog breeding business. Because the parents had been writing off significant losses (and receiving a tax break for the losses) while no real income had been generated, they were subject to hobby loss rules.

The parents brought in their attorneys and CPAs to deal with the sheriff and the IRS. There were fines and penalties to pay on both fronts. One of the CPA's assistants who knew Bobo and Morton found the whole situation hilarious. He dubbed them the 'Hobby Loss Twins' which, to Bobo and Morton's chagrin and anger, made the rounds around town.

And with their dog breeding business suddenly shut down, Bobo and Morton needed to find something new to do...

Hobby Loss Rules

When getting into business you must distinguish between a legitimate business and an activity that is considered a hobby or a business that is not at all profitable. The IRS has been targeting hobby losses for many years.

Losses from hobbies cannot be written off against other income. Look at it from the IRS point of view. If you love breeding horses, and make no money at it, why should you get a write off? If your new business makes a profit, then you don't have to worry about the hobby loss rules. On the other hand, if the new enterprise consistently generates losses (deductions exceed income), the IRS may step in and say it's a hobby rather than a business.

There are two ways to avoid the hobby loss rules. The first way is to show a profit in at least three out of five consecutive years (two out of seven years for breeding, training, showing, or racing horses). The second way is to run the venture in such a way as to show that you intend to make it profitable. The IRS regulations say the hobby loss rules won't apply if the facts and circumstances show that you have a profit-making objective.

How can you prove that your objective is to make a profit? As a start, you can do so by running the new venture in a businesslike manner. More specifically, the IRS and the courts will look to the following factors:

- how you run the activity.

- your expertise in the area (and your adviser's expertise).

- the time and effort you expend in the enterprise.

- whether there's an expectation that the assets used in the activity will rise in value.

- your success in carrying on other similar or dissimilar activities.

- your history of income or loss in the activity.

- the amount of occasional profits (if any) that are earned.

- your financial status; and whether the activity involves elements of personal pleasure or recreation.

The classic "hobby loss" situation involves a successful business person or professional who starts something like a horse ranch or a farm. But the IRS's long arm also can reach out to more common situations, such as business people that start what appears to be a bone fide sideline business.

Before starting your business speak to your CPA to make sure it is considered a legitimate business in the eyes of the IRS. While hobbies can be a source of relaxation and satisfaction we don't want the IRS to deem your business that you work hard in to make successful a mere hobby. And as you are starting to realize right at the start you may need the help of...

Your Professional Team

Hiring professionals to do what they do best frees you up to do what you do best. And while you may not need all of them before you set up shop, it is not a bad idea to know who you will need and want on your team before the day-to-day demands of your business overwhelm you. Remember that corporate veil? Utilizing the expertise of the right professional team will help you make certain your business is complying with local and federal requirements. As an example, they'll help you avoid the hobby loss rules.

You want a professional team on your side who understand your business and work well with you and with each other. You want professionals who can guide you through the startup phase and who can then assist you in growing and expanding your company, deal with contracts and customers, get your message out and protect your assets. The following are some (but not all) of the experts who make up the professional team.

Banker

Banks have a host of services for businesses of all sizes. Knowing a banker (not just a teller at the counter) at your business bank is important. A good banker on your team can provide you with ideas and programs for your growth.

Establishing a relationship with a local bank can help you network in your business community. And having a previously established relationship with a banker will help when you are ready for a business loan or line of credit. Bankers can keep you up to date with other financial products that might work for your business, from merchant banking services to having the bank put together your payroll system.

Ask to meet with a vice president or a private business banker. Get to know them and keep in touch. It can't hurt to have a banker on your side. At the start, you will open a bank checking account for your business and get checks imprinted with your company name. Banks can also provide credit cards for your business, which is a great way to start building credit for your business for the day when you start looking for loans and other forms of financing.

Insurance Agents

At the start, shop your insurance needs around. Insurance rates can vary greatly and you don't want to overpay. Once you are comfortable with your agent, you can save yourself time and effort if you use one insurance agent for all your insurance needs. As well, discounts are available if you go through one company. Every two years or so sit down with your agent and go through your coverages. Are you paying too much? Has the value of your business or property gone up? Are you not properly covered for certain risks? Do a risk assessment review with him or her to make sure your business (and personal) needs are being met.

Attorneys

For all the lawyer jokes (and I tell a few myself), please remember that a good attorney can be a lifesaver for your business. From discussing the right entity choice and checking on name availability to handling the formation of the company and filing the required paperwork, your attorney is going to be a big help when you are starting out. You can use your attorneys to help you prepare the documents you will use when running a day-to-day business, including the contracts and agreements you'll have with vendors and suppliers or customers. Your attorneys can assist you with proprietary information and intellectual property, protecting your ideas and filing for patents or copyrights and trademarks. If you have the misfortune of having a run-in with the government (as we'll discuss ahead) an attorney specializing in such issues can be a very big help. As an overall strategy, for specialized advice, the attorney you choose should be well versed in the field or industry in which your business will operate.

Starting out, as with choosing an accountant, you're going to want to ask friends and family and other business owners for recommendations and referrals, and interview attorneys to find one who will be right for you and your business. Your current banker, accountant or insurance agent, if you already have such professionals on your team, may be able to refer you to an attorney who's right for you.

You also need to keep in mind the business license requirements for the type of business you're starting up. (Recall our last case where Bobo and Morton weren't properly licensed and were assessed large fees and penalties.) Almost every business you can operate requires a business license in the city in which you'll be working. In some locations, you may also need to have a county and/or state business license. Each license requires an annual fee and some paperwork. Your attorney can help you with these requirements.

Accountants

Your accountant works with your books, with the finances of your business and your livelihood, so you definitely want to hire someone whose skills and judgment you trust. While you're still starting up, your accountant can help you:

- set up your books and bookkeeping system.
- prepare the balance sheet and projected profit and loss statements needed for a business plan.
- advise you on quarterly tax requirements.
- help you set up financial timelines to assist with startup costs.

After startup, your accountant may continue to assist you with bookkeeping, payroll and financial management. At all times you want your accountant (and all your professional team members) to maintain matters in confidence. In the case of Bobo and Morton where the CPA's assistant dubbed them the Hobby Loss Twins and spread word of their misadventures around town you have a serious breach of confidentiality. The assistant and his CPA firm could be sued for such behavior. I have many clients in smaller towns and rural areas who do not trust their local professionals to keep a secret. In many cases they end up using professionals in a larger metropolitan area.

With all your professionals make certain that confidences are maintained. Of course, a good professional will not have to be told this basic principle.

Your Business Name

Before incorporating you should check to see if the business name you want to use is available. There are three searches you must do.

1. Corporate Name

Whether you are forming a corporation, LLC or LP you will need to check and see if the name is available for use as an entity name. This involves visiting the website of the Secretary of State in the state you want to incorporate in and searching for name availability. (You should search for name availability for any state you want to qualify to do business in as well, as we will discuss ahead.) Also know that some states won't allow certain words such as 'financial' or 'insurance' in the corporate name without having a special license in the field involved.

Be careful on this part of the search. States are very lenient in name availability, which is understandable since they want as many formations and filing fees to be sent in as possible. If the name is not a direct match, they'll let it through.

So, for example, you may find that the proposed business name of your new computer consulting firm—Xcel Computing, Inc.—is available with the state. But what if there is another computer consulting business in your area named Xcel Consulting, Inc.? The state won't mind. They want the fees. But will Xcel Consulting have a problem with your new name? Of course they will. There will be confusion in the marketplace and they will stand to lose business with you operating under a similar name. (Of course, you may benefit initially from the confusion. But if Xcel Consulting is not good at what they do eventually the negative word of mouth will be confused with your company, too.)

Xcel Consulting may have the right to send a cease and desist letter stopping you from using Xcel Computing. What if this arrives after you have spent $20,000 on a logo and signage and printing? You may be out that money. The point here is that you can't rely only on the Secretary of State's website for name availability. While they won't allow you to form as Xcel Consulting because it is already directly taken, they will let you form Xcel Computing, even though that name will get you in trouble on several different levels. So we have to do some more searches.

But first, there is the issue of forming in a good state, like Nevada, and then qualifying to do business in another state like California. You should see if the name is available in both states. If it is not you have two choices for proceeding. One way, in our example, is to use another name in California. So if Nevada allowed Xcel Computing, Inc. but the name was taken in California you could qualify the company to do business in California under a different name. But technically your official corporate name in California would be fairly unwieldy: Xcel Computing, Inc. doing business in California as Xcel Consulting, Inc. Do you want to put that on every check and document? The second method is much easier: Find a name that works in both states.

2.   Domain Name

Almost every business has a website nowadays. It is the new business card. It is a way for the public to review and gauge you. And in terms of building business credit many lenders will require that you have a website as an indicator of your seriousness towards business.

It is best if your domain name is identical to or at least very similar to your business name. As you probably already know, it is very easy to see if a domain is taken. Just type in www._____.com, with the blank space representing the name you are considering. With so many domain names taken, if it is clean and the exact name you want, it may make sense to buy it right then. Even if you change the name later you have only spent $20 or so to tie it up.

3. Trademark Search

The trademark search is the most important search you will conduct. This is because a trademark trumps a corporate name and a domain name. A trademark is king of the hill here.

An example explains why. Suppose in your home state the name McDonald's Healthy Mush is available for use as a corporate name. Suppose you can obtain the domain name www.mcdonaldshealthymush.com. All is good so far. When you go to uspto.gov (the U.S. Patent and Trademark Office's very helpful website) and do a trademark search you find a number of McDonald's marks but nothing under McDonald's Healthy Mush for the category of nutritious, groovy oatmeal. You may think you are good to go.

The problem is that McDonald's, the massive hamburger chain, maintains and asserts a very strong trademark protection for their name in all categories of food. If you use their name in any phase of food production or sales (even if your own name is McDonald) they will have their attorneys demanding that you cease and desist and will promptly take you to court if you don't. (That is how the big companies do it, and so would you in their shoes.)

So the fact that you can incorporate under the name McDonald's and get a domain name based on the name McDonald's is of no consequence. The trademark, which protects your name to the exclusion of others when you do business with the public, is the hurdle you want to clear.

We will discuss trademarks again in Chapter Nine. You also can download a free eBook *Winning With Trademarks* from www.corporatedirect.com. For now know that you want the corporate name, the domain name and the trademark all to be clear when starting your business. This may mean coming up with a more unique name than you at first anticipated. But if unique is memorable, and is remembered, that is a good thing for you in your new business.

Rich Dad Tips

- Before you start, work with your team to choose the right entity.
- Choice of entity is a key foundational step not to be ignored or taken lightly.
- The company name you choose is very important. Do the necessary research to make sure you can control your name.

You are now ready to move forward...

Chapter Two

A.D. (Activation Day)

Today is the day you form your entity. It may be after you consult with an attorney, as our three teams will do ahead. It may be that you know exactly what you want.

Before you rush head long into it let's explore the tax side of things a little bit more. It will help us see why Alana and Sherri and then Tom and Nancy chose the entities they did. Of course, on this matter, Bobo and Morton's case is a little different, as we will see.

Taxing Matters

By choosing to use a good entity for your business, as a traditional C corporation, an S corporation, an LLC or an LP, you've made a choice that will help to protect your personal assets and those of other shareholders, members or partners in your company. You've also chosen an excellent entity for tax savings. If you were starting business as a sole proprietorship or general partnership there's very little you'd need to do to prepare for paying your business taxes. Everything you made in your business would be income and everything you made would be taxed, at a fairly high tax rate.

In a sole proprietorship or general partnership all of your income is subject to payroll taxes (or self-employment taxes) of 15.3% on the first $110,010 (at this writing) and 2.9% on anything above. Know that with the good entities there are ways to minimize these payments.

As well, while you're working with your team of professionals to put together your good entity, there are several decisions you need to make with regard to financial record keeping and preparing for the tax periods that are yet to come.

Elect a System of Accounting

You must elect a system of accounting for your business and, once selected, you need to stick to that system. The IRS does not want to play catch up in figuring out how you're keeping your books, and to keep it simple, there are only a handful of systems allowed. The two main systems are the cash method and the accrual method. In addition, the IRS permits a hybrid method of cash and accrual, and may permit other forms of accounting allowable under IRS code. But let's stick with the main ones.

The cash method accounts for income and outflow in real time. Income is recognized when received by the business. Expenses are considered deductible when paid. So work invoiced or billed in one financial year (i.e. December) and paid in the next (January) is not taxable the year it was invoiced but rather in the year that the money was actually received (January). Expenses coming due in one financial year and paid in the next are considered deductions in the year they were actually paid, not the year they were invoiced. So by real time we mean that income is recognized when it is really received and expenses are recognized when they are really paid.

Under the accrual method, income is recognized when it's earned, whether or not the funds are actually received. Similarly, expenses are deductible when incurred, whether or not it takes some time to actually pay them off. So a business with a calendar (December 31st) year-end which sends out invoices in December and is paid in January is still responsible for taxes on the amount invoiced for the calendar tax year that ended in December. Again, under the cash method, taxes on the invoiced amount wouldn't be due until the invoiced amount was actually received. So accrual is not real time receipts but rather real time billed. I prefer the certainty of receiving cash over the hope of billing for it.

Most businesses elect the cash system of accounting unless inventory is a large part of the business. No matter which method is chosen, the IRS requires business owners to make a choice and, once that choice is made, you need the IRS's permission to change it.

In order to keep the corporate veil intact, decisions such as electing a system of accounting need to be an actual election, a vote taken or a decision made during a documented meeting of members of the LLC or shareholders of the corporation. Include such decisions in the minutes of the meeting and keep the minutes in the corporation book. Election of the professional team the business is working with, the system of accounting, opening and closing bank accounts, applying for loans and credit are all decisions that need to be recorded and maintained in the corporate minutes. Those decisions made by shareholders, members, managers or directors outside the annual meeting are made as resolutions, which need to be recorded in a written document as well and kept with the corporate meeting minutes. Decisions that need to be documented include:

- Initial election of type of business entity
- Determination of shareholder-employee or member-employee salaries
- Choice of accountant and bookkeeper
- Opening of bank accounts
- Sale of stock
- Issuing dividends
- Purchase or sale of equipment
- Purchase of real property

We will be dealing with the important topic of documentation throughout the book.

Choose Your Tax Year

Another choice you'll be making during this time is your fiscal year. You can choose to have your company's fiscal year end at the end of any month, but be aware that federal taxes are due 2.5 months after the end of your fiscal year, not 3.5 months as personal taxes are. So if you elect a calendar year (January through December and ending on December 31ˢᵗ) as your corporate fiscal year, your federal return will need to be filed March 15, not April 15. And as with personal taxes, a six-month extension is available by filing IRS Form 7004, which will probably extend the filing period for your state income tax as well. State income taxes are required for corporate entities in every state with some notable exceptions, including Nevada and Wyoming. Remember that an extension is for filing the tax return, not for paying the estimated taxes due. (You extend, you still pay.)

However, if you're making quarterly estimated payments to the IRS, this shouldn't be such a shock at the end of the year. While federal tax payments for Social Security and Medicare are required to be made quarterly with IRS Form 941 (unless you're informed by the IRS they find your paperwork too much nuisance for too little income from you, and you file annually with a Form 944), you can also choose to make payments on a monthly, biweekly or weekly basis. Sometimes it's less painful to pay more often and in smaller increments.

Be sure to work with your CPA on these matters to get them right. Failure to pay or even falling behind on your payroll tax obligations can lead to personal liability and serious penalties. We will consider such a case further ahead.

IRS Definitions and Requirements

The IRS defines a corporation as an entity formed under state law by the filing of articles of incorporation with the state. Articles of incorporation need to be date stamped (or file stamped) by the Secretary of State's office in order to be official.

The IRS defines S corporations as corporations that elect to pass corporate income losses, deductions and credits through to their shareholders for federal tax purposes. Shareholders of S corporations report the flow through of income and losses on their personal tax returns and are assessed tax at their individual income tax rates. This allows S corporations to avoid double taxation on the corporate income. S corporations are responsible for tax on certain built-in gains and passive income.

The IRS code really doesn't define LLCs. As such, the IRS allows them the flexibility to be taxed however you, the LLC owner, wants. You can choose C corporation, S corporation, partnership or, if one member, disregarded entity taxation. Your election will be filed on Form 8832.

The following is a quick comparison of federal tax requirements for traditional C corporations, S corporations and LLC entities.

C Corporation

- Files IRS Form 1120.

- Balance sheet required on tax return.

- Must use double-entry bookkeeping system.

- Corporation must file all necessary employment tax returns.

- Pays tax on all profits. When shareholders take profits as dividends, distributions are taxable on shareholder's tax returns (double taxation).

- Some C corporations are defined as personal service corporations (such as professional corporations for physicians) and these are generally taxed at a higher rate.

- Tax elections are at corporation level.

- Allocation of income/deductions not permitted.

- Tax responsibility does not flow through to individual shareholder level.

- Shareholders who work for the corporation are considered employees (shareholder-employees) and need to draw a reasonable salary which is subject to payroll and withholding taxes. Dividend distributions, however, are not subject to social security tax.

S Corporation

- Must make the election (Form 2553) for IRS to consider an S corporation.

- Files IRS Form 1120S.

- Must use double-entry bookkeeping.

- All S corporations are required to file payroll tax and reporting forms for shareholders functioning as employees.

- Income and expense flow through to shareholders and are not taxed at corporation level.

- Tax elections are at S corporate level.

- Shareholders who function as employees must receive reasonable compensation (wages) and payroll taxes must be paid. Dividend distributions are not subject to payroll taxes.

- Profits flow through to shareholders and are taxed at individual levels (no double taxation).

LLC

- IRS form to be used depends on tax classification. If an LLC doesn't file a Form 8832 and elect the tax classification, default rules apply. Under IRS default rules, a single member LLC is considered a disregarded entity for tax purposes and taxed as a sole proprietorship, required to file a 1040 Schedule C, and subject to self-employment tax if the business has a net income over $400. A two member LLC defaults to be taxed as a partnership.

- Can elect to be taxed as a sole proprietorship, partnership, S corporation, C corporation or if one member is a disregarded entity, with tax obligations flowing directly onto the member's tax return.

- Bookkeeping is determined by tax classification.

Startup Expenses and Tax Advantages

Before you ever quite get the business off the ground—or while you're still contemplating your options—there are tax advantages available to you. Startup expenses are a good percentage of costs at the beginning of your business and include equipment, supplies and location, and also expenses incurred by investigating a business you want to purchase or create. Startup expenses also include the services performed by your professional team of accountants, attorneys and advisors who assist you in setting up the company, including legal fees for preparing your legal entity, filing fees paid to the state for official records and the like.

Startup expenses paid before the business is actually up and running can't be taken as deductions or losses, but during your first tax year you can write off $5,000 and over the next 15 years the rest of the expenses can be deducted, starting with the first month of operation. According to the IRS, the $5,000 deduction is reduced by the amount of total startup costs if those costs are more than $50,000, in which case the remaining costs must be amortized.

In order to utilize your startup expense deductions, you'll need to choose the write-off election. To do this, attach IRS Form 4562 to your first annual return. (You can file Form 4562 for both organizational and startup costs). As well, for more information on these and other important tax issues please see Tom Wheelwright's *Tax-Free Wealth* (BZK Press, 2012).

As soon as you decide you want to go into business, start keeping records. The more you document, the better your ability to take the tax deductions and credits your business deserves. The better you document your financial transactions and decisions, the better you protect your corporate veil—and allow it to keep protecting you.

Key Tax Issues of Corporate Entities

The biggest advantage of a legal entity over a sole proprietorship or a general partnership is the corporate veil. This is what protects corporate shareholders and LLC members from personal liability for business debts. In order for a creditor to get as far as an owner's personal assets, the entity veil has to be pierced, which means the creditor has to prove the corporation or LLC didn't act like a separate legal entity by filing the correct IRS paperwork, adhering to the tax laws and following other legal formalities. You want to maintain this veil of protection and thus you will follow the rules. So for all you extreme and unchained rebels out there: Please channel your boundless energy into your business and not against the rules which, if followed, will actually help you.

S Corporation

The advantage of an S corporation over a C corporation is the flow-through nature of the entity. (Know that an LLC can also be a flow-through entity and that an LP must be taxed in such a manner.) Profits are taxed not at the entity level but rather at the shareholder level.

For startup businesses that expect to incur losses early, an S corporation may be a better entity choice than the C corporation. S corporation shareholders are able to deduct a share of those losses on their personal income tax returns to the extent of the number of shares they own and to the extent of the amount of any loans they have made to the business. C corporation shareholders aren't allowed to take these deductions. Then again, the C corporation (but not the shareholders) can use their losses to offset future gains.

In an S corporation, once the business begins making a profit, those profits are taxed as income to shareholders at their individual tax rate, even if the profits are not distributed. So if your one person company has a profit of $50,000 at the end of the year and you need that money in the company for next year's expansion you'll pay tax on a $50,000 gain. (One solution may be to flow through enough money to pay the taxes. So if your tax rate is 28% you'd distribute $14,000 from the Company to you to pay the 28% tax on a $50,000 profit.) Know that S corporation income is reported on your individual return.

A key advantage of the S corporation has to do with Social Security withholding taxes. (In some situations they are called FICA taxes, in others self-employment taxes. We will generally refer to these monies headed to our bankrupt Social Security system as 'payroll taxes'.) Shareholders in an S corporation who take a salary can also take distribution of excess profits without paying payroll taxes. However, the salary the shareholder receives must be reasonable. Too low a salary coupled with higher distributions of profits can signal to the IRS that a shareholder is avoiding paying the Social Security system its 'fair' share and trigger an audit. If the discrepancy between the low salary and the high amount of distributions is too great, the IRS may disallow the distribution and consider all monies received to be salary, with taxes to be owed on that amount (along with penalties and interest).

The chart below helps to explain the concept. In example A, the owner pays herself a very low salary of $10,000 and thus only pays payroll taxes of $1,530. The company makes a profit of $1,000,000 and while the owner will pay regular income taxes on the flow through distribution she won't pay any payroll taxes on that amount.

The IRS will make a very reasonable argument when reviewing this case: Could you hire someone else to run your business for $10,000 a year to make you a million dollar profit? Of course, the answer is no.

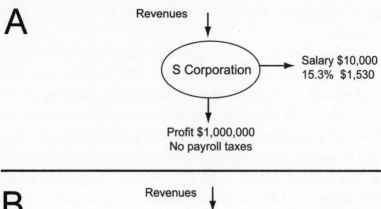

A

Revenues

S Corporation

Salary $10,000
15.3% $1,530

Profit $1,000,000
No payroll taxes

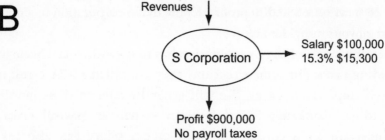

B

Revenues

S Corporation

Salary $100,000
15.3% $15,300

Profit $900,000
No payroll taxes

Which is why Example B is closer to the economic and market reality of the transaction. In today's market you would more likely have to pay someone at least $100,000 a year to manage a business that now produced $900,000 in annual profits. Notice the difference for the Social Security system. Instead of just $1,530 a year Social Security gets $15,300 a year. They want that money. They need that money.

So be careful on what you take for a salary. Don't make it too low, or too high. You just need to be on the cheaper side of reasonable. There is a website called salary.com which offers comparisons for salary levels in various industries. And work with your CPA to arrive at a reasonable salary amount.

C Corporation

Unlike the S corporation, a C corporation is taxed as its own taxpayer, separate from the shareholders owners. Just as an individual's tax return is determined by figuring income, credits, losses and deductions, a C corporation's taxes are figured the same way. The C corporation pays a tax on income. If any money is later distributed to the shareholders they will pay an income tax on those distributions individually. Double taxation is a disadvantage of the C corporation.

Another disadvantage for some is that losses for the business are held at the corporate level in a C corporation. While the business can use the losses to offset later profits, unlike an S corporation the losses do not flow through to the individual shareholder. For businesses that may incur losses during their startup and for the first few years, the S corporation will flow through the losses to the shareholders. The C corporation will not. The losses are trapped, if you will, in the entity. A C corporation can be a disadvantage this way, but maybe not. It depends on your strategy and situation.

Two factors minimize the C corporation's double taxation and the losses held at corporate level. First, a C corporation's first $50,000 income is subject to only a 15 percent tax. This may allow the corporation to keep more money inside the company for expansion. Second, if most income the C corporation receives will be payable as salary to the shareholder-employees, the corporation can deduct the salaries and pay a lower tax on its income. But if the shareholders take excess profit as dividends, those funds are taxed to the shareholders as income which, again, involves paying a double tax on the same dollar of income. So, it is important to work with your tax advisors on which way is best for you.

LLC

The LLC, if you so choose, can be a flow-through entity (with either partnership or S corporation taxation) where taxes are not taken at entity level. Or it can be taxed as a C corporation if you'd like. So you have a great deal of taxation flexibility with an LLC.

One disadvantage of operating a business (versus real estate) through an LLC is that current regulations require that payroll taxes be paid on all earnings. As well, a single member LLC may be considered a disregarded entity with all taxes paid at the individual level. Again, payroll (self-employment) taxes would be due on all such income.

But there are many other advantages to the LLC, as well as the other entities, which we explore through our three teams as we go through this book.

Knowing this, what entities did our actors choose?

Alana and Sherri

The two sisters met at the Law Offices of Boyden & Zook to determine which entity to use for their salon business. Alana's friend Jay was a handsome, single attorney in his mid 30's. He quickly got down to business with his new clients.

Jay told them they had a number of choices: LLCs, LPs or C and S corporations. The key, Jay said, was to pick an entity that offered limited liability protections and allowed them to minimize payroll taxes. He explained that while most people didn't realize it, payroll taxes, which are supposed to fund the Social Security and Medicare entitlements, are huge. On the first $110,010.00 of income (as of this writing) they are 15.3% of your payroll. After $110,010.00 in income (again, at this writing—but it keeps going up) they would continue to pay the 2.9% Medicare component on all salary payments, plus an additional 0.9% Medicare surtax for high income individuals ($200,000 for single employees and $250,000 for marrieds).

Sherri had questioned the 15.3% figure. On her paycheck from the jewelry kiosk at the mall the amount deducted was only 7.65% of her salary. Jay explained that the employee's wage was reduced by that amount and then the business paid on top of the employee's wages the same 7.65% amount, thus a total of 15.3%. The important thing to realize was that when you were both the employee and the owner, as the sisters would be in their business, you paid both halves. So your payroll taxes were 15.3%.

If you were paid a salary of $50,000.00 from the business the amount going to the government was not just your half (or $3825.00) but as an owner the full amount, or $7,650.00. That is a lot of money year after year going into a system that is technically bankrupt. Jay advised them to look at their next Social Security statement. In the body of the letter the government admits that the system is not solvent.

So the girls, Jay explained, wanted an entity with taxation that would allow them to minimize payroll taxes. That entity he explained was the S corporation. With an S corporation you can pay yourself a reasonable salary (and pay the 15.3% on that salary amount) and then flow any profits above your salary to yourself as dividends, without payroll taxes. (Of course, on all of it you pay your regular income taxes. At a top income rate of 35% plus payroll taxes of 15.3% you are at a hefty government take of 50.3%, with state taxes not even included.)

An example helps explain all of this. Suppose the ladies were doing well with their salon. They are earning a salary on all of the work they do directly but on top of that they make money, as most beauty parlors do, by renting out chairs to other stylists and by selling shampoos, lotions and other high profit margin beauty products. The money coming into the salon is as follows:

Alana	$55,000.00
Sherri	$55,000.00
Other Salon income	$30,000.00

On their $55,000.00 in salary income because they are both owners and employees they will pay $8,415.00 in payroll taxes. On the remaining $30,000.00 in income, from chair rentals and beauty product sales they will not pay $4,590 in payroll taxes because the income is not derived from salaries. Instead, it is generated from rentals and sales in the salon.

Jay explained if they set up as a general partnership with both of them as owners or if they set up with one of them as owner through a sole proprietorship the owner(s) would have to pay $4,590.00 in extra payroll taxes on the $30,000 in other salon income. Alana noted that that was a lot of money year in and year out. Choice of entity, as she was coming to appreciate, was important.

Jay continued by noting that while he liked LLCs for their asset protection there were regulations holding that a business LLC would also have to pay the $4,590 in extra payroll taxes. But he had a solution, which he would get to in a minute.

Jay then discussed the difference between an LLC and an S corporation for asset protection purposes. There were two types of claims to deal with. Attack #1 was brought by a customer against the business. It was an inside attack brought directly against the business. Attack #2 was brought by a claimant independent of the business, for example, a car wreck victim. This attack is an outside attack. Someone who has gone to court and won a claim against you for something unrelated to the business can then try and get at your assets, which includes your ownership of the business.

A car wreck victim whose claim exceeds your insurance may want to collect by getting at your business assets.

Jay drew a picture to explain.

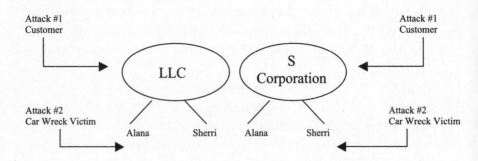

In Attack #1, a customer could get a judgment against the entity and reach the assets inside the entity, be it an LLC or a corporation (either C or S). Before Alana could finish saying, "That's not asset protection," Jay explained that it was important to realize what the claimant couldn't get. While they could get what the entity owned—in their case beauty supply inventory, equipment and a customer list—they couldn't get what was outside the entity—their house, their individual bank account and other personal assets. The asset protection came from using the entity to protect the customer's claim from reaching their assets outside the entity.

Jay went over it three more times so that the sisters grasped the concept. He noted that they didn't teach this in school, although they should. This was much more important, he felt, than a quadratic equation. (When was the last time you used $ax^2+bx+c=0$?) And because choice of entity was never, ever taught, you had to go over it a few times to really get it.

Again, in Attack #1, the inside attack, a successful claim against the company (by an angry customer or a bullying vendor) would be satisfied (paid off) with company assets but not their personal assets. On the other hand, Alana noted, if they had used a sole proprietorship or a general partnership all of their personal assets would be exposed to such a claim. Sherri agreed that by using the wrong entities they could lose it all.

Jay was glad they now understood Attack #1 and moved on to Attack #2. This Attack, he noted, had nothing to do with the business. It was one brought by someone who, for example, got into a car wreck with one of the sisters when they weren't doing any business driving. In the event their insurance company didn't cover the claim the car wreck victim could seek to get at their business assets by gaining control of their interest in the company.

The difference in how this was handled by each entity was significant. With an LLC formed in a strong protection state like Wyoming or Nevada, the claimant could only get a charging order. This is a court order 'charging' the car wreck victim with the right to recover monetary distributions. If no distributions were made, the claimant had to wait to be paid. Claimants, and their contingency fee attorneys, do not like to be put into this position. Importantly, Jay noted, the claimant did not have the right to get into the business and make decisions and vote to sell off all the assets to pay his claim.

Jay then discussed what could happen with an LLC formed in a weak protection state like California or New York. In those states the claimant could reach inside the LLC and sell all the assets. When Alana again said, "That is not asset protection," Jay agreed. If you were going to form an LLC the choice of state of formation made a big difference.

Jay then discussed how Attack #2 would be handled in an S (or C) corporation. In that scenario the judgment creditor could reach and control the shares of the corporation. If Sherri were sued and the judgment creditor got control of her shares equaling 50% of the company all sorts of problems could ensue. First of all, Alana would suddenly have a new and, in almost all cases, uncooperative partner, a partner who wants to sell the company and get their money as soon as possible. Secondly, with a

50/50 split between Alana and the judgment creditor they would be in a deadlock situation where nothing would ever be resolved. Both Alana and Sherri clearly saw that a corporation was not the ideal choice and asked what could be done.

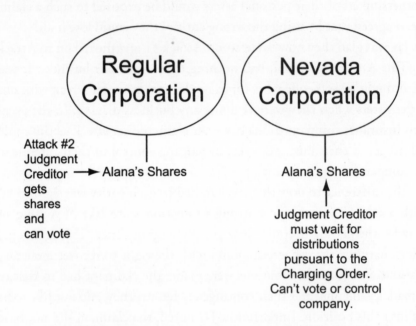

Jay noted that Nevada was the only state to allow charging order protection for corporate shares. The remaining 49 states did not protect corporate shares. But he had a plan, which he explained to the sisters. Jay noted they wanted asset protection and payroll tax minimization. An LLC formed in a strong state offered the best asset protection and S corporation taxation offered the best way to deal with payroll taxes. What if they could combine the two?

Alana and Sherri were puzzled. "How can you do that?" Sherri asked.

Jay explained that with an LLC you could file a Form 8832 with the IRS and elect to be taxed as a corporation. Then you filed a Form 2553 to be taxed as an S corporation. You could have your cake and eat it too.

Alana and Sherri thought about it for a minute and found that they liked the idea. A Nevada LLC for asset protection taxed as an S corporation for payroll tax minimization.

Jay also talked to them about the name they would use for the new business. Sherri said they liked the name SalonAlana because it rolled off the tongue. Jay also liked the name and asked if they had done a trademark search. Alana said they couldn't afford $1500 for a full name search. They had checked the U.S. Trademark office website at uspto.gov and had not found a conflict. They were able to get the domain name salonalana.com, and felt that that was a good sign.

Jay said that official government website search was a good indicator but not a definitive one. The girls understood. They would take that risk and go ahead with the name SalonAlana. Jay then asked them if they were certain of this, and they were. With that, Sherri and Alana instructed Jay to begin the LLC formation process and left happy that they were acting on their dreams.

When Sherri got home her husband Clint asked what they decided to do. When she mentioned they were forming an LLC taxed as an S corporation he immediately scowled. His lawyer buddy Wilson down at the lodge had said they should set up as a C corporation. Clint said that would be the best way to pay for their health insurance.

Sherri defended Jay's decision as Clint became more obstinate that he was right. Finally, she told Clint to call Jay and hear what his thoughts were. Clint said he didn't want to speak to no lawyer. Sherri patiently said that he had already talked to Wilson about it, why not also speak to Jay. She noted that while Wilson was a personal injury attorney Jay focused on business matters. Clint's response was to proclaim that all this didn't matter in the long run because they weren't going to succeed anyway. He left in a huff. Sherri was left to ask herself, "Why is he acting this way?"

The next day Sherri was running errands and still asking herself why her husband was so against her starting a business. At the grocery store Sherri ran into a girl friend who had successfully become an entrepreneur. Sherri asked how she dealt with people who didn't like the idea of a start-up. Her girlfriend said that was one of the hardest things she faced. Many friends and family members didn't want you to succeed because your success would only highlight their own lack of advancement. These people would discourage you and keep you down at their level because they were too afraid or lazy or whatever to rise above where they were. If they were to wallow so would you.

Sherri then asked the entrepreneur friend how the issue was resolved. Her reply was blunt: "I had to find new friends."

Sherri didn't like the sound of that.

Tom and Nancy

After their horrendous experience with Steve and the Righteous Rock Quarry case, Tom and Nancy Green were ready to move forward. The attorney who helped them through the engineering malpractice case mentioned an associate in the firm named Katherine could help them set up the right entity.

So Tom and Nancy met with Katherine in her office. They had brought Dooger and left him on a leash tied to a pine tree in front of the law office. All the secretaries and paralegals went outside to pet the loveable Great Dane. Everyone around town was fond of Dooger.

Tom, Nancy and Katherine reviewed the pros and cons of the various entities and the three of them kept coming back to a unique one of them— the professional corporation.

A PC, as they were known, was available to licensed professionals such as doctors and lawyers. Each state had their subtle variations but typically shareholders could only be professionals licensed to do business in one or more states by a state licensing agency. In some states the only way to do business through an entity was with a PC. Since Tom and Nancy were both licensed engineers they would both qualify to be shareholders of a PC.

Katherine discussed using a Professional LLC (or PLLC) for their consulting business. She said the law surrounding professional limited liability companies for professional activities was unsettled. California had just started to allow them and other states still did not permit their use. If they would ever engage in a long-term consulting business in another state (over 30 days, generally) they would have to qualify to do business in that state. Because every state allowed PCs and not every state allowed PLLCs it made sense to use a professional corporation. (In some states PCs are known as a Professional Association [PA] or a Service Corporation [SC]).

Katherine noted that forming a PC was very much like forming a regular corporation. The one additional step involved obtaining and filing a certificate of good standing from the state licensing division. She indicated that the specific division for engineer licensing was usually very cooperative with this.

Katherine then explained an important feature of the PC (which also applied to a PLLC). The entity did not provide protection from a claim of professional negligence. If a client like Steve at the quarry sued again on a malpractice claim they would have to rely on insurance. She suggested that Tom and Nancy have a $5 million E & O (errors and omissions) policy to cover any future claims. She also suggested putting all of their other personal assets in other protected entities in the event a claimant wanted more than the insurance coverage, or in the event their insurance company found a reason not to cover them.

Tom mentioned that they owned a fourplex in their individual names. Katherine explained that this asset needed to be protected for two reasons. First, if they left the property in their individual names and were ever sued by a tenant, the tenant could reach not only the fourplex but all of their other assets. Conversely, in a case like the Righteous Rock matter, if the claimant ever obtained a judgment against them, assets in their individual names could be easily reached. They should put the fourplex into a separate LLC formed in their home state, and then have the home state LLC owned by a Wyoming LLC for maximum asset protection. (This strategy is discussed in Chapter 3 of *Start Your Own Corporation*.) Tom and Nancy agreed to this strategy for the fourplex.

Moving back to their engineering business, Katherine noted that the PC would protect them from other business claims, such as a trip and fall at their office or a claim from a vendor. In those cases, the PC limited their liability. But, she said, to be clear, on a claim of personal negligence they were personally responsible no matter what entity they used. And so insurance was a must.

Nancy asked how the PC would be taxed. Katherine indicated they could choose between S corporation or C corporation taxation. She reminded Tom and Nancy that there was double tax with a C corporation—once on corporate income and then again on dividend distributions. She further noted that if all of the activities of the company were for professional services (i.e. law, health, accounting or engineering) they would be treated as a Personal Service Company and taxed at a flat 35% rate, without a graduation of tax rates as in a regular corporation. On the other hand, with an S corporation the profits flowed through the PC and were only paid at the shareholder level.

Nancy asked about health insurance. She had some medical issues and wanted to be sure she was covered. Katherine said that there was a small advantage with a C corporation. A C corporation could deduct health insurance premiums as a business expense. With an S corporation it was also an expense to the business but for those shareholders owning 2% or more of the shares (which would include Tom and Nancy at 50% each) the premium payments would be counted as personal income to them. So, for example, if their health premiums were $5400 a year in a C corporation that amount could be written off as a straight business expense and thus reduce the corporation's profit. In an S corporation the business could pay for it and write it off but the $5400 would show up as income on the Green's personal return. At a 35% tax rate they would pay $1890 in extra taxes.

But Katherine then showed how much they would save by only being taxed once in an S corporation instead of twice in a C corporation. Assuming a 5% state tax and the highest federal income tax rate of 35%, on net income of $200,000 the following is how C vs. S corporation taxation plays out:

	C Corp	S Corp
Net Income:	$200,000	$200,000
Corporate Tax:		No corporate tax
State Tax 5%	- 10,000	
Federal Rate	- 60,000	
(Applied on net after state taxes, blended rates)		
After Corporate Tax Profits	$130,000	$200,000
		- 10,000 State Tax
Dividend Tax	- 26,000	- 66,500
Federal/State		
	$104,000	$123,500

The example drove home the point for Tom and Nancy. While they may lose almost $2,000 by being taxed on health benefits in an S corporation they would save almost $20,000 a year by being taxed as an S corporation instead of as a C corporation.

The choice for them was easy. They instructed Katherine to form a professional corporation taxed as an S corporation under the name Green Engineers, P.C. They also had her form a Wyoming LLC to own a newly formed home state LLC to hold the fourplex for maximum protection.

Bobo and Morton

After the Sheriff and the IRS shut down their dog-breeding operation, Bobo and Morton struggled to find a new business activity. Their wealthy, distant parents did not have any ideas this time. The two families had certainly benefitted from the hobby losses while they lasted. But to help the boys actually make money was a different matter.

The Trentham and McGill parents did not see much of a future for Bobo and Morton. Early on they had shuttled them from boarding schools to summer camps and back so they wouldn't have to be with them. And the other Trentham and McGill siblings looked down their aquiline noses on their younger brothers. While the older brothers and sisters were attending well regarded colleges and making their way into lucrative careers they disdained and were embarrassed by, in their highly jaundiced view, their indolent little brothers.

The only champion Bobo and Morton really had was Maddy McGill, Bobo's uncle's wife. Aunt Maddy was not a blood relation but she was more warm blooded than the icy blue bloods of her husband's family. Aunt Maddy had always taken an interest in the two boys. She always made time to catch up with them. She was the only person to ever buy a whippet from them—their only sale in two years' time.

Aunt Maddy invited Bobo and Morton over to her property for lemonade. After the obligatory small talk she inquired what the boys would do next.

Bobo and Morton had no idea.

Aunt Maddy did have an idea.

While they appreciated her thinking of them, the boys were down on themselves. Having barely graduated from high school, they really weren't qualified to do much of anything.

Aunt Maddy cheered them up. A friend's daughter who knew all the families had just set up a computer installation and repair service. It was a brilliant move, and good for both the business owner and the customers because everyone trusted each other. Bobo and Morton could do the same sort of thing and the business she had in mind would be perfect for them. She told them that they were both trustworthy, pleasant to work with and their clientele would accept them because they knew their families.

The boys were puzzled. What kind of business was this?

Aunt Maddy proudly exclaimed, "House-sitting." The boys were at first reluctant. "Sitting at houses?" Bobo asked. Aunt Maddy was certain of it and the boys gradually warmed to the idea. Many of their families' friends had large estates that needed to be watched over. Many had multiple properties outside the area and were gone from their local estates for extended periods of time. Having some unknown person handle the duties was anathema to most. Aunt Maddy pointed out that Bobo and Morton were already in The Club. Clients would feel much more comfortable working with them.

And so their next business was to be formed. A business where profits would actually be made. A business they could be proud of.

Shortly thereafter, Bobo and Morton went to visit the attorney for both families. Parker T. Ruxton was the silver-haired senior partner of a very large, prestigious and overly wood-paneled law firm. He agreed to see Bobo and Morton only because he cared deeply about keeping the Trentham and McGill business for himself. He cared not for Bobo and Morton. After cleaning up the dog breeding mess he was further confirmed that the two were weak seeded dolts unworthy of their station.

When he met with the boys Ruxton's tone and demeanor was condescending, sarcastic, patronizing and dour. While many entrepreneurs would not put up with such an egotistical and officious team member, Bobo and Morton just assumed that all attorneys acted that way and stayed on.

Ruxton said they would need a corporation to do business through. Because they were both just over 18 they could now own and manage a corporate entity. A friend of Morton's had told him that to sound smart he should ask the question, "Should it be a Sí or a Yes corporation?" But when he did, Ruxton demeaned Morton for asking such an ill-informed question. It was not Sí or Yes, but rather C or S. Morton couldn't tell a difference. Bobo said they sounded the same.

Ruxton cut off any further discussion. They would be a C corporation. He had prepared one under the name Glockenspiel Ventura, Inc. Bobo said he didn't like that name and wanted to change it.

Ruxton, knowing full well that by amending the articles of incorporation the name could easily be changed, told the boys it couldn't be done. In truth, several months back, his paralegal had mangled the spelling on the corporate name. The filing was for their firearms client, who wouldn't pay for the mistake and made them start over, leaving this entity unpaid for and on the shelf. The corporation had passed the 75-day limit for an S corporation filing. So Ruxton took the oddly named C corporation and foisted it on the boys, and charged the families $10,000 for his twenty minutes of trouble. It didn't matter, Ruxton thought at the time. The ignorant boys would only make trouble, not money...

Rich Dad Tips

- Be sure to consider the tax consequences when choosing your entity.

- With our Social Security system technically insolvent you want to explore ways to legally minimize payroll taxes.

- A good CPA is a good team member to have on your team right from the start.

Now that we have our entities let's get started...

Chapter Three

Day One

Records

On Day One you've got to think about setting up your bookkeeping and tax system. Federal and state taxes fall into a pattern of quarterly and annual requirements and before you know it they will be due. So start working on this on your first day.

Good records and a great team working with you are your best defenses against repercussions from mistakes. A bookkeeper or CPA on your team can handle quarterly tax requirements and paperwork. The expense is worth it for the peace of mind—and to free you up to do what you really want to do. Even though you're still completing the initial paperwork to flesh out your entity and kick off your business, taking the time to make the right choices in your accounting and record keeping can pay off in saved time and money once your business is up and booming.

Apply for an EIN (Employer Identification Number)

Once you've filed your incorporation papers and they've been approved by the Secretary of State, your corporation needs to file for an Employer Identification Number, or EIN. An EIN is a permanent number assigned to your business which is used for official corporate business such as opening bank accounts and paying taxes. Think of an EIN as a Social Security number for your business. If you've hired a professional team to set up your corporation or LLC, they may apply for the EIN for your business. Be sure to confirm that they are doing it.

The IRS allows businesses to apply for an EIN online, or by phone, fax or mail. If applying online, the EIN is assigned immediately upon completion of the interview-style application that walks you through type of business, identity of business, authentication, addresses, details and confirmation of the new EIN number. But even though receiving the number is immediate, it can take up to two weeks to be added into the IRS database and until it is added, the number can't be used for filing returns.

Start Your Record Keeping

Once you're up and running, having a system in place for keeping track of tax records will make day-to-day business run smoother. Some of the documents you'll be providing your CPA for your tax returns include financial statements and your financial records you're keeping either through a manual system or on a system such as Intuit QuickBooks. You'll also want to keep track of bank statements, equipment bought and sold by the corporation during the year, loans and detailed information about them, and detail on the estimated tax payments you've made to both federal and state tax entities. Keeping track of this information as it flows in and out of your business makes putting your hands on it at tax time less taxing and far less of a headache.

And now, back to one of our teams...

Tom and Nancy

Tom and Nancy's first day was a good one. Eight months previous they had put in a bid for the civil engineering of a small sewer plant in Chase Fields. They had not heard anything since and had forgotten about it. That morning they received a call saying they had won the bid. Tom mentioned they were now a professional corporation and asked if the Chase Fields contract could be in their corporate name. The project manager said that was not a problem and asked them to come in and sign it.

Tom, Nancy and Dooger the Great Dane drove down to the construction office. After letting Dooger romp around the lot, the humans got down to the signing. The contractor said he liked their company name—Green Engineers—and commented how funny it was that amongst all the green environmental wannabes their last name was actually Green. The project manager wrote a check out to Green Engineers, P.C. for the first progress payment.

Tom and Nancy were driving back to their home office in a good mood. They had their first job since the lawsuit and a check in their new corporate name to prove it. Nancy suggested they stop by their bank and cash the check. They could certainly use the money.

When they entered the bank and presented the check to the teller there was confusion. Tom and Nancy had an account opened in the name of their living trust, The Green Family Living Trust. But the teller noted this was made out to Green Engineers, PC. Did they have an account in that name? Tom explained that they had an account at the bank. What else did they need?

The branch manager quickly came over. In a somewhat smug manner he explained that because the check was made out to a corporation they would need to open a corporate account. To do that they would need to bring in a copy of the corporation's articles of incorporation filed with the state and the company's EIN. Nancy asked what that was. The manager explained with exasperation that the Employer Identification Number, or EIN, was issued to corporations, LLCs and other entities by the IRS. It was akin to a Social Security Number for a business. Under the rules, they couldn't open a corporate bank account without one.

Nancy grew a little exasperated herself. They needed to cash the check right away. The manager said Nancy could go online to the IRS website and promptly get an EIN. Or the attorney preparing their corporation could get it for her. But until then, they couldn't cash the check. At that point Dooger, who had been waiting outside, burst in through an open door and created a big commotion. The teller, who always had a cookie ready for the lovable dog, happily squealed his name. The branch manager, however, was quite upset by it all, and so Tom and Nancy decided to leave with the cookie munching pooch in tow.

After leaving the bank, Tom called their attorney Katherine to inquire as to the status of the filing and how they could cash the check. Katherine replied that she had just received in record time the license documents from the State Engineers Division she needed for filing a professional corporation. She was sending it all in that day and she estimated that it would take another week to ten days to get the corporate paperwork back from the Secretary of State's office. Until then, they couldn't cash the check.

Tom and Nancy finally gave into the fact that they weren't going to get at their money right away. Katherine then explained there was a procedure for getting money out of a corporation. They would either do it as a salary payment (with payroll taxes and income taxes withheld) or as a distribution. In either case, they had to follow proper accounting procedures. Katherine asked if either of them had any bookkeeper experience. Nancy knew where the conversation was headed and said they would be hiring a bookkeeper.

As they continued driving home, Nancy asked Tom to drive through a commercial district near their neighborhood. Nancy had seen the bold red sign many times as she drove by. Now it was time to stop in at....

Betty's Bookkeeping

Corporate Formalities

As we've discussed, corporate formalities are important. By following these simple rules you can avoid being held personally responsible for future company blues. So you will hold your initial corporate meeting and record what happened (which writings are called 'corporate minutes'). These corporate minutes are easy to prepare. (Note how they are not called 'corporate hours.')

You can hold your first corporation, LLC or LP meeting on Day One or it may occur in the first 10 or so days after your entity is filed with the

Secretary of State. Exactly when it occurs initially is not as important as it is that it does occur shortly after you are formed. Take the time to flesh out your corporation on paper. It is through all this paper that the corporate veil is raised, so it's well worth your time.

Important papers to have in your corporate minute book (a binder holding all your corporate papers) includes:

- Articles of Incorporation (for a corporation) or Articles of Organization (for an LLC)

- Bylaws (for a corporation) or Operating Agreement (for an LLC)

- Shareholder or Member minutes

- Board or Manager minutes and consents

- State filings

- Actions of the incorporator

Amendments to any corporate documents such as bylaws or articles of incorporation need to be made by vote of the owners, or in some cases the board of managers. The vote should be recorded in the meeting minutes. In *Start Your Own Corporation* we discussed the components listed above. As a refresher, we have included some more information on these important documents on our website at www.CorporateDirect.com.

Some businesses will require even more documents, such as:

- Licenses

- Permits

- Registration forms

- Contracts

- Employee records

- Intellectual property records

- Stock records

Your professional team can help you determine what licenses and permits are required for your business in your location. Or you can start by calling your city (or county if you are in an unincorporated area) business license department. Politely explain you are starting a business and want to follow all the local rules. (They love hearing that.) They usually will explain everything you need to know over the phone.

In addition, if you're part of a professional organization or trade group, you may have access to a wealth of information on continuing education requirements, licensing and permitting required for your specific business, and perhaps leads on accountants and other professionals who work frequently with others in your field. When you're just getting your business started, this type of information is very valuable, and can save you a great deal of time and trouble at the start.

Now that you have a keen appreciation for the required corporate formalities at the start, let's see how our next team is proceeding.

Alana and Sherri

The sisters' attorney Jay called to say some papers were ready to sign. They were the meeting minutes for their initial LLC meeting and they were important in providing limited liability protection. He said he also needed to talk to them about a buy-sell agreement.

Alana and Sherri were seated in a large conference room. The sisters were surprised at how quickly the LLC was formed. Jay responded that they had formed in Nevada, a strong protection state. For a small fee, which Jay said he graciously covered as he smiled at Sherri, he could expedite the filing and form an entity within hours. Sherri thanked Jay for his special consideration and extra effort.

Jay then had them sign the IRS Form 8832 electing to have their LLC taxed as a corporation and Form 2553 to have it be taxed as an S corporation. He also asked them to sign the minutes of the initial meeting, which read as follows:

WAIVER OF NOTICE OF FIRST MEETING OF MEMBERS
OF
SALONALANA, LLC
A Nevada Limited Liability Company

We, the undersigned, being all of the Members, do hereby waive notice of the time, place and purpose of the First Meeting of the Members of SalonAlana, LLC, a Nevada Limited Liability Company.

We do further agree and consent that any and all lawful business may be transacted at such meeting or at any adjournment or adjournments thereof as may be deemed advisable by the Members present thereat. Any business transacted at such meeting or any adjournment or adjournments thereof shall be as valid and legal and of the same force and effect as if such meeting or adjourned meeting were held after notice.

Place of Meeting: Law Offices of Boyden & Zook

Date of Meeting: March 4, 2012

Time of Meeting: 10:00 a.m.

Dated: March 4, 2012

_____

Alana Cambridge representing
The Cambridge Family Trust, MEMBER

_____

Sherri Marks representing
The Marks Family Trust, MEMBER

MINUTES OF FIRST MEETING OF MEMBERS
OF
SALONALANA, LLC
a Nevada Limited Liability Company

The First Meeting of the Members of SalonAlana, LLC, a Nevada Limited Liability Company, was held on the 4th day of March, 2012, pursuant to waiver of notice and consent to the holding thereof executed by each Member of the Company. Present were all the Members, listed as follows:

Alana Cambridge

Sherri Marks

Sherri Marks was elected temporary Chairman and Alana Cambridge was elected temporary Secretary, each to serve only until the close of the meeting.

The Chairman reported that the Articles of Organization of the Company had been filed with the office of the Nevada Secretary of State on March 3, 2012, and have been issued file number LLC55555-55 by the State of Nevada, and that as a consequence, the Company is duly and validly existing and in good standing under the laws of the State of Nevada and qualified to proceed with the transactions of business. The Certificate of Organization of the Company then being exhibited, on motion duly made, seconded and carried, said Certificate of Organization was accepted and approved.

The Chairman called for the nomination and election of Company Officers. Upon nominations duly made and seconded, the following were elected and qualified:

NAME	OFFICE
Alana Cambridge	Operating Manager
Sherri Marks	Operating Manager

The Secretary presented to the meeting the following:
1.   Copy of the Articles of Organization.
2.   Copy of the proposed Operating Agreement of the Company.

Upon motion duly made, seconded and carried, the following resolutions were adopted:

RESOLVED, that the Articles of Organization and the Operating Agreement be, and are hereby approved, ratified and adopted by the Members.

RESOLVED, that the specific form appointing the registered agent and specifying the principal place of business supplied by the Nevada Secretary of State be, and is hereby adopted as the official resolutions and list of this Company.

RESOLVED, that the Operating Managers be, and are hereby authorized to pay all fees and expenses incident to and necessary for the organization of this Company.

RESOLVED, that the Operating Managers be, and are hereby authorized and directed on behalf of the Company to make and file IRS Forms 8832 and 2253 to gain S corporation taxation for the Company, and, to make and file such certificates, reports, or other instruments as may be required by law to be filed in any state in which said Officers shall find it necessary or expedient to file the same to register or authorize the Company to transact business in such state.

RESOLVED, that the Operating Managers be, and are hereby ordered to open a bank account in the name of this Company with Massivco Bank for deposit of funds belonging to the Company, such funds to be withdrawn only by check of the Company signed by one of its Operating Managers.

RESOLVED, that the actions taken by Alana Cambridge and Sherri Marks, and prior to the organization of the Company, but for and on behalf of the Company, are hereby approved, ratified, and adopted as if done pursuant to Company authorization.

RESOLVED, that the fiscal year of the Company shall commence on January 1st, and end on December 31st of each year hereafter.

RESOLVED, that Corporate Direct, Inc. be, and is hereby appointed registered agent of this Company, in charge of the principal office and so authorized to discharge the duties of registered agent.

RESOLVED, that the Secretary forthwith supply a list of Members to the registered agent for filing with the Secretary of State as required by law, and be it

FURTHER RESOLVED, that the Secretary forthwith supply the registered agent with a copy of the Operating Agreement to be kept on file at the principal office as required by law.

There being no further business to come before the meeting, upon motion duly made, seconded, and carried, it was adjourned.

_____

Alana Cambridge, Secretary

After reading the above carefully, Alana said she had read somewhere LLCs didn't need to have meeting minutes. Jay explained that certain entity promoters had put that word out over the internet to sell LLCs to busy (or, as Jay said, lazy) business owners who did not want to be bothered by an annual requirement. In point of fact, many states now required written documents for LLCs to prevent the piercing of the corporate veil and imposition of personal liability. And, he noted, they certainly wanted to have meeting minutes if the IRS ever showed up.

After Sherri and Alana signed the required entity documents Jay discussed the need for a buy-sell agreement. A buy-sell was a contract that dealt with issues related to changes in ownership. Jay explained that especially when you had a 50/50 split in ownership, as the sisters probably would, and the possibilities for future deadlocks, it was important to have, as he called it, a will for the business. Unlike how it sounded, a buy-sell did not really deal with buying and selling things. Instead, a buy-sell provided how things would be dealt with if one of them left the business, got divorced, died or was disabled, events called 'triggering events.' Jay explained that the time to sign it was now, when everyone was optimistic and fresh into the business. A year or more down the road, when partners have their own jaundiced view of their contributions versus their other partner's efforts, it was hard to get anyone to sign a buy-sell agreement.

Jay explained that if an owner was to leave a corporate entity as a result of a triggering event or because of differences with other shareholders that could not be resolved, a buy-sell agreement would be used by the remaining owners of small, closely held businesses to cover the buyout of shares. He clarified that generally with a large, publicly traded company, where shares can be freely sold, a buy-sell agreement wasn't really necessary.

But in a smaller setting, with a buy-sell in place, a procedure for valuing the stock had to be put in place. Thus, when a triggering event did occur, there was a way to value a purchase of corporate shares or LLC interests.

Silently, both Alana and Sherri could see the need for a buy-sell. In the event of a divorce, death or disability, neither one wanted to suddenly be partners with the others' spouse. Sherri thought Alana's husband Will was without will, and just plain lazy. Alana did not like Clint, period. She could not imagine doing business with such a coarse and intolerant character.

Jay continued explaining that in a divorce a buy sell would require that a spouse who did not work in the salon would not be allowed to retain ownership. In a divorce, only the sister, and not their ex-husband, would be an owner.

Because of this type of provision, it was necessary for their spouses to sign the buy-sell agreement. While there were many variations of it, Jay showed them the form he used (in this case for Sherri and Clint):

SPOUSAL CONSENT

A. The undersigned, as a registered holder of membership interests of the LLC pursuant to the Buy-Sell Agreement dated March 4, 2012, hereby acknowledges and agrees that he/she has read and is familiar with this Agreement and that he/she and his/her heirs, executors, administrators, successors, assigns agree to be bound by the terms of this Agreement with respect to any interest in the LLCs membership interests actually or beneficially owned by him/her.

B. Clint Marks, being the spouse of Sherri Marks, hereby acknowledges that he has read and is familiar with the provisions of the Buy-Sell Agreement dated March 4, 2012, and agrees to be bound thereby and to join therein to the extent, if any, that his joinder may be necessary. The undersigned hereby agrees that his spouse may join in any future amendment or consent on his part and further agrees that any interest which he may have in the membership interests in the LLC owned directly or beneficially by his spouse shall be subject to the provisions of this Agreement.

_____	_____
Clint Marks	Sherri Marks
_____	_____
Date	Date

Alana and Sherri liked the idea of a buy-sell agreement. They each took one home to review and show to their husbands.

Clint scowled when he saw the Spousal Consent form. He grabbed it out of Sherri's hands and went down to the lodge to talk to his attorney buddy, Wilson, about it. When he returned he was tipsy and loud. He yelled that Wilson said he should never sign such a thing. He yelled that her damn attorney was trying to drive the family apart. Sherri ran upstairs with their young daughter Ellie and locked the door.

The next day Clint's father-in-law Big Jim paid him a visit. Clint was reminded that Big Jim was signing the personal guarantee for the lease of the salon space. Big Jim also firmly reminded Clint that he didn't like seeing his daughter upset. At Big Jim's very forceful suggestion that he do it immediately, Clint signed the Spousal Consent.

It was an act that would have consequences.

Bobo and Morton

Aunt Maddy called to congratulate the boys. With their corporation formed they were officially in business. Prudently, she asked if they needed a special permit or license from the county. Morton said they had learned their lesson from the dog business on that one. Bobo had called to learn there was nothing special required to be a house-sitter. Aunt Maddy was happy to hear that because she had their first client lined up. They were surprised at how quickly Bobo's aunt was proceeding. She gave them the address and a few words of encouragement.

Bobo and Morton drove their Ford F-150 into the country. They drove past financial wizard Frank Fodom's incredibly large country estate. Everyone crowed about how much money Frank Fodom made them in the stock market. Bobo and Morton could only wonder if they would ever have enough for a basic savings account.

Bobo and Morton drove up to the Muller estate, which featured 17 bedrooms and a large circular driveway. They had no idea what to do. Aunt Maddy had said to just introduce themselves. Beyond that they didn't know what to say or how to explain this odd corporate name that was foisted on them.

Mrs. Muller's maid opened the door and escorted the boys to an expansive living room filled with expensive furniture and art works. Eventually, Mrs. Muller, a 75-year grand dame dressed in casual elegance, entered the room.

After chatting about their families and what was happening at The Club, Mrs. Muller eventually inquired about their service and the contractual terms. Bobo stammered about house-sitting when she was gone—taking care of any plants and animals, making sure all was safe and secure. Mrs. Muller asked what their fee was. Morton had no idea of what they should charge and embarrassedly asked her what she thought would be a fair price. When she named her rate the boys were quite surprised. They could do it for that.

She asked for their cards and contract. Bobo admitted they had only been incorporated the day before and didn't have it yet. She understood and asked for the name of their business. When Morton shyly said "Glockenspiel Ventura" Mrs. Muller brightened. "What a creative name" she said. "I have two glockenspiels."

Morton nudged Bobo before Bobo stumbled into asking what a glockenspiel was. Morton then asked to see her glockenspiels. They were led into a large conservatory filled with all sorts of musical instruments. When she said, "There they are," the boys had no idea which one it was. Morton asked if she might play it for them.

Mrs. Muller went up to a small percussion instrument that looked like a xylophone. Instead of bars made of wood the glockenspiel's keys were made of metal and laid out like a piano. She grabbed two metal headed mallets and began to play. The sound was pure and bell-like, like a carillon.

Mrs. Muller surprised Bobo and Morton with her musical knowledge. Morton thought she must have partied somewhere in her youth. She told the boys that a glockenspiel was used in a number of songs by the Canadian rock band, Rush, one of Bobo's favorite groups. Her favorite song with a glockenspiel was the Beatles' "Being for the Benefit of Mr. Kite" where it helped to create the circus atmosphere of the song.

Mrs. Muller then showed the boys around the estate and explained their duties. She was leaving for the Caribbean in two weeks and would need them to start then. She expected cards and a contract before she left.

At the door she complimented them on their business name. "It says you are bell men in a very oblique and creative way." She said she had two other friends to refer them to if they performed well on this assignment.

Bobo and Morton left in a daze. Mrs. Muller paid well, she had others to refer and, incredibly enough, she liked their name. It was a good first day. Bobo jokingly asked how long it would last.

Rich Dad Tips

- To properly raise the corporate veil of protection you must follow the corporate formalities, which importantly includes holding an initial meeting.

- Buy Sell Agreements are very important to consider at the start. (For more information on them see Chapter 17 of *Start Your Own Corporation*.)

- You will need to get an EIN (Employer Identification Number) as soon as possible for your banking and financial needs.

You are in business. Now you need to start keeping track...

Chapter Four

Day Two

Keeping Your Books

Bookkeeping may not be your forte, or even something you want to do, but keeping financial records doesn't have to make you miserable. For businesses, the basics are these: every transaction involves money in or money out. Income is all money that comes into your business. Expenses are all money that flow out of your business. As long as the two balance, the basics of your bookkeeping are in order.

Your business expenses will include any payments you make to acquire inventory, expenses related to actually doing business, including marketing and advertising, creation of a product, shipping and receiving, research and development—in short, the costs of doing business.

Other expenses of running a business include hiring your professional team, paying employees, paying for business licenses and overhead. Many of your business expenses are tax deductible, meaning you get to write them off to reduce your net income. Tax deductible expenses can be based on depreciation—those items like major pieces of equipment that lose value after a certain amount of use or a certain period of time and are thus written off over several years or more. They can also be written off quicker as a fully deductible expense. These are expenses incurred in operating your business, and are deductible immediately which helps to reduce your net income.

Some items that depreciate (and must be written off over time) include:

- Vehicles your corporate entity uses
- Tools, office equipment, office technology
- The property in which your business is housed (not the land on which it is located)
- Furniture for the office
- Machinery used in production

Some items that are deductible (and reduce net income in the year incurred) include:

- Fees for services from your professional team
- Advertising
- Bad debts (can be written off)
- Mileage or actual expenses for vehicle use
- Utility bills for your business site
- Maintenance of your business site
- Rent for your business site
- Property tax
- Subscriptions to professional publications
- Wages

Work with your bookkeeper or tax advisor to make sure you are properly deducting and depreciating expenses. The more you can deduct (versus depreciate) the more you will reduce your profit (and thus pay less in tax) this year.

10 Steps for Payroll Compliance

To comply with all of the rules and regulations on payroll withholding and reporting you will need to follow the ten steps listed here:

1. File IRS Form SS-4 to get your federal Employer Identification Number ("EIN").

2. With your EIN and articles of incorporation open a bank account.

3. Get each employee an IRS Form W-4 (Employee's Withholding Allowance Certificate) and have them fill it out. Keep this on file. (All of the IRS forms referenced in this book can be found at IRS.gov.)

4. Visit your state's employment division office, register your business and make the required unemployment insurance payments.

5. Institute a payroll plan for making payroll tax deposits on a regular basis. Either a staff member or an outside service must be responsible for this.

6. File the Employer's Quarterly Federal Tax Return (Form 941) at the end of each quarter (March 31/June 30/September 30/December 31).

7. At the end of each tax year report your federal payroll tax payments on either Form 940 or 940-EZ.

8. At the end of each year report each employee's annual wages to the IRS (always required) and state (if required) on Form W-2.

9. At the end of each year file and report payment of $600 or more to each independent contractor on Form 1099-MISC.

10. Take a deep breath. Acknowledge that while this is a lot of work every other legal business out there is going through the same thing. They are doing it. So can you.

Payroll definitely requires good bookkeeping and a healthy paper trail. Whether you are hiring a bookkeeper or a bank or payroll service or not, you must make certain that all of the employee payroll-related documentation is on file. The W-4 and I-9 forms signed by employees when they're brought on board must be on hand. The W-2 sent to employees on wages earned or the 1099 forms sent to independent contractors for services performed for the company each year must be sent out, and a copy kept in your files. (If this seems like a lot to do already—we are just getting into it. There are many more requirements ahead. Are you liking the idea of a bookkeeper to handle it all?)

Bookkeepers work in a variety of ways. Starting out you may need one to work one or more hours a week for you. As you grow, the hours will increase. At some point you may want to hire an in-house bookkeeper that works only for you.

No matter which option you choose, please know that you will never pay your employees in cash. You will always pay your employees by check from the corporate checking account, preferably with the sort of check that leaves a stub with duplicate information in your corporate checkbook. Document everything! The more you document, the more you protect your business.

Your corporate entity is responsible for paying half of the employee's federal withholding taxes, including the 940 FUTA (Federal Unemployment Tax Act) and the quarterly FICA (Federal Insurance Contributions Act) taxes. (Your quarterly payments may only be due annually if your tax liability is less than $2,500 per quarter.) While the other half comes out of the employee's wages, when you are the owner of the business and work in the business you are really paying both halves, or a full 15.3%. That is a huge amount of money, especially considering it is going to a system that is by all objective measures technically bankrupt. Pay attention to these payments, and always seek ways to legally minimize them.

You'll need to determine the gross wage, less FICA taxes, federal income tax withheld and any state income tax. In addition, most states impose their own employer-paid taxes for employment security, workmen's compensation and the like. There's a lot of paperwork and there are a lot of deadlines. Hiring a bookkeeper to handle this portion of your business frees you up to actually run your business. Remember the concept of opportunity cost. The more time you are doing bookkeeping the less opportunity you have to go out and make money.

Hiring the right bookkeeper is important...

Tom and Nancy

Tom and Nancy returned to the office of Betty's Bookkeeping. Betty had been running errands the day before and they were instructed to come back the next day. Which they did, with Dooger. The Greens tried to keep the Great Dane in their Prius but the dog bounded out and immediately made his mark on Betty's lawn. Betty, looking out her front window, was not pleased. After getting Dooger back in the car, the Greens entered the office.

Betty was in her early 40's but looked much older. Her face was deeply lined and she had the husky voice of a chain smoker. She always had a cup of coffee at her side and her less than straight teeth were a dullish yellow.

She promptly got down to business. She offered a full to partial bookkeeping service, depending on the needs of Green Engineers, PC. If they wanted to use a QuickBooks accounting program at their office she could back them up and do the payroll reporting and reconciliation of bank accounts. If they wanted her to do all the data entry and handle the QuickBooks accounting she could do everything for them. It was their choice.

Tom and Nancy agreed that Betty should do it all. They had not been very good at keeping up with all of it in the past. Even though they were highly trained engineers they never really grasped the concept of double entry bookkeeping where the assets and liabilities had to equal out. Now that they were a corporation it would be even harder.

Betty agreed that being a corporation required a few extra steps. It wasn't that much more work, she said, but it did involve some specialized knowledge, which she had. When Nancy asked for references Betty sat back. She said her clients liked their privacy and did not want to be called. She said she had one client who was cooperative enough to field such a call. Betty gave Nancy the number and name of Dave's Plumbing.

Tom had heard of the business. He then asked if Betty was bonded. She quickly replied that she was, and that she had E & O coverage as well. (E & O, or Errors and Omissions insurance, covers professionals against malpractice claims.)

Tom and Nancy thanked Betty for her time. They would call her later in the day with their decision. Once in the car they discussed the issue of hiring her. Tom noted that her office seemed to be neat and well ordered. She appeared to have control of the business, instead of the other way around. Nancy had been put off by her answer about references. She thought that had been a little odd. At the same time, Betty was conveniently located, being less than a mile from their home office. And they needed help right away to get their check cashed.

That afternoon they placed a call and hired Betty's Bookkeeping.

Alana and Sherri

Big Jim was looking at retail lease space for his daughters. Alana and Sherri's first choice was to be in the town's big mall, which was a regional draw. But there was already a large salon in the mall and he knew the lease terms would be onerous.

So Big Jim focused on space in the smaller malls and strip centers which were clean, well lit, had good parking and were on busy streets. If he was going to sign the personal guarantee on any lease his girls were going to be located in a spot where they had a fighting chance to succeed. He had decided not to use a commercial real estate broker due to the personal guarantee issue he was facing. While he didn't know for sure, he felt as if some brokers wouldn't go to bat for him on any attempts to limit it. So he was going it alone.

Big Jim narrowed his focus to two centers that fit his requirements. Because the lease market was soft and landlords had to currently be more flexible to obtain tenants he wanted to be able to play two owners off against each other. At the same time he was realistic from his experience as a supermarket store manager that landlords could be difficult, even obstinate, no matter what the market conditions.

He first called on Pennoyer Neff, who owned the Crossroads Center, a newer retail site on a busy street. There was a 1,500-square-foot space in the center that would serve Alana and Sherri's needs. Big Jim shook Mr. Neff's hand and got down to business. He mentioned the center could use a strong salon. The other tenants would certainly benefit from the foot traffic. Mr. Neff was matter of fact about the space. The minimum term was five years with a personal guarantee and an initial per-square-foot rate that increased every year. A Common Area Maintenance (CAM) fee for landscaping, exterior wall repairs, parking lot maintenance and the like was due every quarter. While a deposit equal to two months' rent was due, the first month's rent would be free so they could set up in the space. Big Jim said the lease would be in the name of his daughter's LLC. Mr. Neff said it would have to be in their individual names. When Big Jim suggested certain other concessions besides the first month's free rent (which was usually always given) Mr. Neff would not budge. Big Jim could play the game. He thanked Mr. Neff for his time, mentioned he had an appointment at Frenchman's, and abruptly left.

Big Jim's next visit was to Frenchman's Corner, originally the site of a historic stage coach stop and now an older mid-sized mall. Oscar Acquirre, the mall's manager, was effusive in welcoming Big Jim into his office. After discussing the terms, Big Jim sought some concessions. He wanted three months' rent free and he wanted the personal guarantee to drop after the first two years. If his daughters were in business after two years he said they would be there for the next twenty years. There was no need for more than a two-year personal guarantee. When Mr. Aguirre said those terms were beyond what they offered, Big Jim mentioned that Crossroads Center was considering the same terms. Saying he had an appointment, Big Jim thanked the mall manager for his time and departed.

That afternoon Big Jim received two calls, one from each mall representative. Both Mr. Neff and Mr. Acquirre indicated there could be some room to negotiate.

As it turned out, on a five-year lease the Crossroads Center gave him two months of free rent and agreed to lease to SalonAlana, LLC, the entity, instead of to Sherri and Alana as individuals. Big Jim would personally guarantee the lease for the first two and half years. Once his girls were halfway through the five-year term, his personal guarantee dropped off and just the business, not Big Jim personally, would be responsible for the remaining lease payments.

That night at dinner Big Jim received big hugs from his girls. They were very pleased with the space. The Crossroads Center was perfect for them.

When Clint muttered to Will that their father-in-law had snuck out of the full, promised personal guarantee, Will responded, "Why shouldn't he?"

Personal Guarantees

A personal guarantee (or a commercial guarantee) is a contract between a lender, lessor or vendor and an individual for the extension of credit or services to the individual's business. If the business (be it a corporation, LLC or other entity) doesn't pay or defaults then the individual who signed the guarantee becomes personally responsible for the obligation. There is no corporate veil to deal with in that case. The lender doesn't have to worry about getting at any corporate assets. With the guarantee they have a clear shot at the individual.

Lenders and others insist upon a personal guarantee for a variety of reasons. One is to motivate management to stick with the business. Nothing quite keeps your attention as the prospect of losing all of your personal assets if the business fails. A personal guarantee also acts as a secondary collateral (an individual's net worth) to the primary collateral of all the business' assets. It is prudent, from a lender viewpoint, to ask for them. And most lenders will be very upfront about such requirements.

But not all businesses are so forthcoming. Some will hide personal guarantees in contracts and not notify you of all the significance of the section. As an example, a client of mine recently came to me about the following language buried in a lease agreement.

"To induce Lessor to enter into this Lease and purchase the Equipment for Lessee and knowing that Lessor is relying on the guaranty as a precondition to entering into this Lease, I, the undersigned, individually, absolutely and unconditionally guarantee to Lessor the prompt payment when due all of Lessee's obligations to Lessor under the Lease. Lessor shall not be required to proceed against Lessee or the Equipment or enforce any other remedy before proceeding against me. I agree to pay all reasonable attorney's fees and other expenses Lessor incurs in enforcing this guaranty and Lease. I consent to any extension or modification granted to Lessee, and the release and /or compromise of any obligation of Lessee or any other obligors and guarantors shall not in any way release me from my obligations under this guaranty. This is a continuing guarantee and shall bind my heirs, successors and assigns, and may be enforced by or for the benefit of any assignee or successor of Lessor. This guaranty shall be governed by the laws of the State of New York. ALL DISPUTES RELATING TO THIS GUARANTY SHALL BE LITIGATED EXCLUSIVELY IN THE FEDERAL OR STATE COURTS LOCATED IN THE STATE AND COUNTY OF NEW YORK notwithstanding that other courts may have jurisdiction over the parties and the subject matter, and I freely consent to the jurisdiction of such courts, including without limitation, the Civil Court of the City of New York. LESSOR MAY PROPERLY SERVE ME WITH LEGAL PROCESS VIA CERTIFIED MAIL TO MY ADDRESS BELOW. I WAIVE, INSOFAR AS PERMITTED BY LAW, TRIAL BY JURY IN ANY LITIGATION ARISING FROM OR IN ANY WAY RELATING TO THIS LEASE OR GUARANTEE. I agree not to pursue a claim against Lessor or its assigns as part of a class action, private attorney general action or other representative action, to the extent permitted by applicable law. I expressly authorize Lessor or its agents or assigns continuing authority to obtain an investigative credit report from a credit bureau or credit reporting agency and conduct credit checks concerning my credit history, and acknowledge that Lessor may furnish information relating to this Lease and guaranty to a credit reporting agency. Disputes or inaccuracies regarding information Lessor furnishes to a credit reporting agency shall be sent to Lessor at the address listed below."

Did you feel your family assets slipping away in there? In the case where the above language was used, the leasing company representative was in a false hurry and had my client rush to sign and initial several places on the form. The personal guaranty section, which was never identified or discussed, was one of the hurriedly signed portions of the agreement. The consequences are dramatic. The leasing company never provided the services promised, but has leverage with my client's personal guarantee. It makes the case more problematic. Please be careful when signing such agreements. Understand whether there is a personal guarantee or not in any contract you sign.

One way to avoid signing personal guarantees for your business is to have good business credit associated with your business. If your business has a track record of paying its debts and has built up its business credit profile you may be able to avoid a personal guarantee altogether. For more information on building business credit see Chapter 11 of *Start Your Own Corporation*.

Stationery

When you are in business you need to convey a professional appearance. Business cards, letterhead, envelopes and the like can do this for you. But remember, in designing them, all of them must include the corporate element of your business name (Inc., LLC., Co.). You want to be very clear in all your dealings that you are acting on behalf of your business, not yourself. Even when it comes to signing your name on any business documents, be sure to sign your name followed by your corporate officer designation (Joe Blow, President, XYZ, Inc.) to deter any confusion as to whom is being obligated—your company, not you.

Bobo and Morton

Bobo and Morton knew they were on a deadline. Mrs. Muller expected business cards and a contract by the end of the week. While they certainly wanted the work they also thought she was kind of cool and wanted to meet her expectations of them.

They first began working on a business card. Bobo and Morton had the same computer skills as everyone else their age did, which meant they were pretty adept. They could get a business card done.

Bobo wondered: Should it have a glockenspiel on it? Like himself, perhaps not everyone knew what one was. Morton thought that would be random, in a good way. House-sitting, glockenspiel, bellmen. Not everyone would get there, but that was OK. At least they were stuck with a name that no one would forget.

On their computer, Bobo laid out the card:

**Glockenspiel
Ventura**

Morton Trentham
(555) 555-1234
Bobo McGill
(555) 555-9871

They did not list a street address since they hadn't thought through where their office would be. Would it be each of their apartments, their cars, or where they were housesitting? They decided to figure that out later.

For two reasons, they decided to list both names and their cell numbers on the card. First of all, they would only have to print one card. And secondly, since they wanted to focus on customer service and satisfaction, with one card they were able to tell clients to call either one of them on their cell phones at any time.

They needed one opinion before printing. Aunt Maddy was happy to see them. She had been concerned about the company name of Glockenspiel Ventura when she first heard it but it seemed like they were making it work for them. She liked the way their card was laid out and thought it was good to go.

Aunt Maddy then discussed their other needs. They would need to open a bank account and get a bookkeeper. Bobo and Morton looked at each other wide eyed. They hadn't even thought of that.

Aunt Maddy said a good bank, and even more so a good bookkeeper, were critical to their success. She wasn't going to let them go to just anyone. She and Bobo's uncle used only the best and most reputable for their businesses and investments. She would arrange for them to meet the right people.

Rich Dad Tips

- Keep your books straight right from the start. You will save time in the long run.

- Payroll compliance is a must. The government is very strict about receiving what they perceive as their money.

- Think twice before signing a personal guarantee.

And now you are ready to hire...

Chapter Five

Day Four

How to Deal with All of the Employee Issues

Our teams have accomplished a lot in several days. There is more to come.

But for Day Four we are going to step away from our actors and focus on issues that will affect some of you immediately and some of you eventually—dealing with employees.

There are five main issues to consider in this area. First, at the very start, do you hire employees or independent contractors? (Be careful.) Second, when hiring employees what is involved in an employment agreement? Third, what employment law issues do you need to know? Fourth, what employee benefits can you offer? And finally, what are the issues with employee turnover?

Employee vs. Independent Contractor – Which is Better?

Now that your Company is incorporated and you're ready to begin operating, the next step is to think about employees, and how to fit them inside your business with the minimal amount of headache.

First up—should you hire employees or engage independent contractors?

You know what it means to be an employee. Chances are you've probably been one. But, once you step over to the employer side of the working relationship, it's a whole new ballgame.

As an employee, your responsibilities include things like showing up for work on time, performing the duties assigned to you, and generally giving an honest day's work for an honest day's pay.

As an employer, however, you have to think about things like: payroll, remitting state and federal taxes, workers compensation premiums, health care plans and benefits, pension and 401k benefits, salary and performance reviews, paid holiday and overtime, vehicle allowances, sick and holiday time, assuming liability for certain acts of your employees (i.e., if they cause an accident driving the company van to make a delivery, guess who gets sued), severance pay, and on and on. Often-times this is going to effectively mean you either roll up your sleeves, train yourself and go to it, or, alternatively, you bring someone in to do this for you. However, as a small start-up business, bringing someone in to manage your employee administration may not be economically possible. After all, you're just beginning and your efforts really need to be on growing your business.

The alternative is to turn away from a traditional employer-employee relationship to one of Business/Independent Contractor. There are advantages and disadvantages to this type of scenario.

An independent contractor is just as it sounds. A contractor is someone who is contracted to perform services for someone else under a written or oral agreement. The "independent" part of independent contractor means that you, as a party to a Service Contract, pay this individual a flat fee based on whatever terms you negotiate, and they assume all responsibility for their own tax, healthcare premiums, workers compensation, and unemployment insurance. An independent contractor is specifically designated by law to not be an employee, and so your company takes on none of the obligations, liabilities or responsibilities associated with traditional employer/employee relationships. You can also write in specific indemnification clauses into your Service Contract, whereby you offset liability arising from certain acts of an independent contractor from attaching to your company. In many cases, people who are working as independent contractors have formed their own companies, in which case you would hire that company, and, by association its employee(s), perform whatever functions you agree to.

The drawback to this type of relationship comes mainly from IRS treatment of independent contractor relationships. Even though you and this individual have contracted out of the traditional employer/employee responsibilities and obligations, as far as the IRS are concerned, if an individual fits into certain criteria then they are deemed to be an employee, regardless of contractual arrangements. The IRS freely admits that self-employed independent contractors are not as tax compliant as are W-2 employees. (Remember, the IRS has better leverage over W-2 employees due to payroll withholding procedures.) The misclassification of workers (as the IRS calls it) whereby employees are allowed to be the more challenging independent contractors it is claimed costs the US Treasury over $1 billion per year. In practical terms, this means that where an independent contractor fails to remit their taxes and statutory deductions out of the flat fee that you have negotiated to pay them, the IRS can and will come looking to you to make good if they consider the independent contractor to be classifiable as an employee.

In the last few years the IRS has stepped up the number of employment tax audits. (We will discuss audits further in Chapter 14.) If they come in and find that you have misclassified employees as independent contractors the penalties can be steep. Tax adjustments can range from 10% to 40% of the previous three years salaries depending on whether the IRS asserts the misclassification as willful or not. (Was it an accident or intentional?) The IRS has offered amnesty programs for employers who want to 'correct' their practices. Be sure to speak with your tax professional about such programs.

For now, it is important to understand that the criteria used by the IRS to determine employee vs. independent contractor status is as follows:

Employee	**Independent Contractor**
• Works for you (the Employer) 100% of their time, at least during the length of time it takes to achieve a specific goal.	• Works for you (the Business Owner) on a part-time basis, and may also be working for other companies or individuals at the same time.

Employee	Independent Contractor
• Hours and days of work are scheduled by you.	• Is given a goal and a deadline, but no specific schedule is set.
• Is trained by you, and must perform work in a particular fashion, sequence or method.	• Is responsible only for the attainment of a goal, without specific requirements on how the goal must be achieved.
• Is provided with tools and materials, and must work on your premises.	• Provides own tools and materials, and may work from home, own location, etc.
• Must perform the work personally.	• May hire assistants or sub-contractors to accomplish the goal.
• Is paid hourly, weekly or monthly.	• Is paid on a per-project, commission basis, or invoices you for time worked.
	• Holds their own business licenses, permits, etc.

So, in order to make the argument that you are contracting with individuals on an independent contractor basis, you must ensure that, at a minimum, you enter into an Independent Contractor Service Agreement, and that independent contractors all submit invoices to your company to cover work they perform. If your contract with these individuals contains most or all of the points mentioned above, then you stand a better chance of successfully arguing that you are not an employer.

A sample form of the Independent Contractor Service Agreement and Employment Agreement may be found among the supporting documents at www.CorporateDirect.com.

Employment Agreements and Considerations

Employment Agreements will likely feature prominently in a start-up company's business plan, especially in connection with your "key" management or technical employees.

Traditionally, there are two types of employment groups associated with start-up companies: "Regular" employees and "Key" employees. Regular employees work under you, or other management, have a minor to moderate level of responsibility, and are paid accordingly. On the other hand, key employees are those you need to get your business plan off the ground. They are highly-skilled in either technology or business operations and are essential to your Company. They are likely to receive a considerable amount of money for their services, or, in many start-up companies where cash is not available, they receive a large allocation of founders shares in return for all or a part of their contributions. The relationship of key employees to your Company is probably closer to that of a business partner or founder than it is to that of regular employees. Regular employees may also receive a stock allocation or option to purchase stock in your company, but it is usually a considerably smaller amount than that granted to your key employees.

For new companies, the use of carefully crafted Employment Agreements may be the only way that you can attract the talent you need to get your business off the ground. Highly knowledgeable individuals, possessing extremely marketable skills have likely invested their own time and money to obtain those skills and knowledge, and will be looking to secure their own future and ensure fair compensation for their services. In these instances, it is quite likely that they will be looking for a significant stock allocation in addition to financial compensation.

Having Employment Agreements in place with your Company's key employees may also be a condition of attracting venture capital. (Of course, some of this information may not directly apply to those of you who are sole owners and are not raising outside moneys. But it is still important to know for the future.) Prospective investors, especially those you are seeking a large capital investment from, will be looking to see that you have secured the talent required to put your business plan into effect. A new company with a great idea, but which is relying on a single person to put this idea into effect, and the single person in question is not under contract or obligated to stay with your Company in any way, is not an attractive proposition for a potential investor.

A carefully crafted Employment Agreement can secure other things besides guaranteed service and peace of mind for investors. Through the use of confidentiality and non-competition clauses, your Company can be protected from employees selling your valuable information and processes to a competitor, or worse, breaking away to form a new company to compete directly with your Company, based on ideas developed with your Company and marketed at your Company's existing customer base. Through the use of ownership clauses, you can ensure that the software or products you are paying people to develop for you, remains your Company's property.

Even in cases where you don't have any employees, and the bright shining idea that is your Company is you, an Employment Agreement can still be desirable, or necessary. Remember, investors are investing in your Company, not you personally, and, by investing in your Company, are also purchasing a degree of control over how your Company operates. Therefore, they will want some type of assurance that the products or technology you are developing belong to the Company, and not to you. Another point to consider is how you are to be paid for your efforts. Having an agreed-upon amount which you will receive for the products and services you are contributing to your Company is, again, reassuring to potential investors. It would not be prudent to invest in a company in which there was no guarantee that the products or services, which attracted such an investment in the first place, could be removed at any time. It would be equally imprudent to invest in a company where there was no method to control what funds went to company development and what funds went into someone's pocket.

Who Should Sign an Employment Agreement?

As set out above, it is desirable to enter into Employment Agreements with all of your Company's key employees. These should include, but are not limited to, yourself and your partners or other founders of your Company, scientific personnel, software and hardware developers, financial officers, accountants, lawyers (if your Company has in-house counsel) and sales managers (particularly those with in-depth knowledge of and significant contacts in your Company's target industry).

What Should go into an Employment Agreement?

What goes into an Employment Agreement will depend on whom your Company is contracting with. However, there are certain basic elements which should be contained in every Employment Agreement.

Job Title and Scope of Duties

What is this individual going to do for your Company and how specific do you need to be?

Although a job title may on the face of it be fairly easy to apply, when considering what the scope of someone's duties will be you must consider how specifically those duties should be set out, and whether you need to leave some room for a job to change and grow. If the job title's scope is too narrow, the risk is that you will constantly be renegotiating your Company's Employment Agreements, particularly in a start-up situation where the chances of positions expanding beyond their original scope are high. If the scope is too broad, however, the risk comes when you try to narrow the scope at a future date, particularly where you are looking to remove certain responsibilities from an employee. An employee who disagrees with having responsibilities removed may argue that the legal concept of "constructive dismissal" applies and take legal action against your Company. (Constructive dismissal means making unilateral [i.e. one-sided] changes to an employee's position, duties or wages—usually involving reduction or removal—which fundamentally alters their job). Alternatively, an employee in this situation may argue that your Company has breached the Employment Agreement, and by doing so, has nullified the entire Agreement, including the portions relating to confidentiality and non-competition. It is always a good idea to include in any Employment

Agreement a clause that states that a company's Board of Directors is the final policy-maker and may choose to amend employment duties as they feel to best benefit the Company as a whole.

Where the Employment Agreement being created is for you, as the founder, additional consideration needs to be given to ensure that you do not lose control over your Company to incoming investors. You may wish to consider including a clause limiting the amount by which your position can be changed by the Board of Directors. You may also wish to establish a separate Shareholders Agreement with these individuals, which would cover other facets of your relationship with these investors, including control issues, veto powers, etc., and use that Shareholders Agreement to ensure that you do not wind up in a situation where you lose shareholder control over your Company and then are terminated from your position within the Company, effectively removing you entirely from the operation. You may also want to consider a voting trust, which is discussed in Chapter 15 of *Start Your Own Corporation*.

Term of the Employment Agreement

There are several ways to approach the idea of how long an Employment Agreement should last. With certain key employees, it may be best to limit the term of the Employment Agreement to a specific time, in which a specific project or goal is to be achieved. Alternatively, you may wish to make the Employment Agreement renewable yearly, or bi-yearly, depending on your Company's specific requirements. Where you anticipate the employment relationship as being long-term and continuous, you may wish to allow for that in the Employment Agreement. You may also elect to add a clause to the Agreement whereby the Employment Agreement is for an initial term of one year, and automatically renews for additional one-year terms until terminated by your Company or the Employee. It is generally preferable to have key employees contracted for a longer term, as opposed to a month-by-month basis, as again, your Company is trying to promote an image of stability to investors.

Hours of Employ

In addition to setting out the job title and scope of duties, it is also important to note in the Employment Agreement that while an individual is working for your Company, they are to devote their full time and attention to carrying out those duties. Again, you need to guard against becoming too narrow—for example, scientific and high-tech employees will often times be involved in conferences and seminars, writing papers, and information exchanges with other members of their scientific community. If employees are not permitted time for these other opportunities, the risk exists that their knowledge will become stagnant and of less value to your Company. On the other hand, an employee who is never at work isn't much help, either. You need to consider where balance will be achieved, and tailor the Employment Agreement to each individual situation. You may wish to consider a clause limiting the amount of time which may be spent on these outside activities, or that attendance or participation in certain activities must be subject to prior consent by your Company. This is particularly important in the case of part-time, or consulting employees, who may work for several other organizations simultaneously. The more organizations an employee is working for simultaneously, the more difficult it becomes to properly ensure that your Company's trade secrets, proprietary processes and methods are not being transferred or modified to suit these other organizations.

Paid Employment Expenses, including Travel and Relocation

If you are anticipating that an employment position with your Company may require travel and/or relocation, it is important that this be addressed in the Employment Agreement. A proper schedule and method of reimbursement must be set out, and adhered to by both sides. If receipts and documentation is to be required for reimbursement, this must be made clear.

Salary and Other Benefits

In addition to the monetary portion of an employee's salary, there may be other benefits to consider, i.e., stock allocations or options to purchase stock in the future, medical and dental health plans, pension schemes, profit-sharing arrangements, paid vehicle allowances, etc. It is a good idea, particularly in a start-up situation, where your Company does not have significant cash on hand to pay large salaries, and is depending on stock allocations and options, to tie these to continuing service by employees, or upon milestones reached. A more detailed discussion on Employee Benefits is found later in this chapter.

Key Man Life Insurance

It may be to the benefit of your Company to consider life insurance on key employees, particularly in the case of a Founders Employment Agreement. Under such a policy, the Company may be designated as beneficiary, or you may wish to consider having your Company's investors as beneficiaries where the insured person is irreplaceable, and your Company is not likely to succeed without them. Where such a clause is requested though, you must ensure that the employee in question agrees to undergo any required medical examinations, etc., and to perform such acts and things and sign any documents required to put such a policy into place.

Assignability

Any Employment Agreement should contain a clause allowing your Company to assign the Employment Agreement to an affiliate, associate, subsidiary or successor company to your Company. You do not want to be in a situation where your Company is being purchased by another company but a reluctant key employee whose services are essential to your Company refuses to work for the successor company.

Confidentiality and Non-Competition

As discussed earlier, it is vital for start-up companies to protect their intellectual property, patents, trade secrets, products, methods of production and business model from being either provided to existing competitors, or from being poached by your own employees into new spin-off operations. An Employment Agreement should be fairly specific as to what is considered "confidential" information, and should also set out a clause whereby an employee acknowledges that breaching this confidentiality clause could leave them open to prosecution by your Company.

Non-competition, on the other hand, must be tailored a bit more specifically. For example, hiring a software engineer to write a certain piece of software for your Company does not mean that this person may realistically be barred from ever writing another piece of software for another company, even if that company is in a similar business venture. What your Company may be able to do, however, is set a reasonable time and/or geographical limit before that individual is permitted to engage in conduct which could be seen as in direct competition to yours, either directly, by creating their own start-up business, or indirectly, by working for a competitor, and potentially utilizing all of the knowledge gained at your Company to assist the competition. It is important, however, when considering this provision to obtain proper legal advice on what is considered "reasonable" and what is considered "excessive". Most courts hold that, as a matter of public policy, it is good for society for people to work. And so the Courts are not fond of employers who try to limit in draconian fashion, future activities of employees. For example, a requirement whereby a former employee is not permitted to engage in their profession for several years following termination of their employment with your Company, or where they are not permitted to work in your Company's state and six surrounding states, will likely be overturned by a Court, and may even result in extra penalties being assessed against your Company. You cannot prevent an employee from practicing his trade, especially where knowledge and skills have been obtained over a lengthy time prior to employment with your Company. You can, however, seek to minimize to a reasonable degree, what that employee can do with the knowledge gained during their employment with your Company.

Development and Ownership of Inventions, Trade Secrets and New Business Ideas

Again, as set out above, where your Company is engaging individuals to help it develop a business, expand on an idea, and create new products, services or ideas for your Company, it is very important that all parties be clear on who owns what. An Employment Agreement should have a section requiring an employee to acknowledge that ideas, inventions and improvements created by that employee which (1) relate to your Company's existing, proposed or contemplated business, or actual or anticipated research; (2) result from work done by the Employee, using your Company's equipment, including software platforms; and (3) result from the Employee's access to your Company's trade secrets, assets, information, etc., belong to the Company, and not the employee. You should also follow up this clause with a clause requiring an employee to specifically assign all of his or her right, title and interest in and to such idea, invention or improvement to your Company.

Termination

It's going to happen, sooner or later. The best way to protect your Company from future wrongful dismissal lawsuits is to set out a termination clause, identifying the circumstances under which an employee can be terminated, how much notice is required, or what appropriate payment in lieu of notice will be. In this clause, you should set out a "neutral" termination section, whereby either you or the Employee can choose to terminate the employment relationship for no cause, by providing each other with sufficient written notice. A section allowing for "natural termination" should be included, whereby either party can choose not to renew the Employment Agreement following the completion of its term. There should also be a "for cause" termination, in which you set out specifically what is unacceptable conduct and what will result in immediate termination or termination on sufficient notice. It is also a good idea to set out a section dealing with what would constitute a breach of the Employment Agreement by your Company, which should typically be limited to failure to pay salary.

Where the Employment Agreement is being drafted to cover you, as a founder, you may wish to include other events which would constitute a breach by your Company, including fundamental changes to your job responsibilities and functions mandated by the Board of Directors which would constitute constructive dismissal.

In situations where stock allocations have been made, or more particularly, in situations where options to purchase stock have not been exercised, or have not entirely vested, it must be made clear what happens to unexercised or unvested portions. "Vesting" is a term used to describe how ownership of shares is transferred in a situation where a stock grant is made over a period of time. For example, a yearly allocation of 120 shares per year, vesting on a monthly basis, would mean that 10 shares per month would "vest" into an employee's name. Accordingly, should this employee leave after six months, a total of 60 shares would have vested in his name, and he would lose his entitlement to the remaining 60 shares. In addition, you may wish to consider a clause whereby all stock sold to an employee during the course of their employment is subject to repurchase by your Company, at a favorable price, or at the purchase price. A repurchase clause is found most commonly in privately-held company situations, where it is a company's best interests to have shares held by as few shareholders as possible. You may also wish to consider a repurchase formula in Employment Agreements entered into between you, as a founder, with your Company, particularly in instances where you are being bought out by investors. Alternatively, if your Company is considering going public then you, as founder, may wish to add a clause allowing you to retain your shareholdings and liquidate them into the public market following the completion of the going public process. It may be advantageous to you to try and tie a stock repurchase formula to a non-compete clause in a Founder's Employment Agreement.

Another point for a founder to consider including in an Employment Agreement is a requirement for a valuation of your Company's business to be performed prior to investors seeking to buy out your interest and terminate your working relationship with your Company. Having a valuation conducted by a third-party ensures that your shareholding and contribution may be fairly valued, and you get fully compensated for the time and effort you have put into building your Company.

A sample Founders/Key Employee Agreement is found at www.CorporateDirect.com. We have also provided in that section a sample form of Employment Agreement which may be used with key employees, as well as an Independent Contractor Service Agreement, which is discussed later in this chapter.

Employment Law Primer

We talked briefly in the "Employment Agreements and Considerations" section about certain things your Company should and shouldn't do in order to avoid being the subject of a wrongful or constructive dismissal lawsuit by former employees. The following is a very brief primer on fundamental employment law concepts to give you an idea of what exactly you are getting yourself into. As with everything else in this book, this section is not meant to take the place of proper legal advice, nor is it overly detailed. It is meant simply to cover the major laws in place surrounding the Employer/Employee relationship.

The Fair Labor Standards Act (the "FLSA")

This is a federal-level law, which governs things like minimum wage, equal pay, overtime, child labor and what records a company is required to keep regarding its employees. The FLSA covers companies who engage in commerce, production of goods for sale, handling, selling or moving of goods with a minimum gross sale value of $550,000 (whether or not the goods were manufactured by them). Several exemptions exist, including the "white collar" exemption applicable to executive, professional and administrative employees. As well, the FLSA does not apply to independent contractors, which leads to the misclassification of workers issue all over again. Know that exemptions and independent contractors are construed very narrowly by the courts, meaning they will find a way to classify workers as employees. Courts look to the "economic reality" of the arrangement to apply coverage.

Assuming your Company comes under the FLSA, minimum wage requirements will apply. The minimum wage is set by the federal government from time to time. As of the time of writing it was $7.25 per hour. (Know that some local jurisdictions may set a higher—or 'living'—minimum wage.) If you are operating a business where employees may receive tips, you may claim that up to 50% of their minimum wages may be paid by way of tips that they receive, but you must be able to prove that overall, wages and tips included, your employees received at least the minimum wage.

Overtime is also payable, once an employee has worked more than 40 hours in a work week. Overtime is traditionally calculated to be 1.5 times the employee's regular wage, but there are exceptions to this rule, depending on the employee's specific classification. Before modifying the traditional 1.5 calculation, it is best to contact the Department of Labor to determine whether you have any employees who can be reclassified at a lower rate.

With respect to coffee and lunch breaks, the rule of thumb is, where the break is 20 minutes or less in length, the time is considered to be on the clock, and payable by your Company. On the other hand, meal breaks of 30 minutes or longer in length are not considered payable, as long as your employees are relieved of all duties during this time, and are not required to remain "on the job" and eat at their desks or workstations.

The FLSA also provides that employees receive a Form W-2 on a yearly basis, which is a record of hours worked, wages received, and statutory deductions made. So, good record-keeping is essential, as you must be able to produce these records, complete and intact, should the Department of Labor come looking.

Child labor laws are strictly regulated under the FLSA. Children under the age of 16 are generally prohibited from being employed, although there is an exception for children of a business owner. In addition, children are prohibited from performing hazardous work such as mining, or from being around hazardous work-sites, such as heavy manufacturing or machining, transportation, warehousing or construction.

I-9 Employment Eligibility Verification

All employers must fill out and keep a Form I-9 for every individual (whether a citizen or not) they hire to work in the USA. The intent is for the employer to examine the employment eligibility and identity documents of the employee, determine whether they appear genuine and thus establish that the worker can accept U.S. employment.

The Civil Rights Act of 1964 (the "CRA")

The CRA is another federal law which guards employees from being the target of discriminatory practices by an employer, including discrimination based on race, color, gender, religion or national origin. A sub-section of the CRA deals with the treatment of pregnant women in the workplace, prohibiting employers using someone's pregnancy as a reason to deny them a job, or for removing them from a job at a certain stage of pregnancy, unless that employee is physically unable to perform the work due to their pregnancy. Sexual harassment is covered under the CRA, requiring an employer to provide a safe, harassment-free workplace. The CRA also provides for protection from "retaliation" by an employer against an employee who raises a complaint, as well as protection for any other employees assisting an employee with a discrimination complaint.

Age Discrimination and Employment Act (the "ADEA")

As employment law has advanced significantly throughout the past few decades, the ADEA was written to cover those individuals who were found to not be covered by the CRA. Prior to the enactment of the ADEA, age had never been considered an applicable factor upon which to base a claim of discrimination. However, massive changes in the workplace led to situations where qualified individuals were denied employment because younger, cheaper, and less-qualified help was available, or, individuals over a certain age were prohibited from applying for certain positions, which had been reserved for younger individuals. The ADEA provides that companies may not discriminate against individuals in either hiring or firing, where age is a motivating factor. In addition, the ADEA also provides that a company generally may not force a person to retire, although there are certain compulsory retirement provisions applicable to executives who are 65 years or older, and have held an executive-level position for a minimum of two years preceding their retirement.

Americans with Disabilities Act (the "ADA")

Another entry into the employment law forum is the ADA. Under the ADA, individuals with disabilities such as blindness, deafness, speech impediments, cerebral palsy, epilepsy, muscular dystrophy, multiple sclerosis, AIDS, cancer, heart disease, diabetes, mental retardation and emotional illness are protected from discriminatory hiring and firing practices by employers. However, in order to rely on the ADA, disabled persons must be able to show that they are qualified, and physically capable of performing the work required, or would be capable of performing it with reasonable accommodations and adjustments by an employer (i.e., installing ramps for wheelchair access, etc.). On the other hand, where an employer can show that employing the individual in question would be enormously costly, in terms of modifications required, to the point where the cost of hiring the employee would far outstrip the value of the work to be performed, then an exemption to the ADA may be available.

The Occupational Safety and Health Act (the "OSHA")

The OSHA was enacted to protect employees from being forcibly exposed to harmful substances while working. OSHA rules apply to industries such as manufacturing, restaurant, agriculture, medical byproducts and waste, and the like. Employers are required to provide a safe and healthy working environment, and to minimize the risk to their employees, through the use of protective equipment such as masks or breathing apparatus, or through the design of the workplace itself, i.e., exhaust/ventilation systems. (We shall deal with OSHA again, the author wrote ominously.)

Workers Compensation

Even with the best efforts on the part of an employer and its employees, accidents in the workplace can and do happen. Workers Compensation is designed to protect employees from being impoverished due to their inability to work following a work-related accident. It requires an employer to take certain steps, which include (a) obtaining an insurance policy to cover workplace accidents (the most popular method of complying with Workers Compensation requirements); or (b) establishing individual self-insurance funds, either on an employer-by-employer basis, or in collective groups of employers. Employers who do not have adequate Workers Compensation coverage may find themselves the subject of a lawsuit if an employee is left unprotected following a workplace-related accident.

As Workers Compensation is not applicable to independent contractors or subcontractors, it is important to be clear, when preparing any sort of Employment Agreement or Independent Contractor Service Agreement, of what the exact status of the would-be employee will be. Courts do not look favorably upon employers who attempt to reclassify employees as independent contractors to avoid paying Workers Compensation benefits.

The Employee Polygraph Protection Act of 1988 (the "EPPA")

An Act for every situation, a situation for every Act. Under the provisions of the EPPA, subjecting job applicants and employees to lie-detector testing, although a novel way of interviewing, is illegal, unless it falls under a specialized exemption, for example, employees who will be dealing with certain controlled substances.

The Electronic Communications Privacy Act of 1986 (the "ECPA")

Wiretapping or other monitoring of an employee's conversations and actions whilst on the job is illegal without the express consent of the employee (which tends to defeat the point). Nevertheless, for situations where you will want to visually monitor employees (i.e. banks, jewelry stores, etc.), or monitor by telephone (i.e. telemarketing, customer service, etc.), you will need to clearly explain what you are doing and obtain their consent ahead of time.

The Family and Medical Leave Act (the "FMLA")

Under the provisions of the FMLA, employees may take up to 12 weeks per year of unpaid leave in order to deal with family or medical reasons. The act covers employees seeking leave for childbirth or adoption, caring for an immediate family member with a serious health condition, or being unable to work due to a serious health condition. Employees are required to provide thirty (30) days' notice prior to taking leave under the FMLA, although obviously, this will not always be possible, given the nature of the family or medical emergency.

Again, we remind you, this is a brief overview to introduce you to certain employment-related issues which may arise in your Company. It is not, nor is it intended to be, complete or to replace proper legal advice and assistance.

Employee Benefit Plans

An Employment Benefit Plan can be a crucial element in attracting the talent that your Company needs to grow and thrive. Oftentimes in the case of start-up companies, there is limited cash flow, and so a degree of flexibility and creativity is called for to make up for this.

Employee benefits may be broadly defined into two distinct areas—traditional benefits, such as health and dental plans, pension plans, vacation and sick allowances, and equity benefits, such as stock option grants, incentive stock option plans, profit sharing formula, and performance bonuses. When considering how to implement employee benefit plans, it may be to your Company's advantage to consider two separate plans, one covering the traditional benefits, which will be available to all employees, and the second one covering equity benefits, which may be available to select employees only.

The following is a brief overview of elements to consider including in your Company's employee benefit plan. We have divided these elements into the "traditional" and "equity" sections, as discussed above. Because of the various tax implications involved in many elements of an Employee Benefit Plan, we recommend that you not attempt to implement one into your Company without individual legal and financial advice from your lawyers and accountants.

Traditional Health Insurance Plans

At this writing there is a great deal of uncertainty with regard to the government and health care. Until there is greater clarity we will advise on what historically has been done. Health insurance plans may be purchased through most insurance companies, in varying levels of coverage. Elements of a health insurance plan may include HMO coverage, dental and vision coverage, short-term and long-term disability coverage, life insurance, prescription reimbursement, "cafeteria" style medical plans, and emergency hospitalization coverage. The levels and complexity of packages offered varies widely, and will require some time and effort on your part to review and consider the most appropriate plan for your Company. Monthly premiums for coverage may be paid wholly by your Company, or apportioned to some degree between your Company and its employees.

The costs of implementing health insurance plans are tax-deductible for your Company, and are tax-deductible for most employees, as well. Where Group Insurance is included in a health insurance plan, however, it becomes subject to government regulation.

Supplemental Compensation Benefits

These are additional benefits from which employees may make a selection, with their premium rates being adjusted accordingly, based on the benefits they select. Supplemental Compensation Benefits may include things like interest-free loans, company car (for use on company business only), financial or retirement planning and counseling or fitness or other club memberships.

Tax-Qualified Retirement Plans

A tax-qualified retirement plan is an employer-funded plan, whereby the Company makes contributions on behalf of its employees, usually to a separate entity which then manages and invests the funds. The payments by the Company into the plan are tax-deductible at the time of payment, and do not become taxable until the employee withdraws the funds, at which time the employee is responsible for payment of the taxes. A defined benefit pension plan (where annual contributions are mandatory) and a defined contribution plan are two types of plans used by larger companies. While from a taxation point of view this type of plan is attractive to a company, due to the tax deductible status of the contributions, it is subject to detailed government regulations, review and continued monitoring by both the IRS and the Department of Labor.

Simple IRA

For businesses with fewer than 100 employees, the Savings Incentive Match Plan for Employees ("SIMPLE") IRA is easy to establish and administer. Unlike other retirement plans there are no complicated reporting requirements. SIMPLE IRAs allow individuals to determine how much they want to contribute and where the money is invested (within certain limits). At this writing, employees can defer up to $11,500 (or 100% of their compensation, whichever is less) along with a $2500 catch up contribution for employees 50 or older. Every year, the employer must decide to do either a non-matching contribution of 2 percent of an employee's compensation or a matching contribution of the lesser of the employee's salary deferral or 3 percent of the employee's compensation.

Simplified Employee Pension Individual Retirement Account (SEP IRA)

This plan is easy to set up and has low administrative costs. It is funded by the employer and established through an IRA. The employer can make tax deductible contributions of up to the lesser of 25% of earned income or $50,000 (at this writing). The employer determines how much will be contributed each year, as well as whether any contributions will be made at all. The same formula must be used to calculate the contribution amount for all eligible employees, including owners. Assets in the plan grow on a tax deferred basis.

401(k) Plans

Taking its name from subsection 401(k) of the Internal Revenue Code, 401(k) plans have become a widely utilized retirement vehicle for small businesses. It is estimated that over 60% of American households nearing retirement age have a 401(k) account.

There are two types of 401(k) plans. The traditional plan allows the employee to decide how much they want to contribute from their paycheck on a pretax basis. The employer is entitled to a tax deduction on any matching contributions made for the employee's benefit. The employees choose where to invest their monies, usually in a mix of mutual funds. Some plans allow employees to use 401(k) monies to purchase their company stock. Employees are usually free to re-allocate their investment choices within the plan. Money accumulates tax free in the account until it is withdrawn at retirement (after age 59 ½) at which time income taxes are paid.

The second form is known as the Roth 401(k) plan. In this version, after tax money is used to fund the plan. Once in the plan the money accumulates tax free. Importantly, once the money is withdrawn at retirement no further taxes are paid. The idea is that you paid your taxes when it went into the account so there is no tax on the way out.

The maximum limit on 401(k) contributions at this writing is $17,000 per year with a $5,500 catch up for those over 50. The limits are indexed for inflation and tend to rise every year.

Be sure to work with your advisor on maximizing benefits.

IRAs for your Business

A final point should be made about retirement plans. There are promoters all over the internet advocating that you can start and/or fund your own business or real estate venture using your personal IRA account. You can turn it into a 'checkbook IRA,' they will happily assert as they charge you large fees. They will have you transfer your IRA monies to a self-directed IRA account and claim that you can then direct the money to be used to invest in your new business or loan monies to an existing business.

The IRS calls this a prohibited transaction. Does that sound like a good thing?

The intent of IRAs is to accumulate monies for retirement, not to engage in self-dealing transactions. As such, the following transactions are not allowed:

Prohibited Transactions

Defined in IRC 4975(c)(1) and IRS Publication 590, these rules were established to maintain that everything the IRA engages in is for the exclusive benefit of the retirement plan. Professionals often refer to any out of bounds transactions as "self-dealing" transactions. This section of the code identifies prohibited transactions to include any direct or indirect:

- Selling or leasing any property between a plan and a disqualified person. (Disqualified persons are defined below and most notably include you.) Your IRA cannot buy property you currently own from you.

- Lending money or extending credit between a plan and a disqualified person. You cannot personally guarantee a loan for a real estate purchase by your IRA or loan money to your personal business.

- Furnishing goods or services, between a plan and a disqualified person. You cannot use personal furniture to furnish your IRAs rental property.

- Using property owned by the plan for your benefit. Your IRA cannot buy a vacation property that you or family members will use.

- Receiving any consideration. You cannot pay yourself income from the plan from profits generated from your IRAs rental property.

Disqualified Persons

A disqualified person (IRC 4975(e)(2)) is defined as:

- The IRA owner
- The IRA owner's spouse
- Ancestors (Mom, Dad, Grandparents)
- Lineal Descendants (daughters, sons, grandchildren)
- Spouses of Lineal Descendants (son or daughter-in-law)
- Investment advisors
- Fiduciaries—those providing services to the plan
- Any business entity i.e., LLC, Corp, Trust or Partnership in which any of the disqualified personas above hold 50% or greater interest.

If you engage in a prohibited transaction, which includes the promoter's claim of a 'checkbook IRA' you can supposedly control, you can lose your IRA's tax free status—the entire IRA becomes taxable based on the total account value at the start of the year in which the transaction occurred. An early withdrawal penalty of 10% may also apply.

So play it safe. Let your retirement plans do what the law intends.

Employee Turnover

Many small businesses will (or should) know what it costs to employ an individual in a given year. The entrepreneur will be able to quote the wage, insurance, payroll taxes and benefits costs for that employee in the current year. "My head of sales costs the company $96,000 per year in salary, insurance and all the other costs of payroll," you will say. "Soup to nuts, she is 96k."

But what does it cost if she leaves?

What many fail to appreciate are the very hard costs involved when that employee exits the company, and a replacement must be found. It is estimated that employee turnover costs 30 percent of the individual's annual compensation. Knowing the money (and time) involved will allow you to be better at retaining good employees, and budgeting for replacements in the normal course of business.

What are the costs to consider? There are three of them.

Exit Costs

When a key employee leaves, specialized knowledge within the company may be lost. You may have to hire that talent to fill the void (at perhaps a higher price than before). As well, if the departing employee developed positive relationships with the Company's clients, some of those clients may follow them out the door.

Knowing the cost to replace talent and the loss of business from departing talent should be factored into any equation of employee turnover costs.

Absence Costs

When other employees must now cover for the void created by a departing employee, the costs of an absent employee really begin to add up. Overtime pay may go up, productivity goes down and so does employee morale. Some employees are now pulled into hiring and training roles, diluting their job effectiveness as they are absent from their core responsibilities.

Recruitment and Hiring Costs

The costs to advertise for new recruits, review resumes, conduct background checks, hold interviews, negotiate employment offers and the myriad of other activities associated with bringing aboard a new employee are very real. So are the hiring costs of training and integrating the employee into the Company. It may be six months or more before they are productive.

That is a cost to factor in. So are the costs of new business cards, new IT account set ups and Human Resource department interactions.

It is estimated that fifty percent of all employees are dissatisfied with their current job. If given the right opportunity they would move to a new job. That is a very high number. Employers wishing to retain talent and maintain consistency for their clients are advised to appreciate the costs of employee turnover. It may be that incentives to retain existing employees are more cost effective than first appreciated.

Rich Dad Tips

- Work with your controller or CPA to be certain you are properly classifying workers as either employees or independent contractors.

- Always consider using an employment agreement with provisions for confidentiality and noncompetition.

- There are a number of federal and state laws governing employment relationships. You are expected to know them all.

With the employment issues now appreciated, let's get back to our teams...

Chapter Six

First Week

Capitalizing Your Business

An important early step is to capitalize—or fund—your business. While you want to keep your business and personal assets separate, you have to put something in to get the business started. If you end up making a personal loan to your corporate entity in order to get the ball rolling and have some operating capital, make certain you keep records of those loans and that the corporation pays you back, whether in stock or cash. Be sure to have full financial records of that transaction, as well.

One reason it's important for your business to have enough capital on hand to meet short-term obligations is that courts frequently pierce the veil upon a showing that the corporation didn't have the funds at the time of contracting. If this happens, a court may find the corporation exists only to shield the owner's personal assets. Along with maintaining proper corporate records, an excellent way to prevent a piercing is to have money in the corporation to meet its obligations. Know that some states have capitalization requirements. In Texas, for example, you must capitalize your Company with at least $1,000 when starting up. Know also that courts will pierce the corporate veil for a failure to capitalize the Company and issue stock.

Transferring assets into your entity is a good way to show its own separateness, its own financial identity. (And know that it's hard to prove you're separate from your business when you're "sharing" your personal assets with your own business.)

It is not particularly difficult to transfer assets. Simply make a list of what items you are transferring (say, your computer, printer, office furniture and the like) along with each item's current value and present value and when each was purchased. You can then prepare a bill of sale for the entire list. From there, you simply need the transfer approval at the meeting of your Board of Directors. You can have your company pay you in stock (to help your initial capitalization) or set up a loan, whereby the company pays you back the value of the items over time.

Alana and Sherri

Jay had suggested that Alana and Sherri capitalize their business with at least $10,000. The attorney for the girls felt that they should have enough money on hand to be able to operate the business for three months without a client walking in the door. By their calculations, with rent, utilities and all, and without salaries, $10,000 was the right number for a three-month run without customers.

They also discussed how to bring in certain items they would need for the salon. Sherri had a nice computer at home that she could contribute. Alana had purchased some display cases, which could hold shampoos and beauty supplies, at a garage sale that she could bring in. Jay agreed that these contributions would help the business (since it wouldn't have to buy the items) and discussed how to paper all the transactions.

First, regarding the money transaction. There were two or three ways to bring it in. Sherri was surprised. Was it two or three?

Jay smiled at Sherri. There were two definite ways and a third hybrid way. The first way was to use the $10,000 to buy stock in the company. They had to buy at least some stock in the company to be in control. The $10,000 could cover that. The second way was to loan the $10,000 to the company. This means that when there was money available, the company would pay them back principal and interest. As such, they would get their

$10,000 back (the principal loan amount) and any interest they charged (say 10% or another $1,000.)

Sherri asked what was the third way. Jay explained it was a combination of the two. So, for example, in their case, Alana and Sherri could each put in $1,000 to buy their LLC interest and then loan $4,000 each and be repaid from later profits. In this way, they used enough money to buy ownership (which is required) and loan the rest for later repayment. Alana and Sherri liked this approach.

Jay then discussed how to handle contributing equipment (the computer and display cases) to the company. It was best handled through a simple bill of sale whereby the individual transfers the property to the company in exchange for stock or a loan. Jay felt that capitalizing the company with the $1,000 in cash and the equipment would be sufficient. The ladies agreed.

Sherri and Alana then said that they wanted to benefit their father. Big Jim had signed the personal guarantee for the Crossroads Center lease. As thanks, they wanted to issue him certificates for 4% of the LLC. Jay said that was a nice gesture and certainly could be done.

It was agreed that Jay would prepare the documents and forward them to the sisters.

In a day, Sherri received the following documents:

MINUTES OF SPECIAL MEETING OF MEMBERS
OF
SALONALANA, LLC

The special meeting of the Members of SalonAlana, LLC, a Nevada limited liability company, was held at 10:30 a.m. on the 11th day of March, 2012. The following members were present at said meeting:

Alana Cambridge
Sherri Marks
Jim Holcomb

Alana Cambridge called the meeting to order, and announced that the meeting was held pursuant to a written Waiver of Notice and Consent to the holding thereof. The waiver and consent was then presented to the meeting and upon motion duly made, seconded and unanimously carried, was made a part of the records of the meeting and ordered inserted in the minute book immediately preceding the records of the minutes of this meeting.

The first item of business was approval of the lease. After reviewing the terms and after further discussion it was

RESOLVED and in unanimous agreement by all the members that the Crossroads Center lease is approved.

The second item of business was the capitalization of the Company. The members reviewed the attached promissory notes and bills of sale. After discussion it was

RESOLVED and in unanimous agreement by all the members that the Cambridge Family Trust and the Marks Family Trust shall each contribute $1,000 in cash and loan $4,000 to the Company for their interests in the Company, and that Jim Holcomb shall contribute his personal guarantee for the lease of Company retail space for his interest in the Company.

The next matter discussed was the membership of the LLC.

Upon motions duly made and seconded and unanimously carried, it was

RESOLVED and in unanimous agreement by all of the members that the Members of the LLC shall be The Cambridge Family Trust with a 48% membership interest, The Marks Family Trust with a 48% membership interest and Jim Holcomb with a 4% membership interest. The Manager is hereby authorized and directed to issue Membership Interests certificates to the following Members, representing the interests set out at follows:

Cert No:	Name	Number of Membership Interests:
1.	The Cambridge Family Trust	48%
2.	The Marks Family Trust	48%
3.	Jim Holcomb	4%

There being no further business to come before the meeting, upon motion duly made, seconded, and unanimously carried, the meeting was adjourned.

Respectfully Submitted by

_____

Alana Cambridge

PROMISSORY NOTE

$4,000   March 11, 2012

UPON DEMAND, for value received, SalonAlana, LLC, a Nevada limited liability company, whose address is _____ _____, ("Maker") promises to pay to the order of Alana Cambridge, ("Lender") the principal sum of Four Thousand Dollars ($4,000) together with interest thereon at the rate of 5% simple interest per annum.

As security for the repayment of this Promissory Note the Maker agrees to grant to Lender a UCC-1 lien over the Maker's personal property.

Maker waives demand for payment, notice of nonpayment, presentment, notice of dishonor, protest, and notice of protest. If Maker fails to make payment upon demand as required by this Promissory Note, Maker relinquishes all rights to property secured by the UCC-1.

All remedies hereunder or by law afforded shall be cumulative and all shall be available to the Lender in connection with this Note until the liability of the Maker herein created has been paid in full. In the event of any dispute, the prevailing party shall be entitled to attorney's fees and costs. Exclusive venue shall be _____ County, State of _____.

IN WITNESS WHEREOF, the Maker has executed this Note the day and year first above written.

SalonAlana, LLC

_____

By: Manager

BILL OF SALE

In consideration of the payment of five dollars ($5.00) and other good and valuable consideration, by SalonAlana, LLC (the "Purchaser") to Sherri Marks (the "Seller"), the receipt and sufficiency of which is hereby acknowledged, the Seller does hereby grant, sell, assign, transfer, convey, set over and deliver to the Purchaser this date, all of the Seller's right, title, and interest in the assets described hereto (the "Assets") as:

One Dell Computer System.

All of the Assets are transferred to the Purchaser, its successors and assigns, to have and to hold for its own proper right, use and benefit forever.

Except as otherwise specifically provided, the Purchaser covenants with the Seller, its successors and assigns, that the Purchaser is subject to a UCC-1 financing statement in favor of Seller for said Assets. Purchaser shall not sell, transfer or assign the assets until Seller shall discharge and release the UCC-1.

Date:_____

SalonAlana, LLC
A Nevada Limited Liability Company

By: _____   _____
    Alana Cambridge, Manager   Sherri Marks, an individual

As Sherri reviewed the documents at her kitchen table, Clint entered the kitchen with a beer in his hand. He demanded to see the latest set of papers from the "damned lawyer". Sherri was put off and tried to leave the room. Clint grabbed her folder from behind and dug through the papers.

Clint was furious when he saw the Bill of Sale. He yelled at Sherri for giving away the family computer to this losing business.

Sherri kept walking. She knew what she had to do. She would not confront Clint while he had been drinking.

Tom and Nancy

Tom and Nancy had a large check from the Chase Fields sewer system contract but couldn't cash it. They needed the money, but because they had tried to open the account too quickly the bank had become guarded with them. They were not as accommodating as one would think with a new client trying to deposit money.

The next time they went to the bank, the unctuous branch manager insisted that Tom and Nancy's banking resolution was not acceptable. The manager snidely suggested that the Green's attorney prepare a more comprehensive resolution. Tom grew angry and asked why he should have to pay an attorney to get a bank account open.

With that the branch manager said their behavior was unacceptable and showed them the door. As they were leaving, Dooger, who had been waiting outside, burst through the bank's front door and, in his zeal, knocked the branch manager to the floor. The tellers, who all loved Dooger, (and apparently not the branch manager) were laughing uproariously. The Greens quickly departed the scene, and Tom muttered under his breath, "Good dog."

The Greens next called their attorney and explained the situation. Katherine's only explanation was that sometimes even the best banks were the worst banks. Katherine said she had a banking resolution that always worked and she suggested that they meet with Mark at Heritage Bank, a good, locally owned bank. They could use her name with Mark and he would get the account open. The Greens agreed and Katherine said the tailored banking resolution would be ready for pick up at her office in half an hour.

Tom and Nancy took the form below to Heritage Bank:

CONSENT RESOLUTIONS OF THE DIRECTORS OF
GREEN ENGINEERS, P.C.
MADE THE 5TH DAY OF MARCH, 2012

WHEREAS Green Engineers, P.C. is a Nevada corporation, duly incorporated/formed under the laws of the State of Nevada on March 1, 2012;

AND WHEREAS Green Engineers, P.C. desires to open a bank account with a recognized financial institution in the United States of America and appoint signing authorities;

NOW THEREFORE BE IT RESOLVED THAT:

1. Green Engineers, P.C. appoint Heritage Bank (the "Financial Institution") as the depository for funds of this business.

2. This Resolution shall continue to have effect until express written notice of its rescission or modification has been received and recorded by this Financial Institution.

3. All transactions, if any, with respect to deposits, withdrawals, rediscounts and borrowings by or on behalf of Green Engineers, P.C. with the Financial Institution prior to the adoption of this Resolution are hereby ratified, approved and confirmed.

4. Any of the persons named below, so long as they act in a representative capacity as agents of Green Engineers, P.C., are authorized to make any and all other contracts, agreements, stipulations and orders which they may deem advisable, from time to time with the Financial Institution, concerning funds deposited with this Financial Institution, subject to any restrictions stated below.

5. Any and all resolutions duly adopted by the business and certified to the Financial Institution as governing the operation of Green

Engineers, P.C. account(s) are in full force and effect, unless revoked, modified or supplemented by this authorization.

6. Green Engineers, P.C. agrees to the terms and conditions of use as may be stipulated by the Financial Institution, and authorizes the Financial Institution, at any time, to charge Green Engineers, P.C. for all checks, drafts and orders for the payment of money that are drawn on the Financial Institution, regardless of by whom or by what means.

7. Facsimile signatures, if any, may be affixed so long as they resemble the facsimile signatures appearing below (or filed with the Financial Institution from time to time) and contain the required number of signatures for this purpose.

8. The persons listed below comprise the exclusive list of authorized signatories for accounts opened with the Financial Institution:

    Tom Green   President
    Nancy Hardcastle Green   Secretary/Treasurer

9. Any of the individuals listed above (subject to any restrictions indicated) is authorized to

    (a) open any deposit or checking account(s) in the name of Green Engineers, P.C..

    (b) endorse checks and orders for the payment of money and withdraw funds on deposit with the Financial Institution. The number of authorized signatures required for this purpose is one.

    (c) Make any and all other contracts, agreements, stipulations and orders which they may deem advisable, from time to time, with the Financial Institution, concerning funds deposited or withdrawn or any other business concerning this account transacted by and between Green Engineers, P.C. and the Financial Institution subject to any restrictions contained herein.

(d) enter into a written lease for the purpose of renting and maintaining a Safety Deposit Box in the Financial Institution. The number of authorized signatures required to gain access to and to terminate the Safety Deposit Box lease is one.

_____

Tom Green, President

_____

Nancy Hardcastle Green, Secretary/Treasurer

CERTIFICATION

I, Nancy Hardcastle Green, certify that I am the Secretary of Green Engineers, P.C., and I further certify that the above is a true and correct copy of a Resolution that Green Engineers, P.C., having full power and lawful authority to do so, has duly adopted and has not rescinded or modified.

_____

Nancy Hardcastle Green, Secretary

The corporate resolution did the trick at Heritage Bank. Their corporate account was promptly opened. They deposited the check into the Green Engineers PC business account. The Greens then immediately wrote a check to themselves to cover their immediate and pressing personal needs.

Nancy next met with Betty to set up their bookkeeping. She explained to Betty that she had written a check to cover their immediate personal needs. Betty understood and said that they needed to set up a file of permanent records for each worker. Whether someone was an employee or an independent contractor who provided limited services, they needed permanent records. If the IRS or state tax agency came to visit for a regular or special tax audit they would want to see them.

Basic employer records included:

1. Names, addresses, Social Security numbers, and dates of employment for paid workers (employees or independent contractors).

2. Forms W-2 and 1099 copies showing payments to workers, including any returns by the post office as undeliverable.

3. Income tax withholding certificates (Form W-4) completed by each worker.

4. Amounts and dates of wage and pension payments to workers.

5. Employee tip reports (if applicable).

6. Fringe benefits and goods or services provided to workers (in addition to cash).

7. Federal Forms 940 (annual) and 941 (quarterly) and corresponding state payroll tax forms.

8. Federal and state payroll tax deposit forms, dated with proof of payment (deposit slip, cancelled check, or financial institution receipt).

9. FICA (Social Security and Medicare) and FUTA (unemployment) taxes paid for each worker.

10. Your individual or business income tax returns on which payments to workers were claimed.

It was agreed that Betty would maintain the files and provide Nancy with a backup disc in case the government ever showed up at her door.

That discussion lead into the next item: Their home office. Tom and Nancy had been working from home and would continue to do so until they could build up the business and obtain office space. They had checked with the local authorities and their neighborhood was zoned appropriately for a home based business.

Nancy and Betty then discussed how the home office would work for them.

Home Office Deductions

Are you afraid to take the home office deduction?

Are you worried that you will be audited?

Have you heard that home office deductions are a huge red flag to the IRS?

Well over two million Americans claim a home office deduction according to the IRS. Do you think the IRS would even release that statistic if there was a problem?

If you do it right there will be no problem. If you do it right you will easily survive the 1 in 50 chance of an audit.

Face it. You've got to conduct your business from somewhere. And a legitimate expense of any business is the rent that's paid for that somewhere. So if that somewhere is from your home, take the deduction.

There are three rules to follow to do it right. They are:

1. It is the principal place of your business.

2. It is separately identifiable space in your home.

3. It is regularly and exclusively used for business.

Let's review them. Rule 1, the Principal Place of Business ("PPOB"), is best explained by examples.

- If your only location is your home office it is your PPOB.

- If you work outside of the house (as a plumber at various jobs, for example) but conduct administrative and/or management activities from a home office, it is your PPOB.

- Similarly, if you are a salesman on the road but bring work home (and don't have an additional outside office), home is your PPOB.

- However, if you do have a separate downtown office but regularly meet patients, customers or clients at your home office, the home office deduction can be taken. (Be sure to keep a log of these meetings in case of a later audit.)

- A separate freestanding building on your property (a studio or a barn) that is used regularly and exclusively for your business—even if it isn't your PPOB and you don't meet clients there—can also be deducted.

Rule 2 is the Separately Identifiable Space requirement. The best (and most common) example is the spare bedroom converted into an office. You remove the bed and the personal items, put in a desk and computer and you have a separate and easily identified home office.

A lesser example is when you occasionally use the dining room table for business. That use would not qualify as either separate or identifiable. (And please don't confuse the home office rules with the business meal rules. This is a huge area for misunderstanding and missteps. When it comes to IRS write offs you are best to just stay away from your dining room table.)

Regular and Exclusive Use is Rule 3. This rule means that you consistently do your paperwork, meet business customers (or both) at your home office. You use the space regularly for business. The exclusive part of the rule is as it sounds. You don't use the space for watching TV or playing cards. It is only for business.

If you fall within the three rules then start calculating your deduction. The IRS allows you two methods to consider.

The one most people use is the square footage method. You divide the number of square feet used for your office by the total square feet of your home. A 150 square foot office in a 1500 square foot house yields a business use percentage of 10% of your rent or depreciation (plus other home related expenses) each year for your home office.

The number of rooms method is also worth considering. Say you own an eight room house and use one room exclusively for business. Your deduction ratio (one of eight) is 12.5%. The size of the room used for your office isn't a factor, as it is with the square footage method. So be sure and run the numbers for both methods to see which one pulls in the higher percentage.

Betty ran through the issues with Nancy. Green Engineers, P.C. would use the Green's house on Elm Street as their home office. It would be their principal place of business since they had no other location. The third bedroom they converted into an office was certainly a separately identifiable space. And the space was to be regularly and exclusively used for business. They would meet customers there. They would do all their engineering work there. It was indeed their office, which happened to be in their home.

Betty calculated that the square footage method would give them their best deduction.

Home Office – Other Considerations

Where you do business will certainly affect costs, but that should not be your only concern. If you're doing business out of your house, you have to take into consideration whether your neighborhood is zoned to allow you to run a commercial enterprise from home. In some residential neighborhoods you can't display signs. Others look at increased vehicular and pedestrian traffic and parking concerns.

If you're selling goods rather than services or storing any kind of chemicals or hazardous materials you may not have the option of a home office. This means you may not be able to run your house painting business out of your house. Your local planning department or zoning board in city or county offices can tell you whether or not what you have in mind is legal. If you're in an apartment or condo, administration for the building should be able to tell you, or at least indicate what governmental body can tell you.

On the flip side, some businesses flourish in the right location. You may find you're more visible in an office building or warehouse or strip mall and that the extra traffic you bring in will more than make up the difference you're paying in rent.

One more consideration if you're thinking about a home office is separating home and home office. That isn't always as easy as it sounds.

The temptation to throw a load of laundry in while returning phone calls or working on a project might not make or break the new business, but your time is better spent pursuing your business, not washing the dog. Even if you're sure you have the discipline to run a business out of your home, you need to take into account whether your family is and whether they'll give you space and time to work.

If all systems still seem go for working from home, consider some of the following:

- For a professional address and consistency if you happen to move to a new house, get a post office box for your business (this also stops customers from coming by without an appointment, at least the first time when they don't know where you live).

- Get a second phone line for your business use.

Working from home allows you to be flexible in your schedule, cuts out any commute time and means you can run back in to "the office" if you forgot something that just can't wait till the next day. Just don't fall prey to the 24/7 aspect of working where you live—just because you're awake doesn't mean you have to be working.

It's a good idea to check in with your insurance agent and make certain your homeowner's or renter's insurance covers any liability you have if someone is hurt coming or going or in your home office. In addition, make certain the equipment, supplies and inventory of your business are covered with a policy that covers business property losses.

If you decide to work at home, make certain you're aware how much you're saving by not paying a lease or mortgage for a commercial space. Otherwise you may be convinced your business is doing well only to realize you'd be going under if you were paying for a location other than your home.

You may decide you'd rather lease or buy a commercial site for your business, especially if you want to control the property, plan to stay in the same location for an extended period of time, and especially if you're locating in an area with appreciating land values. These are all good reasons to buy. Consider leasing if you'd rather not do your own maintenance or if you think you're going to move the business, or if property values in the area you've got your eye on are dropping.

Good Reasons for Working from a Home Office

- Low overhead
- Accessibility
- No commute

Home Office Concerns

- Whether or not you possess the discipline to work amidst the distractions of your life
- Whether your family will respect your working space and working hours
- Whether or not your neighborhood is zoned in such a way you're allowed to have a commercial enterprise in your home
- Make certain you have a homeowners or renters insurance rider covering your home office and your business' inventory and equipment

Good Reasons for Working from a Rented, Leased or Purchased Commercial Location

- Visibility
- A home office/commercial venture may not be permitted in your neighborhood
- Ease in storing inventory or any hazardous materials needed in your work
- Expanding your business and hiring employees

So, as we have seen, there are a number of issues associated with home offices. Be sure to work with your advisors to make the deduction work best for you.

Now, let's consider an important part of any business operation...

Writing Contracts

When running a business it is important to have and use solid contracts. A solid contract is one that is:

1. In writing; and

2. Drafted well enough to accurately state 'the deal;' and

3. Protects your interests.

Many business owners are content to rely on oral contracts. A 'handshake' deal without the need for lawyers and time consuming back and forth negotiations is appealing to many. It is quaint to believe that people will keep their word, uphold their end of the bargain and operate with integrity at all times. We want to believe that of our partners and business associates.

The problem is that at the first sign of trouble a very large majority of people act only in their base self-interest. By not having a written contract detailing responsibilities and consequences, the finger pointing, he said-she said phase begins immediately, only to descend further into a morass of ill will and deep frustration. Who wins in such a scenario? Of course, the lawyers. But remember, those same lawyers now costing each party tens of thousands of dollars would have happily prepared a contract avoiding the whole oral contract mess for a thousand dollars or so.

The best statement about oral contracts comes from filmmaker Samuel Goldwyn, the 'G' of Metro Goldwyn Mayer, the film studio known as MGM. Goldwyn's line: "Oral contracts aren't worth the paper they are written on."

Under the law, certain contracts must be in writing. These include:

1. Contracts longer than one year, and

2. Contracts for the sale of real estate.

Other contracts may be oral but if there is a dispute certain default rules may apply. This means that if the parties start the finger pointing, he said-she said phase, state law (and the judges enforcing it) can ignore the cacophony and apply a default (or substitute or fallback) rule.

An example of this occurs with LLCs and operating agreements. Many states provide that LLCs can freely operate without the need for a written operating agreement. And many promoters sell LLCs for their ease and flexibility and lack of burdensome paperwork. But let's consider how 'easy and flexible' works in the real world.

Joe and Bob form a Nevada LLC. The promoter who sets up their entity says Nevada law does not require an operating agreement (which is true) and so the bother of actually detailing their understanding is left undone.

Joe and Bob orally agree to split ownership, management and profits on a 50/50 basis. Joe contributes 80 percent of the money. Bob contributes 20 percent of the money and the rest of Bob's contribution is based on legwork, sweat equity and time, making the business grow.

After a time Joe decides he wants to sell. Bob does not agree. But there is no operating agreement detailing ownership and management issues. Joe hires a good lawyer who exploits Nevada's default rules in such situations. Absent a written operating agreement stating it's a 50/50 deal, and now that Joe conveniently does not recollect it was ever a 50/50 deal, the fallback rule comes into play. It provides that without an operating agreement management of the LLC is determined according to the member's capital contribution to the company. Because Joe put in 80% of the money he has control. This despite the fact Bob contributed valuable, non-cash sweat equity and had an oral 50/50 deal with Joe. As a result, Joe can sell the company and keep 80% of the profits.

Interestingly, New York, a mature state in these matters, requires a written operating agreement for LLCs. And given the inequities of the results above, you can appreciate why.

The point here is that given how the default rules can apply in any contractual situation (especially to your detriment) you are better off relying on written rather than oral contracts.

What are some key points in a written contract? Since many people are pulling contracts off the internet or from form books, filling them in without the benefit of legal counsel and hoping they will work, let's review some of them. First, please know that my preference is for people to use attorneys in contractual matters involving even the slightest degree of complexity. This is not out of a desire to steer business to my profession. It is instead from witnessing the train wrecks that can occur when laymen act as lawyers and the huge amount of legal fees later spent to clean it all up.

But that won't happen to you, right?

So what needs to be in a contract? There are six main items to consider.

1. Recitals

At the beginning of a contract, recitals are used to set forth the assumptions and factual background upon which the parties are entering into the agreement. Recitals are presumed to be true, which means that later on an opposing party may be prevented from trying to show a fact to the contrary.

For example, among the series of Whereases and Now Therefores in the Recital section, you could see the following:

WHEREAS, Silverheels Inc. has experience in promoting and conducting natural history tours throughout Southern Arizona.

Suppose the other party, Desultory Tours, LLC, gets into a dispute over Silverheels' service. The contractual recital above would prevent Desultory Tours, LLC from claiming that Silverheels, Inc. had no experience conducting natural history tours and thus was in breach of contract. While Desultory could allege Silverheels was negligent in how they conducted tours they would be barred from the bigger claim that Silverheels had no idea what they were doing. Desultory agreed in the recitals that they did. Use recitals to your advantage to expand your protection and perhaps limit the claims of your opposing party.

2. Mandatory vs. Permissive (or Shall vs. Will vs. May)

Is an act to be performed with a contract required or merely permitted? It depends on the words you use. Courts will interpret the words 'Shall' and 'Will' as being mandatory, whereas the word 'May' is seen as merely allowing a certain action. Using the right word is important. Consider and contrast:

"Maria shall maintain insurance coverage at all times." with

"Maria may maintain insurance coverage at all times."

The difference here is huge. If Maria has the right coverage, as the first line requires, your claim shall be covered. If, as in the second line, she may or may not have coverage, it is permissive and up to her, you may or may not be covered.

Put yourself in the best position by utilizing mandatory words.

Interestingly, over the years attorneys have debated which word is stronger: 'shall' or 'will.' As one of my old mentors drilled into me 'shall' is a stronger and more mandatory word than 'will.' I shall always use 'shall.' But I probably will never know the difference.

Conversely, be on the lookout for times when 'shall' or 'will' is used and the word really should be 'may'. In a real estate lease consider:

"Ying may install cabinetry in the leased space, which cabinets shall become permanent fixtures." with

"Ying shall install cabinetry in the leased space, which cabinets shall become permanent fixtures."

In the first example, Ying has permission to install cabinets if he needs them. The term 'permanent fixtures' means that the improvement is permanently affixed to the premises and they will stay once the lease is term is over. If Ying installs them the landlord gets to keep them. In the second version, Ying is required to install cabinets (again, for the landlord's benefit) whether he needs them or not. Can you see the difference one word makes in all of this? Are you sure you don't want a lawyer by your side here?

3. Representations, Covenants and Conditions

These are terms that you will typically see towards the end of a contract. Know that sometimes very material terms are found near the end of a long agreement. Attorneys drafting contracts know you are tired, blurry eyed and numbed by the legalese at this point and may slip in important terms at the back. Stay focused, or come back to it later when you are fresh, so you don't miss anything.

A representation is a statement of fact that is true at the time you enter into the contract and will be true to some point in the future. A covenant is a promise to do or not do an act. A condition is an event, the occurrence or nonoccurrence of which will affect each party's duty to perform.

So how you characterize a clause—as a representation, a covenant or a condition—matters a great deal. Consider these clauses involving the same matter:

1. John represents that he is now and shall be through the performance of this contract a licensed General Contractor.
2. John covenants that he is now and shall remain a licensed General Contractor.
3. This contract is conditioned upon John maintaining his status as a licensed General Contractor.

Which statement is strongest? I prefer number 3, since if John loses his license you have a breach of contract. In number 2, John promises to be licensed. His failure to maintain a license can be a breach, but it isn't necessarily an automatic breach. Number 1 is a statement of fact. In this case, the failure to maintain a license doesn't by itself terminate the contract.

Draft according to your best interests.

4. Contract Termination

How does the contract terminate? Or, to put it in more familiar terms, how can I get out of it?

When one party has a duty to perform, a failure to perform can be a breach of contract. But if the failure is minor (a late payment, for example) the non-breaching party usually may not treat a contract as over. In many contracts you will see a cure provision. Typically, the non-breaching party notifies the breaching party they have thirty days to cure the problem (i.e. make the payment). If after thirty days the problem is not cured, then a full breach has occurred.

Some contracts will state that certain acts or failures to act are a complete breach, thus terminating the contract. They will set out all the remedies the non-breaching party is now entitled to, including money damages.

Be on the lookout for the words 'material breach.' These are inserted into contract clauses so that there can be no argument as to whether a breach is minor or material. It is material and, as you may have guessed, a material breach terminates the contract, with all remedies and damages now available to the other side.

Always look for (or draft in your own) the termination and remedies clause. At the very start you want to know how it will end.

5. Indemnify

Are you ready to reimburse the other side for any damages they suffer? An indemnity shifts the risk of loss from the damaged party (the indemnitee) to the loss assuming party (the indemnitor). Each contract for indemnity will be different according to the setting. A tenant may indemnify a landlord for losses arising inside the premises while the landlord indemnifies a tenant for losses to the exterior of the building. An indemnity can be one way, where, for example, a trucking company indemnitor agrees to cover their negligence in deliveries. The customer gives no reciprocal indemnity back to the company.

Beware of indemnities for consequential damages. Those damages that are supposedly reasonably foreseeable from the triggering event, but never are. A landlord responsible for power supply indemnification could, under such an indemnity, be responsible for the tenant's lost business profits while the power was out. This could add up to significant damages. You may want to have insurance in place to cover such risks. Or make sure the other side has insurance in place to cover the risks they are supposed to be indemnifying for your benefit.

Indemnity clauses are not 'boiler plate,' those standard clauses you see in every contract. Instead, they deal with risks, shift the responsibility for risks, and are thus important to appreciate and understand.

6. Corporate Notice

It is imperative when drafting a contract to be certain that the party is your entity. You do not want to forget the important corporate designations of Inc. or LLC or LP on your contracts.

As an example, a friend in Minden, Nevada, we'll call Paul Smith, had a company we'll name Paul Smith, Inc. He entered into a sales agreement with a vendor without carefully reviewing the document. Instead of the party being listed as Paul Smith, Inc., the contract read Paul Smith. When there was a dispute they sued Paul Smith, the individual, not the company. The court agreed that individual responsibility was appropriate. Nowhere on the contract did it list Paul Smith, Inc. Without such notice the vendor had every reason to believe they were dealing with Paul Smith as an individual. Which, of course, means that Paul Smith was individually liable.

Three little letters in the contract could have saved him from such a problem: I-N-C. It may also be L-L-C or even L-P. Corporate notice is imperative. Include it in every contract.

Bobo and Morton

Bobo and Morton knew they needed to get Mrs. Muller a contract. They had no idea how to write one. Bobo had heard that you could find form contracts on the internet.

Morton found one within three minutes. He spent another minute tailoring it to read as follows:

Service Agreement

Company (Glockenspiel Ventura) agrees to provide house-sitting services to Client. Client (Mrs. Greta Muller) agrees to pay Company for services rendered. Either party may cancel the agreement at any time.
Time is of the essence of this agreement.

_____   _____
Mrs. Greta Muller   Glockenspiel Ventura

Morton thought this wasn't too bad for four minutes work. Bobo had no idea what the last sentence about time meant but it sounded really cool.

They decided to run the contract by Aunt Maddy, who had seen a contract or two in her day. Aunt Maddy was glad to see them, and was especially glad to see the 'first draft' of their contract, as she called it. Bobo's aunt diplomatically suggested that she have her lawyer review to see if there was anything that needed to be included in the second draft. When Bobo said they couldn't afford an attorney she told the boys not to worry, it was her treat. They thanked her profusely.

Bobo asked if the lawyer could keep the last part of the contract, the part about the essence of time, the same. Aunt Maddy said she would see to it.

In a day, Aunt Maddy called the boys back. She explained her lawyer had some spare time and had knocked out a second draft. The contract was now three pages long and had recitals and representations and termination provisions. Time was still of the essence, and the signature block was the same.

Aunt Maddy noted that her attorney said the contract could be twenty pages or longer. But it was felt that for this type of service the people hiring them wouldn't want to wade through a long, verbose contract. So they made a strategic decision to keep it at or under three pages. By using a smaller font size and narrow margins (an old attorney trick and the opposite of what all of us did in school when writing a paper) the contract came in at three pages.

Bobo and Morton then went to see Mrs. Muller. They had business cards and a contract. She was very pleased by their progress and signed up right away. The boys would begin in several days. When she returned from the Caribbean, if they had done a good job, she had other potential clients to refer to them.

Rich Dad Tips

- Your home office deduction, while subject to certain rules, can be very useful. Work with your advisors to get it right.
- Pay attention to your contracts. Done right they are your friends. Done wrong...
- Know that certain contracts must be in writing including contracts for the sale of real estate.

After all this forming don't forget the planning...

Chapter Seven

Second Week

Business Plans

A business plan is not a formal necessity for starting a business, but it sure will help. Most business owners don't want to take the time to plan at the beginning. They want to jump into this thing they're passionate about. They want to get to the selling of cute things, the giving of advice, the making of deals—whatever the passions are that drive their businesses. However, once a business starts, it takes on a momentum of its own. And that momentum often feels like a snowball racing downhill.

Taking the time to create a business plan (or hiring someone to do so) before you start thick into business offers a variety of benefits. It can assist you in your startup, your day-to-day business, in acquiring financing for the business, in working with a business partner, even in determining what you're going to charge for your services. Other benefits include:

- A business plan creates an outline and a narrative for your business.

- Raises questions and guides you through answering them.

- Makes you stop and consider legal and financial considerations.

- Allows you to more clearly communicate your business' possibilities with potential investors, partners and even customers.

There are entire books written about how to write a great business plan (including my own *Writing Winning Business Plans*), but here's a basic outline:

- Cover sheet: business name, address, contact information for the business and the principals
- Statement of purpose: a mission statement for the business, including goals and timelines
- Table of contents of the business plan
- Executive summary:
  - goals
  - corporate structure
  - ownership
  - financials
  - marketing plan
  - operations
- Business background
- Marketing plan
- Action plans
- Financial statements and projections
- Supporting documents:
  - personal financial information including tax returns for previous years
  - copies of existing paperwork such as transfer of ownership for an existing business or a franchise contract
  - leases for physical locations (if applicable)
  - licenses from governing bodies
  - legal documents regarding corporate structure
  - resumes of the principals

Alana and Sherri

Alana and Will were reviewing the book *Writing Winning Business Plans*. On a very basic level it made sense that they should have a business plan. They both wanted to make the salon work and if having a plan brought them closer to that goal all the better.

Will knew that there were template business plans for common businesses—like a beauty salon—that you could buy on the internet. After searching various websites they bought one for $19.99. The software program had all the issues they thought they would need to deal with as salon owners and the ability to format their own specific information into the plan.

Alana and Will weren't sure who besides themselves and Sherri would see the plan. But they felt that by doing one they would at least have a better idea of where they were headed and what to look out for along the way. It took Alana and Will about a week to fill in all the information. They had fun together doing it. And Will asked some pointed questions that forced Alana to think through some potentially sticky issues. When they were done they printed it out and set it on the counter by the phone in the kitchen.

A week later they had a big extended family barbeque at their place. Cousins and kids were running through the house. Sherri and Clint, along with their young daughter, Ellie, showed up, as did Big Jim. The adults had a few drinks and the party in the kitchen grew louder.

Until Big Jim said in his booming voice, "Good on you! You wrote a business plan!" He was holding up the spiral bound plan that had been innocently left by the phone. The party went silent as Big Jim inspected the document. "Good job, girls. Really good job."

The rest of the family crowded around to check out the plan. There were nods of approval and best wishes extended for the new business. Alana proudly said that Will helped them write it.

A few minutes later Clint pulled Will aside. He demanded to know if Will actually helped write the plan.

Will said he did, adding it would help the sisters do better in the business.

Clint asked if he wanted the sisters to succeed. "Of course I do," said Will. "Don't you?" Clint only glowered and walked off.

Attracting Customers and Clients

For some entrepreneurs, going out, meeting new people, networking and finding new clients and customers is the best part of the whole job. Others want to hide under the bed at the mere mention of the word "networking," not to mention "selling."

There's no way around it. If you want to be in business, you need customers. There has to be someone who wants the goods or services you produce, whether you're a multimillion dollar industry in the making or working part time while your kids are in school.

Remember the hobby loss rules?

The IRS distinguishes between a business and a hobby. The burden of proving you're actively engaged in trying to make a profit falls on you as the taxpayer. If the IRS determines you're just dabbling in a sideline enterprise and not in it to make money, you'll lose your business deductions. Actively seeking clients, actually having a client list and work coming in does more than line your coffers; it also protects your business by making it appear to actually be a business, one actively engaged in trying to turn a profit. A hobby, by comparison, generally costs more than it earns, without necessarily having the expectation of making money, or even making back what's been spent.

It isn't always about making money. Sometimes it's about creating the business that's going to one day make the money. A novelist who's selling short stories to make a name for himself isn't making a living yet but he's showing the effort he's putting forth with piles of rejection letters and acceptances in magazines and story anthologies. A dog grooming enterprise just getting off to a start may boast nothing more than a handful of clippers and some strangely sheered poodles, but if there's a paper trail, invoices and canceled checks, a business license with the proper authorities and other evidence the shareholders are trying to make a go of it, then most likely the business will pass the "trying to make a profit" test. According to the Internal Revenue Code §183: Activities Not Engaged in For Profit (ATG), "The taxpayer must devote time to the business in the honest belief that the business will sometime in the future become profitable. It is necessary for the taxpayer to show what their projected profit is expected to be." Customers or clients protect your tax position by proving that, however little your company might be making as a startup, the idea is to create profit.

But if the notion of trying to sell yourself (your corporation and your services) is overwhelming, take it a step at a time. Make it a goal to attend chamber and business mixers, to learn to network and to find customers and clients.

When you're promoting your business, keep in mind some of the basics to set you apart from everyone else. Ideally, you've already listed several of these in the marketing section of your business plan:

- What makes my business different from the competition?
- What do I offer that my competition does not?
- What solutions can I offer to clients and customers to fit their business needs?

Get Known

Next, how can you more broadly make your business known? What's unique about your business, different enough that a local newspaper or magazine would be willing to do a story about you? Are there local or regional events your business fits into or identifies with? Do you offer something specific to the area where you live? Does your business have anything to do with current events? Consider hiring a public relations firm to get the word out about you and your business.

Get Attention

Don't forget advertising, but don't buy ads willy-nilly. Scope out the magazines, newspapers, online and other media channels that most fit your business. Before you pay for an ad, understand the audience of that medium and whether or not they're the right audience for your business. You'll likely only get so much money to spend. So target your spending to reach your best niche market.

Get Together

Learn how to network. If your client base is likely to come from a specific industry, is there an organization or association for that industry that meets regularly? Can non-members attend meetings? If you choose to attend industry association networking meetings, you need to attend at least three to six months in a row. You need to establish a presence. Know that it takes more than one contact—and often as many as four to six—to actually turn a contact into a client.

Once you've met a potential client or customer at a networking event, follow up within a reasonable amount of time, either asking for a simple meeting or suggesting solutions your business has that can assist them. During all of your networking forays make certain you have plenty of business cards. (Again, be sure that your business cards, with your corporate logo, include your corporate designation: Inc., LLC, or LP. Always protect your corporate veil by giving corporate notice.)

Practice your presentation before you're face to face with a potential client or customer. Understand how you sell best. A good book on this issue is Blair Singer's *Sales Dogs* (BZK Press, 2012). You know your business inside and out, but you need to prove that to someone who you're hoping will trust you with their business. Hemming and hawing doesn't inspire confidence. Look your new acquaintance in the eye, don't fidget, and overcome the need to be humble. Explain why your business is special, why what you do is important and why you love doing it—and why you're the right person to provide this service to this customer.

And while you're doing all of this, let the passion that drove you to incorporate your own business shine through. Enthusiasm is contagious. Follow up with a handwritten note on business letterhead thanking them for taking the time to meet you.

Maintaining Existing Clients

Establishing a business relationship with a new client or customer is hard work, and most of the time you'd probably rather be doing the actual work of your business. Which is why maintaining the clients and customers you already have is better than needing to find new ones.

If your business is your passion, doing the work should be more pleasurable than painful. Keep your conversations with clients upbeat and positive and mention everything you loved about the current project for that client. Never complain about the project. (As Henry Ford famously said: "Never complain. Never explain.") If you're having trouble with the task, ask for clarification or guidelines.

When working with your clients:

- Go above and beyond. If you can offer just a little something extra with each project, do so.

- Be consistent. Keep your policies and procedures the same from project to project. (Except if you can find a way to improve!)

- Listen well, ask questions and make sure you understand what the client wants.

- Be on time – or early. Deadlines are hugely important. Getting the work done when promised can be more important than anything else. If you can beat a deadline, great. Otherwise, if you promised it on the fifth, have it done on or before the fifth.

- Follow up. Once you've finished a project, follow up with anything extra you can think of, and make certain your client knows if he or she needs anything else on this project, you'll be glad to provide it.

- Stay in touch. Without bombarding your clients, it's fine to send along a helpful email or a link to an article on a topic regarding their industry, along with a short note that you saw the item and thought of your client.

For every step of the process of finding potential clients, working through projects and invoicing, make certain your corporate identity remains in full view. Invoice with letterhead showing your corporate name, your corporate address and your EIN. Make certain your letterhead, notepaper, business cards and all related materials are clearly marked with your entity designation of Inc. or LLC or the like.

Tom and Nancy

During the Righteous Rock lawsuit Tom and Nancy kept a very low profile. The whole affair was embarrassing and damaging. They did not even circulate among their close friends. Everyone wanted to talk about it—except them.

Now that the lawsuit was behind them and they were incorporated with a new company, it was time to get out. It was time to slowly let people know they were back.

Tom and Nancy renewed their membership with the local Chamber of Commerce. The meetings and get-togethers had always been positive and were often fun. They began going to these meetings and their friends were glad to see them and introduced them to new friends.

They also rejoined their local branch of the American Society of Civil Engineers. The ASCE had workshops and continuing education programs and gatherings for engineers in the area. By showing up to these events they both let their peers know they were back and would some-day generate business from the contacts they had and would make. Tom and Nancy each joined a committee within the Chapter to give back and to further their circle of contacts.

Nancy's friend Gina was in a lead group that met every Tuesday morning. Like most lead groups, there was one person from each profession represented in the group. Gina's group had a lawyer, a real estate broker, an IT consultant, a sign guy and twenty other professionals filling their specific slots. The group did not have an engineer. Gina said the lawyer and real estate broker would welcome having an engineer for referrals. Gina also said it was a great way to meet other local business owners and professionals. Nancy knew this was correct and joined Gina's lead group.

The benefits of these groups were not immediate. Both Tom and Nancy knew it took time. People needed to get to know them and have a sense that they would be around. Flash in the pan types did not do well in this milieu. The slow-and-steady types did.

And over time, Tom and Nancy did well.

Rich Dad Tip

- Almost every profession has its own trade group. Just as the engineers do, lawyers, marketers, restaurateurs and scores of other businesses have groups for learning, sharing and mingling. Some even offer lower rates on group health insurance.

- All that networking requires is a smile and a business card. You may not know it but you are probably good at it.

Vehicle and Transportation Deductions

When it comes to getting from here to there and back again, you have a variety of choices. If you use public transportation as an independent contractor, work with your CPA to save. If your work location changes as you move from project to project working for this company and that company, you can probably claim the deductions for using public transportation. Employees can claim public transportation to and from work as a deduction, but a business owner can't claim commuting miles as mileage. So can a shareholder-employee claim public transportation deductions? A good question. Since the tax laws seem to change in this area, check with your tax professional if you're doing the environmentally conscious thing and taking public transportation.

If you choose to use your own vehicle, you can allow your corporate entity to purchase or lease the vehicle, or you can use your personal vehicle for business use and keep records to track business and personal use. Your corporate entity can also choose to lease the car from you.

If the Company buys the car you use, take advantage of the write offs. For cars that weigh under 6,000 pounds you can depreciate the cost over time. For example, a car put into service in 2011 allows the company to write off $11,060 in the first year, $4,900 in the second year, $2,950 in year three and $1,775 in the fourth and later years. Trucks and vans have their own schedules.

These rules do change so check with your tax advisor for the most current regulations. Also check out IRS Publication 946: How to Depreciate Property for examples and an understanding of this area.

Standard Mileage Rate vs. Actual Expenses

If you own your vehicle and use it for business purposes you can be reimbursed by the company. There are two ways to do it. Figuring out whether to use the standard mileage rate deduction or take actual expenses as a deduction is actually easy—it comes down to which is going to give you a better deduction.

Standard Mileage Rate

The standard mileage rate is now 55.5 cents a mile as of this writing and to determine this number you need to keep a daily account of business miles driven or use the 90-day method to determine average miles driven. You also need your year-start and year-end odometer reading on the vehicle, and for your tracked business and personal miles to add up to that number.

Keep in mind that if you're using this method, commuting to your corporate headquarters is not deductible. Traveling to meet with your professional team, to pick up supplies, to meet with clients or for business travel away from your office, however, are all deductible miles. If you work primarily out of a home office, your miles or cost of travel between that office and other business destinations (meetings, post office, bank, office supply store) should be deductible expenses.

Also keep in mind that if you leave your office, drive to a meeting and then drive home, these are allowable miles. But if you stop between the meeting and home to pick up cat food (or anything else), the miles from the grocery store to home are personal miles and not deductible.

If you're using the standard mileage deduction, you can still deduct:

- Interest on car loans
- Registration fees
- Parking costs and tolls encountered while driving to and from business

But you can't deduct insurance premiums or depreciation. Remember that whatever you do use as deductions is only the percentage of business use for the vehicle; the personal use percentage is not deductible.

Actual Expenses

The second method is the actual expense method. Actual expenses include:

- Gas and oil
- Maintenance and repairs
- Tires and brakes
- Registration and vehicle taxes
- Personal property taxes
- License fees
- Loan interest
- Lease payments
- Depreciation
- Any rent paid for garage space
- Tolls and parking fees

The percentage of business use determines the percentage of actual expenses that can be used for deduction. The math is fairly simple. Here's an example of how it works:

Yearly expenses:

Gas, oil, maintenance, repairs	$4,000
Fees and taxes	$ 300
Loan interest/insurance	$1,800
Actual expenses	$6,100
Total mileage	20,000
Business mileage	14,506

Divide the total mileage by the business mileage for the percentage of business mileage. So, 14,506 divided by 20,000 is 72 percent. For your deduction, 72 percent of $6,100 = $4392.

Using the same figures, if you'd used the standard mileage rate (55.5 cents a mile) for your 14,506 business miles (55.5 x 14,506) your deduction would be $8050.83.

Note that the more economical and environmentally friendly your car is, the lower your actual expenses are going to be and, therefore, the lower your deduction if you choose actual expenses. Standard mileage may work out better for you, so select that method.

There's nothing to prevent you from changing how you deduct for vehicle use. If when you place the car in service to the corporation (and you need to record the date as part of your record keeping) the car is new and gas efficient, it may be best to use actual expenses and write off depreciation for the first few years. As depreciation deductions fall as the car ages, switch to standard mileage rate if there's a better deduction there. There's no penalty for switching systems—just record everything and keep driving.

Just Whose Car Is It?

An entity can either own a vehicle or, if it is owned by an individual, pay for its use.

If the corporation owns the vehicles then it's the corporation that deducts according to actual operating expenses and is limited strictly to business-use expenses for deduction, though it can deduct all operating expenses without regard to the percentage of business use. The personal use portion is considered compensation to the employee, which is properly reported (and taxed) as such.

A shareholder-employee using a personal vehicle should be reimbursed (upon request) by the corporation for business miles at the standard mileage rate. The corporation takes the deduction for vehicle expenses and the employee's reimbursement is not considered taxable income. If the employee or shareholder-employee is required to use a personal vehicle for un-reimbursed business use, the employee may claim an un-reimbursed employer expense deduction on Schedule A of Form 1040.

For a partnership or LLC, the partner or member with un-reimbursed vehicle expenses claims a deduction on Schedule E of Form 1040.

Whether you buy or lease the vehicle makes no difference for determining mileage rate or actual expenses—both apply. However, if you use the standard mileage rate, you cannot deduct the lease payment amount. Also, deductions for depreciation are not allowed for leased vehicles, but the business portion of the lease amount can be deducted.

However you choose to take vehicle deductions for your corporation, remember that record keeping is key—the more and better you document your deductions, your expenses and miles and vehicle use, the better you protect your business and your corporate veil.

Bobo and Morton

Bobo and Morton had a Ford F150 Super Crew pick-up from their dog breeding days. Their parents, the Trenthams and the McGills, had written off the vehicle and forgotten about it. The boys had no intention of refreshing their memories.

But when Bobo and Morton met with Aunt Maddy's bookkeeper the issue came up. Horatio Manfred was a stickler for the correct and the precise. He was proudly bald, wore horn rimmed reading glasses, a bright bow tie and a white starched shirt whose creases could cause a paper cut. There was not one shred of dust in his perfectly ordered office. Aunt Maddy had said there were only two bookkeepers to use in their area: Lisa Shults MacLeod and Horatio Manfred. Their families had always used Horatio Manfred, and so would the boys. Aunt Maddy had said he was tidy in his appearance and his bookkeeping.

As he sat in Horatio's perfect office, Morton wondered to himself if such a neat freak would ever want to take on the messes he and Bobo seemed to create. Horatio Manfred then promptly spoke up and said he liked a challenge now and then. Morton next wondered if this book-minder was also a mind-reader. Then again, Morton silently acknowledged that the two slovenly 19 year olds before Mr. Manfred would probably prompt such a statement.

On the issue of the Ford F150 Horatio asked who paid the insurance on it. The boys didn't know. Horatio peered over his reading glasses and in a less professional setting would have said, "Are you kidding me?" But he continued on and asked who held the truck title. Again, the boys did not know.

Horatio laid out a plan for the boys. He would have the truck title transferred into the C corporation. The corporation would pay for all the expenses—insurance, gas, everything. The boys would record when they used the truck for personal use, which would then be considered as personal compensation to them and a taxable item.

So if they went to a dance they would record in a journal the miles they drove. Horatio then smiled and said that if they went to a dance and handed out a business card then the miles would be for a business purpose. Morton nodded in assent. They would be handing out a lot of business cards.

Horatio said that his service included all billing. The boys were going to be too busy maintaining properties to get the billing out on time. Bobo said he had no idea what billing involved and was glad someone else was doing it. Horatio said for now it entailed the boys turning in time sheets to his office. He would take care of the rest.

Horatio then mentioned that the next step was to offer credit from the corporation and to build business credit within the corporation. The boys were totally confused.

Horatio said that would be for another day. He sent them off to their first job.

When the boys arrived at Mrs. Muller's estate she was watching as her large suitcases were being loaded into a Town Car. She was harried but glad to see them. She needed to get to the airport and had not had time to take the dogs to the vet for kenneling. She noticed their Ford F150 and asked if they could get the dogs to the vet. When Bobo said they would, she told them to add it to the bill and to include their mileage charge.

Bobo asked if Horatio Manfred would know that. Mrs. Muller laughed and said that Mr. Manfred not only knew it but would certainly bill it. She was glad they were in good hands, waved goodbye and sped off to the airport.

Glockenspiel Ventura began its first job.

Rich Dad Tips

- Consider doing a business plan right from the start. It will help focus your attention on what is important.
- As you start out, always think of ways to meet potential clients.
- Work with your advisors to maximize your auto allowances.

And with the first job comes more record keeping...

Chapter Eight

One Month

Tom and Nancy

Nancy was on the phone with her mother. The extended family down in Texas was wondering when she and Tom would be having children. Nancy shrugged off the comment and said they had their hands full with Dooger and a new business. Kids would have to wait.

Nancy concluded the call by saying she had some books to take care of. "At the library?" asked her mother. Nancy laughed. The thought of simply turning all these financial books back to a local branch after a two week check-out period was appealing.

Tom and Nancy drove to Betty's Bookkeeping. Tom wanted to know about their first month requirements. Nancy wanted to discuss their ongoing and never ending bookkeeping requirements.

Betty said that every month business owners had to deposit each employee's withheld income taxes and FICA contributions (Social Security and Medicare) to their IRS-approved bank. Nancy asked if their local bank was IRS-approved and Betty said it was. Most banks got themselves approved as this was an important business banking function—taking in withholding and payroll taxes and forwarding those monies to the US Treasury.

Nancy said that they hadn't started paying themselves yet. They took the one $5,000 payment at week one to pay various expenses but to date hadn't made a payroll payment. Betty said that was fine. When they started paying themselves was when they would have to make the monthly deposits for income tax withholding and FICA payments.

Betty said she would need a Form W-4 filled out for each of them for her records. (Visit IRS.gov for the most current IRS forms.) This form, she explained, was used to calculate the correct amount of tax withholding for each employee. She noted that if someone was single they could still claim more than one exemption. Betty also mentioned that if they hired new employees in the future a W-4 would have to be filled out for each new hire. As well, she needed a Form I-9, the employment eligibility form, for each employee. Betty said it was all just standard stuff.

And in concluding that meeting, Tom and Nancy assumed that all would be properly covered.

Rich Dad Tip

- Remember to verify Social Security Numbers. Not everyone gives out their correct Social. Others make mistakes and transpose numbers.

- You can call the Social Security Administration at 800-772-1213 to verify a worker's number.

- These steps, along with scrutinizing your I-9 forms, is a good way to insure you don't violate any laws against hiring undocumented workers.

Bobo and Morton

Bobo and Morton had done a fine job housesitting for Mrs. Muller. She had told them so by saying that since nothing happened, the plants were alive and the dogs still barked, they had done their job.

Mrs. Muller gave the boys the names of three other friends who were going to Paris and Alaska and all sorts of other places who needed their homes watched over and their animals and property taken care of. The boys were happy that she had faith in them.

Mrs. Muller had two other requests of them. First, she wanted them to take an inventory of all her household assets. Her insurance company insisted that with the size of her estate and the value of her insurance policy a complete inventory had to be done. She would be away again in two weeks and while she was gone she wanted the boys to do a complete inventory of all her furnishings in her 60-room house.

Morton said they would do it but thought it might take a while. Mrs. Muller assured them that they would be paid for the time.

Mrs. Muller indicated the issue of payment led to her second request. Many of the people she would be referring would be gone for several months at a time. Most of them were all members of The Thracian Club and would be good for the money. But to really make this work they would have to be able to extend credit.

Bobo and Morton both looked puzzled. They had used credit cards before but had never thought about being the ones actually giving credit to others. Mrs. Muller clarified that if Glockenspiel Ventura could do the work and then not get paid for 30 to 90 days she could get them more clients. She wondered if the boys would do that.

Bobo and Morton hemmed and hawed as they considered it all. But if they took in more work, they concluded that it probably made sense. Mrs. Muller suggested the boys speak with Horatio Manfred, their bookkeeper, to work out the details.

The grand dame then sped off in her Bentley, leaving the boys to consider the prospects of more work.

Extending Credit

If you're selling a product or service, you may eventually need to extend credit to customers. And knowing the ins and outs of offering credit can mean the difference between that for-profit business and one that's unintentionally not-for-profit.

Before you start extending credit to customers, make sure you have credit applications for them to fill out. Make certain you get those applications returned and fully completed, especially the trade and bank reference sections and the consent for your business to run a credit check. (A sample credit application is found at www.CorporateDirect.com.) Then use the information on the credit application to run a credit check with one of the national credit reporting agencies.

If your customers are individuals rather than businesses, a regular credit application will ask for name and contact information, probably a Social Security Number and personal and professional references. (Know that in some states, such as California, people do not have to give out their Social Security Number in certain situations.)

A business credit application will ask the name and address of the authorized representative of the business, as well as the employer ID number, the type of business entity, parent company if the business is a subsidiary, name and contact information for the principal responsible for business transactions, bank references and trade references. And remember the corporate veil? If you sue a company that has no assets, what do you get? Not much. So be sure and ask: "Is the business big enough to pay us if there's a problem? If not, is the business willing to give us a personal guarantee of one of the owners?"

In Chapter Four we discussed trying to avoid giving personal guarantees. Well, now that you are extending credit the shoe is on the other foot. You want a personal guarantee from the other guy. When you have a personal guarantee the corporate veil of protection the other guy may assert is less of an issue. You have the alternate recourse of going after an individual's assets instead of solely relying on the business' assets. So be sure to ask for a personal guarantee if it is appropriate.

You can also have your customers sign a security agreement. By retaining a security interest in the product you sold if you're not paid you can take back the product. The agent for the business you're extending credit to signs the security agreement and a UCC-1 financing statement. While these forms are online, and available through your Secretary of State's office, it's a good idea to sit down with your legal and financial consultants before embarking on the loaning of credit. Learn the ins and outs, get your hands on the right forms and go forward cautiously.

Credit and Collections

You should also be familiar with some of the laws regulating credit and collections before you extend credit to any of your customers.

The Truth in Lending Act was passed in 1968. This federal act requires all lending arrangements and costs be spelled out clearly for consumers. Most specific requirements of the Act are found in Regulation Z. The Fair Debt Collection Practices Act was added in 1978 to the Consumer Credit Protection Act and is aimed at abusive and harassing debt collection practices. Finally, the Fair Credit Reporting Act regulates the collection, use and dissemination of consumer credit information. For more information on these federal laws see Garrett Sutton's *The ABCs of Getting Out of Debt*.

Getting Paid

It seems simple enough to get paid. You do the work, you submit the invoice. And usually it works that way. But know that businesses go out of business when they don't get paid.

You may expect to receive a blank Form W-9 from the company you are doing business with. This form is used to request your tax ID number (as an entity, your EIN). Your bookkeeper may also send out the same forms to businesses you are doing business with. In all of this form sending, be sure you exercise caution. If you don't know who is asking for your information and why they want it, find out. The information on a W-9 is sensitive and should be kept confidential. It should only be transmitted in a secure manner to those who really need it.

That said, if you're working with the same company on an ongoing basis, make certain you're billing consistently, at regular intervals, rather than hit or miss invoices the billing department won't know to expect. The easier you make it for them to pay you, the more likely the other business is to pay you on time.

If you're not paid within your expected timeline, send a follow-up invoice. Make sure you record your invoices in the same place every time, that they're clear and easy to follow, and that you record payments as soon as they're received. It's not only part of the bookkeeping system you're required to keep, it's also the easiest way to see at a glance if you've been paid.

If the follow-up invoice doesn't reap results, and you've followed up your follow-up with a phone call to the accounts payable department in the other company, you can (and should) take more action, including:

• Mailing a collection letter.

• Asking your attorney to draft a letter of demand.

• Retaining a collection agency.

Your company did the work. You deserve to be paid. You can work with the other company if you want. But just remember that if the bill is not paid within 90 days your chances of ever collecting on it go down dramatically. Let it be known that you cannot do any further work until you are paid. If you need to save face with the customer say that your partner (even if you don't have one) is the one who won't allow any more work to be performed until payment is received.

The real or imaginary 'partner' who won't allow you to work for free is always a great strategy. And it works in all sorts of settings: No discount pricing, no variation on terms, no agreement on delays, etc. I have clients who at the start of their business dealings will say they have a partner (even though they don't) just so they can later use the good partner/bad partner strategy.

When customers ask if they can meet this partner my clients will say the person is a silent partner. They put up the money and don't want to be involved. But, my clients will say, because they put up the money this silent partner has a say with regard to terms, discounts and _____ (fill in the blank as needed.) I have seen a number of clients save face while collecting by using the silent/nonexistent partner strategy.

Building Business Credit

When you're starting out you may not want to risk everything you own on your new business. Because you may not want every last personal dollar going into the effort, building business credit is important.

Business (or corporate) credit, established correctly and used with caution, will allow you to borrow under your corporate entity's name rather than your own, protecting your personal assets and your personal credit score.

Corporate credit also allows you to grow your business. Remember just a few pages earlier when we were looking at your company extending credit to other customers. You were going to run a credit check to see how they measured up. To see if they were likely to pay you what was owed. Well, now the shoe is back again on the other foot. We want you to look good to those who may extend credit to you. And by getting that credit your business will be able to accelerate its growth.

If your business has properly established corporate credit, you've managed to obtain credit through vendors and banks or loan companies that report to the business credit reporting agencies. If you've successfully obtained credit through these organizations, it probably means your business at least appears to have a solid foundation.

Established corporate credit also means you've learned to create the kind of financial statements you need in order to qualify for credit. In addition, you probably have credit reports on your corporation from one of the three major business credit reporting agencies.

Keep in mind that business credit reporting agencies operate differently than those that monitor your personal credit. For one thing, no federal law or regulatory agency oversees the creation of business credit reports, so accuracy is not guaranteed. Some of these agencies also combine your corporate credit rating with your personal, so keeping your personal credit above reproach is important in keeping up your corporate image and your corporate credit.

We have gone into building business credit in more detail in the companion book *Start Your Own Corporation*.

Alana and Sherri

The first month had been a whirlwind of activity. Sherri and Alana had to get into their new space at the Crossroads Center, clean it out and furnish it. They had to get the city license and permits and inspections done so they could open. In three weeks the space looked great, and potential new customers were peering in the window to see the progress and determine when they would be open.

Sherri and Alana had an innate sense of marketing. They planned a SalonAlana Grand Opening Celebration and invited everyone and anyone to attend. It was quite a party. Both Jay, their attorney, and Big Jim, their father, showed up. Alana's husband Will was there. Noticeably, Sherri's husband Clint did not make an appearance. Still, free wine and hors d'oeuvres helped attract a large crowd of well-wishers, local merchants and members of the Chamber of Commerce. The girls had a friend stand at the register during the huge affair to fill in the appointment book. When they opened their doors two days later they had 45 appointments scheduled, and immediate revenues.

This was a good start. But Sherri knew they needed to do more. They needed to have a robust website that would allow for online appointment scheduling and ecommerce sales of their upcoming line of beauty products.

Both Jay and Big Jim, as well as everyone they talked to about websites, said to be careful. Web developers always seemed to over-promise and under-deliver. One month projects always seemed to drag out for expensive months on end.

Jay had given Sherri an article he had written for clients venturing into internet activities. At the time she thought it was very nice of him to take such an interest in her business. Now it was time to read the report.

Steps for Maximizing and Protecting Your Website

1. Register the Site

Assuming you have already obtained the domain name and filed for the trademark, the next step is to register your site with major search engines. (Remember, you want to be found.) Here are some locations for submission:

Google: http://www.google.com/services/biz2.html

Lycos: http://www.domains.lycos.com/

Yahoo: http://search.yahoo.com/info/submit.html

2. Use Disclaimers and Warnings

If your site provides information others may rely on, you may want to include a warning notice and a disclaimer stating that you are not responsible if they do rely on it. The following is one of many examples:

"Warning - The information on this web site is protected by the Copyright Laws of the United States, 17 U.S.C. Section 101 et seq. Reproduction and distribution of the information on this web site without the prior written consent of the owners is strictly prohibited and may subject the infringer to civil and criminal penalties. SalonAlana, LLC. hereby disclaims any and all liability with regard to the accuracy and completeness of the information presented on this web site including, but not limited to, direct, indirect and consequential damages."

3. Use the Copyright Notice

Copyrights protect your written words. You can file for a copyright with the U.S. Library of Congress at copyright.gov. Even if you don't get around to filing (and you should, as it offers greater protections) you should always place a copyright notice, at the very least, at the bottom of your home page.

The notice should read as follows:

"Copyright ©2012, SalonAlana, LLC. All Rights Reserved"

By including this information you are providing the necessary notice to protect your content.

4. Written Agreements with Employees

If you are going to use employees to develop your website you need written agreements with them to protect your position. First of all, the work performed and the materials developed must be described as "works made for hire," meaning you paid them to do it so they don't get to claim the work as theirs. You want the agreement to state that they assign any and all rights to the work to you, the employer. (Without this language, less scrupulous types will claim that they own what they developed. Don't give anyone that type of leverage over you.) You also want the agreement to state that they will keep the information confidential and that your employee won't develop a competing website for a reasonable period of time (usually two years or less).

5. Understand Your Web Development Agreement

If you are paying someone to create and develop your website you will want an agreement in place. You will include the 'work for hire' language and other points found in number 4 above. This agreement (which you may want your attorney's help with) should also make very clear that you own all rights—trademark, copyright, everything—to your site. As web developers in my experience tend to over promise and under deliver you need the agreement to set out dates for completion. Don't pay the entire fee up front. Work to pay the majority of the fees only when the website has been completely constructed to your satisfaction. The agreement should also set forth responsibility and pricing for maintenance and corrections. Work towards allowing your own staff access to the site for corrections instead of paying larger outside service fees.

6. Understand Your Web Hosting Agreement

A key concern is whether you can easily get out of the contract if the web hosting company is not performing to your standards. If you can cancel at any time 'with or without cause' (meaning for a good reason or no reason at all) you will be in better shape than having to wait for a 90 day escape clause to expire. Another issue will be the standards of performance, including speed and back up protections, to be provided. Again, this may be a contract you have your attorney review.

Sherri finished reading the report. She liked how Jay presented everything in a clear and understandable manner. He was totally different than her brooding and beer soaked husband, Clint.

In the last week Clint had been livid about the name of the business. He said SalonAlana gave Sherri no credit. He said his friends thought Sherri just worked for Alana.

Sherri could care less about such appearances. She wanted a solid business that could provide her with a steady income. If a salon named SalonAlana brought in the customers, that was all that mattered. She worried that someday Clint would not be there for her and their daughter Ellie.

All she wanted was a security that did not rely on Clint...

Chapter Nine

First Quarter

Tom and Nancy

Betty at Betty's Bookkeeping called Nancy to discuss the Quarterly Payroll tax payments. Every three months someone from the business (usually the bookkeeper or controller) had to file a Form 941 with the IRS. This form reported federal payroll tax deposits (income tax withholding and FICA taxes) to the IRS.

Nancy said that other than the one $5,000 payment in the first week to pay for expenses they still had not paid themselves. Betty said that was fine. They would file the next quarter.

Importantly, Betty did not file the Form 941 for the First Quarter.

Personal Responsibility for Payroll Taxes

When discussing payroll taxes and your potential personal liability for them it helps to appreciate a very basic point: The federal government sees payroll taxes as their money. When you work, you earn a percentage for the government. They are struggling enough to cover all the Social Security and Medicare promises they have made to America's citizens. The last thing they want is any guff from you which keeps them from getting this money out to voters. That 15.3% of payroll: That is their money. It is not yours. While they'll let you have your share, they'd better get theirs. And they'd better get it like clockwork.

Like any good racket, they can get very angry when they don't get their cut. You don't pay, you don't play. The IRS can, and does, shut businesses down for failing to pay them their money. And they routinely hold officers and directors and others personally liable for unpaid taxes.

But, you say, "I have a limited liability entity. Aren't I protected?"

No, you are not.

You can't hide behind a corporation or an LLC when it comes to payroll taxes. An entity does not shield against the Trust Fund Recovery Penalty (TFRP). The IRS can hold an owner or employee personally responsible for the TFRP. All they have to prove is that 1) the responsible party was supposed to make the payroll deposits and 2) the responsible party willfully did not take care of making the payments.

The IRS does not lose these cases. They have ten years to collect the TFRP. And they can seize almost any assets from any responsible party to get it paid.

As well, the term 'responsible party' is quite broad for the IRS. Not only will they go after the owners of the business but they will pursue bookkeepers and office managers. Outside attorneys and accountants have also been held personally responsible. If you fit into one of the following categories you may be held liable:

- Did you sign or have the authority to sign checks?

- Did you have the power to direct which bills were paid?

- Did you make business decisions for the firm?

- Were you willful in the nonpayment of payroll taxes?

While 'willful' is a strong word in the rest of the legal world (meaning with intent and resolve and purpose) it carries a very weak definition with regard to the IRS and payroll taxes. Willful means you knew payroll taxes were owed (and who doesn't know that?) and didn't do anything about it. 'Willful' for the IRS is akin to 'oops' for everyone else. And know that a lack of money is no excuse for non-payment. When people work the government automatically gets their share. If you can't pay them it's not their problem. If you can't pay them you can find yourself with very big problems.

Please be forewarned.

Alana and Sherri

After three months, SalonAlana was off to a great start. They had excellent word of mouth and a growing list of repeat customers. New stylists were renting chairs from them and the sale of beauty products—shampoos and conditioners and gels that carried high profit margins—was strong. The sisters were actually making money.

Until a letter arrived.

It was a cease and desist letter from a Florida attorney. The letter stated SalonAlana was a large beauty parlor chain in the Tampa area. The company claimed to own the trademark for SalonAlana. The attorney demanded that they immediately stop using their name and turn back the Salonalana.com domain name to them. If they didn't promptly comply the Florida attorney wrote that his client would seek damages for infringement in excess of $150,000.

Sherri and Alana were shocked by this letter. They immediately made an appointment with their attorney, Jay.

Jay was ready for them when they arrived. The handsome attorney had done his research. A federal trademark had indeed been issued to SalonAlana, LLC, a Wyoming limited liability company.

Alana wondered why a Wyoming LLC held the trademark. She thought they were a Florida business.

Jay explained that it was a common asset protection strategy to hold the trademarks, trade secrets, copyrights and patents (or collectively 'the intellectual property' or 'IP') in a separate LLC. He charted out the structure for them:

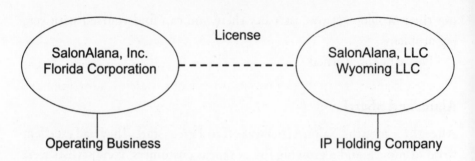

In the event the Operating Business was sued for whatever reason the valuable IP was removed and apart from the main business. A suit against SalonAlana, Inc. in Florida wouldn't directly expose the assets of SalonAlana, LLC in Wyoming. It would be much harder for a claimant to get at the IP because it was segregated into a separate and distinct entity.

That was all fine, Alana noted, but they were worried by all this. They had registered the corporate name in their state. Didn't that give them priority in their state?

Jay explained that a corporate name filed with their Secretary of State's office was very different from a trademark. The corporate name simply allowed them to use a name that didn't conflict with any other business names within the Secretary of State's office. The federal trademark was much more powerful. It allowed businesses to use a trademarked name in all 50 states to the exclusion of all others. Jay explained that while someone could incorporate under the name Coca-Cola in some states, they certainly would not be able to use it when running a business. In vigorously protecting their trademarks, The Coca-Cola Company would see to it that their name was not used in any business capacity.

Sherri then asked about the domain name. They had gone ahead because they had been able to secure the domain name. Didn't that give them rights to the name SalonAlana?

Jay shook his head and explained how it worked. A trademark trumped a domain name. In this case the Florida company had at one point had both the SalonAlana trademark and the www.salonalana.com domain name. But their lackadaisical web person had forgotten to renew the domain name which was right when the girls had been able to get it. "So we get to keep it," asserted Sherri. Jay corrected her impression of it all. The problem, he said, was that the Florida company still owned the trademark and with that they could force a return of the domain name. Again, he stated, a trademark trumped a domain name.

Alana was bitter. Was Jay saying they would have to come up with a new name?

Jay explained that they would.

Sherri said the cost to change the signage on the building, all their cards and flyers, everything, would be over $15,000. She was not happy about this.

Jay said he understood their anger but they really had no choice. He took the Florida attorney at his word that they would seek ten times that amount in damages.

The sisters were both disappointed and bitter. Jay could only say that hopefully something good could come from this. Alana and Sherri did not see anything good at that moment.

Trademarks

A trademark is any word, phrase, slogan, symbol or design which is used to distinguish a product or service. Trademarks are usually a name or logo but they can be other distinguishing characteristics such as the shape of a container or the design and color of a label. Marks that designate services are sometimes called "service marks" but their legal function is the same.

As an example of the difference, consider the Dodge Ram Tough trucks. Whereas "Dodge" is the trademark for a brand of automobile, "Ram Tough" is the service mark for the services offered—durable and reliable transportation. Trademarks and service marks are best protected when they are registered with the United States Patent and Trademark Office ("USPTO").

Once you start looking trademarks can be seen everywhere. As you are driving down the street you may see an "SM," "TM," or "R" symbol attached to the name of your favorite restaurant or retail store. You probably will start noticing these marks everywhere once you finish this chapter and you will come to appreciate that many business owners are protecting their marks. Which, like them, means you need to associate these symbols with your marks to put the world on notice that you claim them.

Any time you claim rights in a mark, you may use the "TM" (trademark) or "SM" (service mark) designation. These marks are used to mark your territory. (Yes, you can think of walking your dog. It is kind of the same.)

You may use the "TM" or "SM" symbols regardless of whether you have filed an application with the USPTO. Know that you may only use the federal registration symbol® once the USPTO actually registers your trademark. You cannot use the ® designation while your application is pending. Also know that you may use the ® symbol with the trademark only on or in connection with the goods and/or services that you listed in the federal trademark registration application.

Trademark notice placements may differ. The trademark that identifies a product or good can generally be placed on the packaging or on the good itself. Since the service mark may not actually sell an object, the mark that identifies the services can usually be seen in the marketing or advertising campaigns.

Trademarks can be stolen, lost and weakened if they are not protected properly. Federal trademark registration is the strongest tool available for protecting trademarks. The benefits of federal trademark registration include:

- Protects customer recognition and goodwill developed in your mark.

- Protects your investment in advertising and promotions.

- Prevents conflicts with other companies that may use your name in the future.

- Reserve names that you intend to use in the future.

- Gain income from licensing the mark to others.

- Give constructive notice of ownership to all later users of the mark.

- Have the right to display the federal registration symbol "®."

- Gain the right to make the mark "incontestable" after five years of continuous use.

- Have a presumption of ownership if the mark ends up in litigation.

- Allows registrants to use the federal courts in a dispute.

A business name, phrase or logo may be federally registered as a trademark if it is fanciful, arbitrary or suggestive. Because they are more likely to be accepted by the USPTO, a fanciful, suggestive or arbitrary business name is a good bet when choosing a potential trademark or service mark.

A fanciful trademark is generally a mark that is without a dictionary meaning. Some examples of this are the trademarks Exxon or Xerox. The first mark in this style was Kodak, a name without any meaning prior to its use as a camera company logo over a hundred years ago. Suggestive trademarks indirectly refer to the goods or services with which they are associated. Greyhound, for example, is a trademark for bus services indicating swiftness.

Arbitrary marks have nothing to do with the goods or services with which they are associated. Some examples of arbitrary trademarks are Apple for electronics, Diesel for clothing and, if the boys ever got to filing for it, Glockenspiel Ventura for housesitting. My son believes that the term 'arbitrary' should be replaced with the more hip and less focused term 'random.' The USPTO has not agreed, but there is no denying that many years ago apples and electronics were random to each other, thus making for a great trademark today.

Descriptive trademarks, names that describe the goods or services with which they are associated, should be avoided. As a general rule the USPTO does not register descriptive trademarks. An example of a descriptive trademark would be naming a restaurant "Fast Food" if you provided food fast to your patrons. You can certainly name your restaurant that but it is so descriptive that it won't get registered as a trademark.

As well, avoid using scandalous, immoral or deceptive names that offend the conscience. The USPTO will not grant such registration, so remember to be politically correct in your filings. As an example, anything with the word 'Mafia' in it will not work. We had a client that wanted to trademark "HMO – Health Mafia Organization". While a humorous take on medical insurance plans, we warned him it wouldn't fly but it was filed anyway. The Trademark Office promptly rejected the application.

A trademark may still be federally registered if it has acquired distinctiveness through "secondary meaning." However, you may not be able to register by simply claiming secondary meaning. Secondary meaning can be described as the degree of customer identification or the status of your trademark compared to others on the market. In other words, the trademark used has become so famous that it has garnered a secondary meaning. The USTPO will decide each trademark based on secondary meaning on its own merits.

The examining attorney with the USPTO will consider the following factors when coming to a decision on a secondary meaning application:

1. How long you have used the trademark;
2. The type and amount of advertising used; and
3. Your efforts to associate the trademark with the goods or services you provide.

You may prove there is trademark recognition or distinctiveness with specific evidence such as the dollar amount of sales generated from the trademark, advertising samples or figures, and consumer or dealer statements recognizing your trademark.

A federal trademark application may be refused registration if a "likelihood of confusion" exists with another trademark or service mark that is in use. Federal trademark law, also known as the Lanham Act, provides that a trademark may be refused registration if it "consists or comprises a mark which so resembles a mark registered in the Patent and Trademark Office, or a mark or trade name previously used in the United

States by another and not abandoned, as to be likely, when used on or in connection with the goods of the applicant, to cause confusion, or to cause mistake, or to deceive" (Lanham Act §2, 15 U.S.C.A. §1052).

Of course, this is why a trademark search should be conducted, so there is no likelihood of confusion at the start.

As Sherri and Alana learned, if you do not do a search to check if a trademark is available for your name, and someone else is using that name, you can run into big problems. The fact that you can get a domain name does mean that you are clear on all trademark issues.

Once you get a trademark you must protect it. The Florida attorney was doing what any company or its representative must do: Protect the mark. If a trademark owner learns of someone else using their mark he must take all steps to protect it—or lose his own rights to the mark. SalonAlana of Florida had to send such a letter to protect themselves.

Mark Searches

A basic search can be done at www.uspto.gov. Please know that if you are really serious about your mark and protecting it you may want to pay a trademark search service to do a comprehensive search and analysis. These can run from $1500 to $3000, and may be worth it depending on what investment you are going to be putting into your mark. As with the SalonAlana example, a comprehensive search before you have developed a market presence with an unacceptable name prevents costly and frustrating name changes later. If you choose a name that is being used by another company, you may be drawn into litigation and forced to change your mark. A mark search can help determine if the name you choose conflicts with any other company's mark.

Searches are also recommended before applying for trademark registration. A search can save a lot of time and money by detecting possible conflicts early.

A common mistake made by small companies is relying upon a state business name search performed by a state government. This is inadequate as a mark search because it is limited to that state's list of registered business names. You must do a search on a powerful computerized database which is much more comprehensive and can detect names used in all fifty states.

The Registration Process

The federal registration process begins with an application to the Patent and Trademark Office. Once filed, the application is examined by a trademark examiner. The examination process may include one or two written exchanges with the examiner. The examiner may reject the application or it may be approved immediately.

Once approved, the application is published for opposition. This allows another party to object to your application. However, most applications do not receive objections. If the mark is not opposed, the mark will be placed on the federal register.

The registration process generally takes one to two years.

Types Of Applications

There are two kinds of applications: In-use and intent-to-use. If the mark is currently being used with a product or service in interstate commerce, an in-use application may be filed. If the mark is not currently being used in interstate commerce but the applicant has a bona fide intention to use it, an intent-to-use application may be filed.

An intent-to-use application allows the applicant to establish an early priority date. Even though the applicant is not using the mark, the applicant can claim priority over all those who were not using the mark before date the application was filed. An intent-to-use application can be renewed every six months up to a maximum of three years.

Getting Started

In order to start the application process, the following information and specimens must be assembled:

- The name, address and telephone number of the applicant. If the applicant is a corporation, you must include the state of incorporation.

- The exact spelling of the mark as it is used in your business. If the mark includes a logo, you will need a clear drawing of the logo that can be placed on a drawing page. The drawing must be clear enough to photocopy and it must be no larger than 4 x 4 inches. If the logo is not available in this form, trademark artists can make the proper drawings.

- A complete list of the goods or services the mark is or will be associated with. The list should be as comprehensive as possible.

- How the mark is used on the goods. For example, printed on the goods, printed on the labels attached to the goods, printed on packaging material, etc.

- The first date of use of the mark anywhere and the first date of use of the mark in interstate commerce. Interstate commerce means selling the goods across state lines or in another country. No dates are needed for an intent-to-use application.

- Three specimens of the mark as it is used with the goods. Specimens of marks used on goods may be labels, boxes, pictures of the goods or the goods themselves if they are flat. Specimens of service marks may be promotional materials such as brochures or advertisements. All three of the specimens may be the same and no specimens are needed for intent-to-use applications.

Costs

The Patent and Trademark Office currently charges between $275 and $375 (depending how you file) for each trademark application. Attorneys charge from $500 on up to prepare the application. Subsequent prosecution of the application, if necessary, is billed at an hourly rate.

Licensing

A trademark owner has the right to sell or license his trademark. This may be an attractive option to trademark owners who have an under-utilized mark with special appeal. Be sure to seek specialized assistance in negotiating and drafting license and assignment agreements.

Insuring Your Business

Just as trademarks are an insurance policy for your business, so must you consider actual insurance policies for protection.

Bobo and Morton

Bobo and Morton sat down to meet with their bookkeeper/advisor Horatio Manfred and Jeff Conte, a well-known insurance broker and another member of The Thracian Club.

Horatio was pleased that the boys were taking on so much business but was also concerned by how much liability they had. After all, while they were house-sitting they were also now taking inventories of estates with furnishings and art work worth a great deal of money. The insurance companies requesting these inventories wanted more and more detailed information. And while Bobo and Morton were looking to computer enable some of the work, they still had to actually handle some very expensive objects. Horatio wanted to make sure they were protected.

Mr. Conte asked if they knew the values of the furnishings and artwork they were dealing with. Bobo said they had just inventoried a house with one Monet, two Manets and three Matisses. They estimated the paintings were worth over $50 million. Mr. Conte asked if they touched the paintings. Morton said they were behind glass in a heavily alarmed space. They had no intention of touching them.

Even so, Horatio indicated that they were dealing with expensive items every day. In the case of a cabinet full of china they had to pull them all out to count and photograph them. Horatio just wanted to make sure the boys were properly covered in the case of any 'slip.'

Mr. Conte understood. He said that it was useful to sit down with their insurance professional every so often to go through a risk analysis. Since people's jobs and responsibilities and liabilities change, their insurance coverage might need to change as well.

After asking a few more questions and understanding more about the actual work of Glockenspiel Ventura, Inc., Mr. Conte said he would come up with some suggestions for better and more comprehensive coverage. Horatio explained to Bobo and Morton that while they might be paying more every year in insurance premiums, they would also (or at least should) sleep better every night.

Bobo and Morton liked the idea of anything that would make a good night's sleep even better.

Business Insurance

Essentially, business insurance exists to protect you against two categories of threats. The first one is the litigious society we live in and the people who make it that way. The second is the world we live in, nature in all its occasionally devastating glory. Business insurance can protect against these risks and in so doing protect the business itself, its assets, its profits and its reputation.

When you are starting up, insurance can be tricky. On the one hand, you don't want to put your business at risk by not having insurance. On the other hand, you don't want all your profits going to pay for a policy that's larger than what you need. This is a good time to consult with members of your professional team—your insurance agent and your CPA.

One option is to insure your company, but with high deductibles. Meaning if there is a claim you are responsible for, as an example, the first $10,000 in costs, with the insurance company responsible for everything above that high deductible amount. If something bad does happen, you're protected after you pay the first $10,000. However, if you never need the policy, you won't have been shelling out all your profits to cover a more comprehensive and expensive policy you didn't need.

The following are some of the types of insurance available to your business:

- Commercial General Liability – A general liability policy insures against risks including bodily injury or property damage caused by the direct or indirect actions of the insured. Make sure that fire coverage is included. And know that these policies generally do not protect against liability for crimes or intentional acts of the insured.

- Product Liability insurance – If you create a product consumed by the public, you have the potential of being sued. Product liability insurance protects you here.

- Professional liability insurance – If you work in a professional capacity, this is the malpractice insurance that covers you for errors and omissions.

- Real property – If you own the facility you run your business out of, or if you work from your home, you will need real property insurance. If you rent space, consider renter's insurance rather than relying on your landlord's policy (which may not cover you at all).

- Business interruption insurance – This covers you if you're unable to work because your business has been destroyed or interrupted for any reason.

- Director and officer liability insurance – This insurance can cover directors and officers for certain acts committed in their capacity as directors or officers. Additional coverage can cover them for acts not permitted or required to be indemnified.

As a startup trying to decide what insurance you can and can't afford, take into account:

- Do you own your own building or facility?
- If you rent business space, do you have renters insurance?
- If you work out of your home, is there a home office rider on your homeowners insurance policy?
- How much have you invested in equipment?
- Do you produce a product consumed by the public?
- Would higher deductibles lower your premiums?
- Do you need liability insurance for yourself of for directors or officers?

While there is no right answer for coverage, all of the above are issues to consider.

As you select your coverage consider the difference between replacement cost or current value. If you insure at replacement cost this means if you lose property, you'll be reimbursed for that property at its cost to replace it and not at depreciated values. Insuring at current value means if your property has depreciated, the insurance company reimburses you at the depreciated amount, which will be lower.

Keep in mind that insurance doesn't work in a vacuum. You need to understand the coverage your policy affords you and you need to keep your corporate affairs in order at the same time. If your liability insurance covers a litigant who was injured on your property, but doesn't cover the punitive damages that litigant is seeking, your next line of defense is your corporate veil. That's what stands between the litigant and your personal assets. If your business is sued, your corporate book and corporate records will come into play. Corporate formalities strengthen your corporate veil, which protects your business and you.

Business Insurance and Tax Considerations for Your Corporate Entity

According to the IRS, you can generally deduct premiums for these types of insurance which are related your business:

- Insurance covering losses from fire, storm, theft, accident or similar events.

- Credit insurance that covers losses incurred from bad business debts.

- Group health insurance plans for employees, including long-term care insurance. Note that a partnership which pays accident and health insurance premiums for its partners can generally deduct them as guaranteed payments to partners, and that an S corporation paying accident and health insurance premiums for its more than 2 percent shareholder-employees can generally deduct these costs but must include them as shareholder wages on the W-2, subject to withholding taxes.

- Liability insurance premiums are tax deductible.

- Premiums for malpractice insurance covering personal liability for professional negligence resulting in damage are tax deductible.

- Worker's compensation insurance set by state law for job-related injury or disease. In a partnership, you may deduct these costs as guaranteed payments to partners. In an S corporation, for shareholder-employees, you can generally deduct these costs but must include them as shareholder wages on the W-2, subject to withholding taxes.

- State unemployment insurance taxes are deductible.

If you haven't met with an insurance professional to analyze the risks you face, the available insurance coverages and the costs involved, now is always a good time to do so.

And now its time to go back to trademark issues...

Alana and Sherri

Alana and Sherri's next two days were extremely tumultuous and very unsettling. Losing the right to use their name felt like getting punched in the stomach for a very prolonged period. They felt weakened and battered.

The sisters' clients loved the name SalonAlana. They loved how it rolled off the tongue. And tongues were wagging with the good word of mouth for SalonAlana around town. And now they had to give all that up.

Worse yet was the reaction of the men in their lives. Their father, Big Jim, was normally very upfront about things. But when he was quite angry he grew very silent. He had guaranteed their lease at the Crossroads Center and had been glad to see the business doing well. It had helped to take the pressure off his personal guarantee. But now, having to change their name after just three months was not a good thing. He felt it put his lease guarantee at risk. And he grew very silent about the whole situation.

Alana's husband Will worried about how it would affect customer relations. Would it look like they had gone out of business by changing the name? Would customers be confused or worried and, as a result, stop coming? They were going to have to do a lot of explaining to overcome this challenge.

Clint was the worst of all of them. He flew into a white hot rage when he heard the news. He cursed that weasel attorney Jay. He should have known the name wasn't available. He yelled that Sherri should have used his attorney friend Wilson from the Lodge. He screamed over the fact that it would cost $15,000 to replace all the signage. They didn't have that kind of money and yet if they didn't do it they could owe $150,000 or more. This whole salon business was ruining their lives. Clint stormed out of the house leaving Sherri and their daughter Ellie in tears. He went on a runner and was not seen for three days.

That was fine with Sherri. She and Alana had to deal with a huge problem. They met it head on.

The sisters had no other choice but to change the name. After an intense eight hours of brainstorming and searching trademarks, domain names and the internet they came up with a new name. It would be

Salon Sen-Sey, which they deemed short for sensational. They could get the trademark and the domain name. They vowed that this would never happen again.

After further brainstorming they came up with a hook for explaining the change of name. It would be because they were having so many new and very talented stylists join them. It wasn't fair to these excellent artisans to limit the name of the salon to one stylist, as in Salon Alana. All the people working there were sensational, hence the new name Salon Sen-Sey.

Alana and Sherri then held a Grand Re-Opening Party. By dealing with their problem head on, by having a reasonable explanation for the change and by having an even bigger blow-out party—with live music and a fully stocked bar—the sisters pulled it off.

Soon enough, clients were saying, no offense to Alana, that they liked the new name even better. And the new stylists, who could be prone to fits of Diva, loved the attention it brought them. Yes, they were sensational and were happy to work at Salon Sen-Sey. There was a huge morale boost inside the business.

There was only one other issue. The Florida attorney for Salon Alana, Inc. had demanded that they change their trade name, the one they did business under, and their entity name, the one filed with the Secretary of State's office.

Alana did not know how to change the names but didn't want to use Jay again. He had let them down. While Jay was Alana's friend, it was Sherri who quickly came to his defense. Jay had asked them about the name and they had told him they were clear. They had told him at the first meeting not to check into the name issue. It wasn't Jay's fault there was a problem. He had tried to help and they told him no thanks.

Alana gradually relented—and found herself wondering about Sherri's feelings toward Jay. Was it something more than professional?

In two days, Alana and Sherri went into Jay's office. He thanked them for coming and said he liked the new name. When he offered to assist with the trademark filing, Sherri took him up on it immediately.

Jay also explained that they would have to change the LLCs name with their Secretary of State's office. This involved amending the articles of organization for the LLC. He had prepared the waiver of notice and the minutes of the member meeting, which read as follows:

WAIVER OF NOTICE OF A SPECIAL MEETING OF THE MEMBERS OF SALONALANA, LLC

We, the undersigned being a majority of the members of SalonAlana, LLC, hereby agree and consent that a special meeting of the Members of SalonAlana, LLC, be held on the date and time and at the place designated hereunder, and do hereby waive all notice whatsoever of such meeting and of any adjournment or adjournments thereof.

We further agree and consent that any and all lawful business may be transacted at such meeting or at any adjournment or adjournments thereof as may be deemed advisable by the Members present thereat shall be as valid and legal and of the same force and effect as if such meeting or adjournment meeting were held after notice.

      Place of Meeting: Law Offices of Boyden & Zook

      Date of Meeting: June 11, 2012

      Time of Meeting: 10:00 a.m.

      Purpose of Meeting: Change name of entity

DATED_____

_____

Alana Cambridge

_____

Sherri Marks

MINUTES OF SPECIAL MEETING OF MEMBERS OF SALONALANA, LLC

The special meeting of the Members of SalonAlana, LLC, a Nevada limited liability company, was held at 10:00 a.m. on the 11th day of June, 2012. The following members were present at said meeting:

Alana Cambridge
Sherri Marks
Jim Holcomb

Alana Cambridge called the meeting to order, and announced that the meeting was held pursuant to a written Waiver of Notice and Consent to the holding thereof. The waiver and consent was then presented to the meeting and upon motion duly made, seconded and unanimously carried, was made a part of the records of the meeting and ordered inserted in the minute book immediately preceding the records of the minutes of this meeting.

The matter discussed was the name of the LLC. The Company had received a cease and desist letter from an attorney in Florida representing a Florida company that owned the federal trademark to the name SalonAlana. As it was determined by investigation that the Florida company had superior rights to the name SalonAlana the members have decided to change the company name to Salon Sen-Sey. After further discussion and review and upon a unanimous vote of the Members in attendance it was:

RESOLVED, that the Articles of Organization be amended to read as follows:

Section One
The Company name shall be Salon Sen-Sey, LLC.

There being no further business to come before the meeting, upon motion duly made, seconded, and unanimously carried, the meeting was adjourned.

Respectfully Submitted by

_____

Alana Cambridge

Sherri and Alana signed the documents and thanked Jay. They were happy to put all of this behind them. They needed to move on and start making money.

Rich Dad Tips

- Trademarks are very important to your business. Please do not take chances with them at the start.

- Insure your business for the risks that exist. Be prudent in analyzing those risks.

- Make sure someone is taking care of the payroll tax deposits within your business. You can be held personally responsible if payments are not made.

And now it is time to realize that not everyone who walks in the door is welcome...

Chapter Ten

Second Quarter

Alana and Sherri

Alana and Sherri had just opened up Salon Sen-Sey for the day when they were visited by an OSHA inspector named Brenda. OSHA, which stands for the Occupational Safety and Health Administration, is the federal government's watchdog for workplace safety. Their Compliance Safety and Health Officers take their jobs very seriously. Some would say very pedantically.

Brenda gained admittance to the salon and began snooping around for violations. There are essentially four classifications of OSHA violations: serious, other than serious ("OTS"), willful and repeat. The penalty for serious and OTS violations is capped at $7,000 while willful and repeat violations are capped at $70,000.

Brenda quickly found two very serious violations. One of the two fire extinguishers did not have a current certification. And one of the two electrical panels had beauty products in front of it.

Sherri was confused. Both of the fire extinguishers would work. The fact that one was out of its certification date didn't mean it wouldn't put out a fire. To prove her point, Sherri removed the out-of-certification fire extinguisher from the wall, took it outside and blasted the pavement with fire retardant.

Brenda acidly noted that Sherri was creating a toxic spill and ordered her to clean it up before another violation was issued.

As Sherri muttered unmentionable words and cleaned up the mess, Alana followed Brenda back inside and took issue with the violation for beauty products placed in front of the rectangular electric panel. How was that a safety hazard?

Brenda would not be engaged in such a discussion. She would only say that those were the rules.

When Sherri returned inside, Brenda offered the two sisters a deal. Brenda said the agency was too busy with cases coming to a hearing. She said that the agency would be willing to reduce the two violations from serious to OTS and waive the two $7,000 penalties.

Sherri and Alana agreed on the spot. They did not have $14,000 to pay the federal government for miniscule, nitpicky safety violations. They didn't have the time to go to hearings and waste time on matters unproductive to their business.

That night, Sherri and Alana related the incident to Big Jim. He didn't like the sound of it. He had dealt with OSHA at the grocery store. He had never found them easy to deal with or willing to compromise. He couldn't put his finger on it but something was up.

OSHA is a federal agency within the Department of Labor. It was established in 1970 and signed into law by President Richard M. Nixon. OSHA's mission is to "assure safe and healthful working conditions for working men and women by setting and enforcing standards and by providing training, outreach, education and assistance."

Some states have their own state level OSHA agencies. The state laws have to be at least as strong as Federal OSHA laws, and in certain cases are more rigorous. A total of 24 states have their own OSHA-approved state plans. The remaining states use the Federal law.

Certain workplaces are exempt from OSHA inspections because they fall outside OSHA scope or are regulated by other agencies. These include:

- Independent contractors and self-employed individuals
- Domestic workers in a person's home
- Workers on small family farms

- Public employees (covered in jurisdictions with state plans)
- Flight crews (covered by the Federal Aviation Administration)
- Miners, transportation and nuclear energy workers (covered by other agencies)

OSHA and its state partners have approximately 2,200 inspectors in the field. In the most recent year at the time of publication there were over 42,000 annual federal workplace inspections and over 52,000 such state inspections. It is estimated that over 100,000 workplace violations are issued each year.

A majority of the worker fatalities each year occur in construction. The leading cause of construction site deaths are falls, electrocution, being struck by an object or being caught in or between an object. If you own any type of construction business know that OSHA will be visiting you.

The government is serious about OSHA's work. There are criminal penalties for assaulting or hampering the work of an OSHA inspector. We will hear back from OSHA later in the book.

Tom and Nancy

Once again, Nancy and Betty spoke about bookkeeping matters. The Chase Fields job was providing Green Engineers with steady payments now. Tom and Nancy had deposited the payments into their business bank account and had started paying themselves a salary. With Betty's help they had withheld money for income and FICA taxes. These monies were being deposited at their IRS-approved bank using coupons for this purpose. Betty explained that the deposits could also be made electronically through the Electronic Federal Tax Payment System (or EFTPS). If they wanted she could call 800-555-4477 to enroll them. Nancy said she would speak to Tom about it.

Betty also explained there were several exceptions to the monthly deposit requirements:

1. Deposits could be made quarterly instead of monthly if total monthly payroll taxes were less than $2,501 per month.

2. A deposit could be made yearly if the payroll taxes were less than $1,001 per year.
3. If total payroll taxes were over $200,000 a year they had to be made electronically through the EFTPS.

It was now time to file a Form 941, the Employer's Quarterly Federal Return with the IRS. With this paperwork completed for the Quarter, Nancy thought everything was fine.

Bobo and Morton

Bobo and Morton invited Aunt Maddy to lunch at The Thracian Club. It was a bluebird day, crisp and sunny blue skies after an overnight snowfall. They sat in the indoor terrace overlooking the water.

Now that the two boys were working full time, and their clientele were members of The Club, it made sense for them to be seen at the scene. And it also made sense to thank Aunt Maddy for all her help by treating her to lunch.

Aunt Maddy was a few minutes late. She had come from Frank Fodom's office, where she and her husband had been signing papers to invest even more money with the Wall Street Wizard. The returns had been very good so far.

Aunt Maddy was very appreciative that the boys were buying her lunch. Not that many people showed gratitude anymore and she was happy that Glockenspiel Ventura was finding work.

Bobo said they wanted to talk to her about gratitude. He asked his Aunt how they should show it. Aunt Maddy said it was a good question— and the right question to ask when starting a business.

Morton said that Mrs. Muller had been very helpful and extremely nice in directing clients their way. What was the best way to thank her?

Aunt Maddy believed that a hand written, personalized thank you note was always appropriate. The best ones could show thoughtfulness, appreciation and gratitude in just a few sentences. The best of the best were memorable. She said Horatio Manfred had just written a very nice note thanking her for referring the boys to his bookkeeping service. Aunt

Maddy commented that she would remember his note, especially when it came time to refer other people to a bookkeeper.

Bobo and Morton nodded. Their parents were always writing and receiving thank you notes. Now they understood why.

Aunt Maddy suggested that after several thank you notes the next level of appreciation could be a lunch or a gift card. Some people even liked having a donation made to their favorite charity.

Bobo and Morton took her suggestions all in. And they felt good knowing that Aunt Maddy thought they were on the right track. They were coming to realize that business gratitude is important for any business—whether a start-up or an established firm.

Business Gratitude

In a society filled with so much negativity isn't it nice to be thanked once in a while? Doesn't it make your day when someone shows genuine gratitude?

There is no need to put too fine a point on it. In a business context, showing your appreciation just makes sense. And without getting overly spiritual, it is good for you to give thanks to others. If your customers choose to appreciate the thought (and they will) it is in turn good for your business. If genuine on the front end, the reciprocity can be powerful for you in return.

Gratitude is a precursor to trust. With trust you have loyalty. And with loyalty you have repeat business and referrals. So start the process. When your customers believe you have their best interests at heart they are more likely to develop a long-term relationship with you. Showing your gratitude is an excellent way to lay the foundation for that relationship. And fostering that appreciation along the way will help cement it.

As an example, I was speaking with my long-time insurance agent over the phone about something and causally mentioned I was working that week on The Wild West Shootout, a charity basketball tournament we hold every year for the Sierra Kids Foundation. When my agent asked about the foundation I explained it was a 501(c)(3) charity that provides scholarships to families with children in the University of Nevada's terrific Early Childhood Autism program in Reno. She liked the idea of helping families through an expensive and challenging process and asked where to send a donation of money.

Now, as I write my checks to Betsi's company for insurance premiums, I recall the kind and spontaneous donation she made to our foundation. I remember it as I write this book and will always remember it. Was the donation a genuine act? Absolutely. Is Betsi in a better position for it? Of course she is.

Gratitude can be a key element in your business's success and growth. No matter how challenging the times or busy you become, never forget it.

Rich Dad Tips

- Be sure to file your Form 941s with the IRS every quarter.
- Whenever OSHA appears at your business, have your guard up.
- Do not overlook the importance of business gratitude.

And you can also be grateful for your own efforts, because...

Chapter Eleven

Year One

Congratulations! You have made it to your first anniversary. Good job! But before the celebrations begin, let's ask some questions related to protecting the corporate veil. (Remember, we don't want to be personally liable in future years any more than in the past.) So, consider these:

- How well have you separated yourself from your business?

- Does your business have a separate bank account?

- If you're working out of a home office, is that office reserved strictly for business?

- Does your business have a separate phone line?

- Are you signing all documents, contracts and agreements with your corporate title?

- Does your corporation or LLC have Articles of Incorporation or Organization filed with the Secretary of State's office? Does your LLC have a written operating agreement?

- Are you filing your list of officers or managers annually with the Secretary of State's office?

- Are your municipal and state business licenses up to date?

- Has the issued stock of your corporation been filed in your stock ledger?

- Do you have a federal tax ID number?

- Are you making quarterly payroll tax deposits?

- Are all bank loans to the corporation documented?

- Are any personal loans to the corporation documented?

- Are annual meetings being held by shareholders?

- Are annual meetings being held by the Board of Directors?

- Are annual meeting of the managers and/or members being held by your LLC?

- Are all corporate resolutions documented in writing and filed in the corporate book?

- Does your corporation or LLC have its own annual tax return?

- Is your corporate entity adequately capitalized?

Annual Filings

The end of your first year is more than just a celebration of your business' first birthday. There are annual filings and meetings due and deadlines that can't be missed. (And know that these requirements exist annually from here on out.) If you've hired a professional team to work with, your bookkeeper, accountant and legal team may be reminding you of what's due and the deadlines for filing paperwork, but you're responsible for your own business and its success. Whether you choose a year-at-a-glance wall calendar, an executive diary, a smart phone or another paperless system of virtual updates, make sure you don't miss annual filings. Some of the annual filings you'll be updating are:

- City business license

- State business license

- Sales tax forms with the state tax department

- List of corporate officers filed with the Secretary of State

Please note that many states, including Nevada and Wyoming, mail out the annual list right before the anniversary date of the entity formation. So if your company was formed in August, the annual list will be sent in July (not January) of each year.

Other year end requirements include updating any information that's changed over the year, including mailing or physical addresses for the business. Many if not most state and federal filings carry stiff penalties for missing a deadline. Some fines are a percentage of monies owed. Others are a simple—and painful—doubling of the fee. Still others continue to accrue on a monthly basis. Businesses have been shut down as a result of missed filing deadlines and related accrued fees. It's not worth it. Invest in whatever system works for you and meet those deadlines.

The end of your first year (be it calendar or anniversary) is also the deadline for the first of your annual meetings of directors and shareholders. Annual meetings and the formal minutes drafted, signed and recorded in the corporate book are some of the most important documents for building and maintaining your corporate veil. These are the actions that prove you are following the required corporate formalities and are thus entitled to the corporate veil of protection.

Even if you're the only employee-shareholder on board, hold your annual meetings and take and record the minutes. It's the law, and the law (in this case) can keep you free from personal liability. Some of my clients who are the sole owners of a corporation or LLC react differently when instructed to have an annual meeting. "You mean I have to have a meeting with myself?" they will say. "People will think that is odd." Please do not worry, people won't think anything of it. You don't have to rent out a hotel room for this meeting, and you can do this in the privacy of your own home. But because this is off-putting to some we provide a service. You fill out a checklist of what happened during the year and we will prepare the minutes. It is just between the two of us. And we'll provide the protection.

Annual Meeting of Board of Directors

The annual meeting of the company's Board of Directors is not optional. Though the Board may meet more often, it must meet once a year. The kinds of items typically addressed at an annual meeting include:

- Electing the Board of Directors
- Changing Articles of incorporation
- Changing Bylaws
- Approving a company policy
- Employee agreement approvals
- Electing company officers
- Setting out or revising company officer agreements
- Approving or changing employee benefits
- Setting a time and place for shareholder meeting
- Adopting obligations, such as contracts, leases, etc.
- Purchase or sale of assets
- Company loans and security of those loans
- Securities (issuing, approving options, warrants or other rights to purchase)
- Stock option plans
- Distributions (including stock splits and dividends)

Shareholder Meeting

Shareholders are required to meet annually to elect and appoint the corporation's directors for the next year. The corporate bylaws can also direct shareholders to meet for specific purposes, and shareholder meetings must take place before sales or mergers involving the corporation.

Prior to any shareholders meetings written notice must be sent to all shareholders. Your corporate bylaws should specify how long before the meeting notice must be sent; state laws will also specify. The norm is that private companies must send notice no less than 10 days before the meeting and no more than 60. Shareholders may waive notice with a signed document. (The same type of waiver was used with Alana and Sherri when they changed their company name.)

Meetings themselves may be waived if shareholders and directors sign a written consent. Consents are documents containing the language or decisions or resolutions the corporation has made. Particularly if you're the only shareholder, consents are a quicker way to document the resolutions and decisions of your business, but check with your lawyer first—not every state allows resolutions to be made without holding a meeting first.

Once again, if you are the sole member of your corporation, you still need to schedule meetings, waive notice and keep records. You must actively protect your corporate veil, even as a sole owner.

Shareholders Special Meetings

In addition to annual meetings, shareholders need to meet prior to sales or mergers of the corporation and for any other reasons set out in the bylaws. Unlike annual shareholder meetings, which cover the election of directors and other general yearly matters, a special meeting is called to discuss a specific topic. No other business beyond the call of the meeting should be transacted at a special meeting.

Minutes of Meetings

Some states require your business to keep minutes of your shareholder and directors meetings. Others don't. In addition, some states don't require LLCs and LPs to hold annual meetings at all.

Whether LLCs or LPs are required to hold annual meetings or not, it's a good idea to hold them. Whether minutes are required or not, it's a good idea to take them. You're protecting your business by following existing and easily anticipated corporate formalities. As well, even if they are not required currently under state law, the IRS during an audit wants to see them. For that reason alone, the better practice is to hold the meetings and prepare the minutes.

When you take minutes of these meetings, you're creating a legal paper trail documenting the actions being taken by shareholders and directors (or manager and members in an LLC). In addition to protecting the corporate veil by maintaining a corporation in good standing, keeping minutes can also head off misunderstandings and miscommunications by keeping every decision in writing.

Tom and Nancy

Nancy brought Dooger by the office of Betty's Bookkeeping. Nancy was there to drop off some tax materials. Betty's assistant was happy to see the big dog and gave him a treat. Then Dooger trotted into Betty's office and tried to cuddle up to Betty, who was not amused.

Nancy explained that Dooger, like many other Great Danes, thought he was a lapdog. Betty shoved the dog off her lap and explained she did not like lapdogs, or any other dogs for that matter. Since the meeting wasn't really going that well, Nancy handed the tax file to Betty and left with Dooger in tow.

Several hours later Betty was preparing the W-2s for Green Engineers, P.C. As she went through the chart of accounts she noticed a $5,000 payment to Tom and Nancy in the first week of business. She hadn't seen that payment before. But clearly it needed to be included on the W-2 statement. So Betty added it to the amount of income reported on the W-2.

It would be another year before the consequences became apparent.

What must be filed after Year One?

By January 31st, employees must be sent an IRS W-2 form. This form is provided by the employer and shows the total wages paid the employee during the year, as well as the total tax withholdings deducted.

Similarly, payments of $600 a year or more for individuals performing services as an independent contractor (and not as an employee) must be sent to the individual on a 1099 Form.

Also due January 31st is Form 940 (or 940-EZ) the Employer's Annual Federal Unemployment Tax Return (FUTA) along with any monies owed. This tax is paid by employers (and not employees) to fund the unemployment insurance system. If your state has its own unemployment insurance program and you've paid it on time you can get a credit on FUTA payments.

By February 28th employers must file a Form W-3 with the IRS, which is a summary of all the W-2 payments. By that date the employer must also send copies of the individual W-2's to the Social Security Administration, which shares information with the IRS.

Also by February 28th you must supply the IRS with copies of the Form 1099s you previously sent out to your independent contractors. Included with these are a Form 1096, Annual Summary and Transmittal of US Information Returns and, for service businesses whose employees receive tips, a Form 8027 Employer's Annual Information Return of Tip Income.

Rich Dad Tip

- If you have questions about all these W-2 and 1099 Forms you can call the IRS at 866-455-7438.

And now let's consider more year end issues...

Alana and Sherri

Clint was furious at the girls and their worthless attorney for the trademark fiasco. Their stupidity had cost the business $15,000 in fees to design a new logo and to change signage, stationery and forms throughout the salon.

Clint was sick of all the time that Sherri devoted to the business, which always meant less time for her to take care of the house and little Ellie. Now he had to work at work and work at home. That wasn't what he bargained for in the whole 'til-death-do-us-part deal.

Clint decided to quell his anger with a few pops at the lodge. Once there he spoke to Wilson, his lawyer buddy, about it all. Wilson said the girls would probably have to hold an annual meeting soon. Wilson didn't like their attorney, Jay, and said he would most likely have them hold an LLC meeting even if one wasn't strictly required. Clint sucked down another beer and asked Wilson if Jay was trying to generate additional fees. Wilson, in a rare moment of candor, told Clint that holding an annual meeting was probably the right thing to do. Courts did like to see that you followed the corporate formalities. Plus, he added, that if Clint attended the meeting he could bring up all the stupid mistakes they had made. Maybe he could get them to shut down the business. That got Clint thinking, always a dangerous proposition.

Clint went home and called his increasingly lame brother-in-law, Will. He asked Will if he was going to attend the annual meeting for the girls' LLC. Will had not heard that there would be such a meeting. Clint implied that they were not telling him things about this business of theirs. Still inebriated he told Will there were issues that he was going to force at the annual meeting. Will said he would check into it. Clint insisted that he not do that. He wanted the girls to give them notice in their own due time.

Will had become increasingly skeptical of Clint's behavior and motivations. He spoke to Alana about the call when she came home. Alana next spoke to Sherri when she was out of her house and away from Clint.

Within 48 hours the girls were meeting with Jay in his office. The attorney quickly explained the situation. Yes, it was appropriate for the LLC to hold an annual meeting of both the managers and the members.

The corporate formalities were best covered when an annual meeting was held. No, Clint was not entitled to attend the manager's meeting. He was not a manager of the LLC and thus did not have standing to attend. Jay said that, of course, Clint could be invited to attend. Alana laughed and said that would not be happening.

A trickier proposition was the handling of the members' meeting. Both Sherri's and Alana's membership interests in the LLC were owned by their living trusts. As such, with Clint having essentially a one half interest in the living trust, he would be able to attend the meeting.

Sherri asked if there was some other way to hold a meeting. Her husband Will had indicated that Clint was seeking to disrupt it and cause problems. Jay responded that Nevada law, where the LLC was formed, allowed for an annual meeting (or a special meeting for that matter) to be held without actually meeting. Meaning it could all be done with a waiver of notice (whereby the members sign a statement waiving the notice requirement) and then a written consent of the actions taken (whereby the members sign a document approving of the actions.) He reminded the sisters that they had done it that way when they changed the company's name several months back. Back then, it was done in a hurry to avoid a problem, with everyone's tacit, implicit and given consent.

This was a different situation. Clint wanted to stir things up. In a 50/50 scenario, could Sherri vote in favor without Clint's consent?

Alana smiled and said they would have a majority. Each sister's trust had received a 48% interest in the LLC. Big Jim, for guaranteeing the loan, had received a 4% interest. If she and Will agreed, and Big Jim did as well, they would have a 52% majority vote. They wouldn't have to worry about Clint or Sherri's interests voting.

Jay smiled. The girls were learning corporate law. He had the paperwork prepared, which read as follows.

WAIVER OF NOTICE OF ANNUAL MEETING OF MANAGERS
OF
SALON SEN-SEY, LLC

We, the undersigned, hereby agree and consent that the Annual Meeting of the Managers of the Limited Liability Company be held on the date and time and at the place designated hereunder, and do hereby waive all notice whatsoever of such meeting and of any adjournment or adjournments thereof.

We do further agree and consent that any and all lawful business may be transacted at such meeting or at any adjournment or adjournments thereof as may be deemed advisable by any Manager present thereat. Any business transacted at such meeting or at any adjournment or adjournments thereof shall be as valid and legal and of the same force and effect as if such meeting or adjourned meeting were held after notice.

> Place of Meeting: Law Offices of Boyden & Zook
> Date of Meeting: March 29, 2013
> Time of Meeting: 10:30 a.m.

Dated: March 29, 2013

_____

Sherri Marks, Manager

_____

Alana Cambridge, Manager

CONSENT RESOLUTIONS OF ANNUAL MEETING OF THE MANAGERS OF SALON SEN-SEY, LLC (THE "LLC")

We, the undersigned, being all or a quorum of the Managers of the LLC, do hereby waive notice of the time, place and purpose of the Annual Meeting of the Managers of the LLC and DO HEREBY CONSENT to the adoption of the following resolutions:

Appointment of Chairman and Secretary of Meeting

RESOLVED, that Sherri Marks be appointed as Chairman of the Annual Meeting and that Alana Cambridge be appointed as Secretary of the Annual Meeting and charged with recording the Minutes.

Approval of Management Activities

RESOLVED, that actions taken in the preceding year on behalf of the LLC be approved and ratified.

Call for Members' Annual Meeting

RESOLVED that the Managers call a Meeting of the Members of the LLC to be held immediately following the conclusion of this Meeting, and present the Members with a report on all business activities conducted by the Managers on behalf of the LLC during the preceding year.

DATED: March 29, 2013

_____

Sherri Marks, Manager

_____

Alana Cambridge, Manager

WAIVER OF NOTICE OF ANNUAL MEETING OF MEMBERS
OF
SALON SEN-SEY, LLC

We, the undersigned, hereby agree and consent that the Annual Meeting of the Members of the Limited Liability Company be held on the date and time and at the place designated hereunder, and do hereby waive all notice whatsoever of such meeting and of any adjournment or adjournments thereof.

We do further agree and consent that any and all lawful business may be transacted at such meeting or at any adjournment or adjournments thereof as may be deemed advisable by any Member present thereat. Any business transacted at such meeting or at any adjournment or adjournments thereof shall be as valid and legal and of the same force and effect as if such meeting or adjourned meeting were held after notice.

Place of Meeting: Law Offices of Boyden & Zook
Date of Meeting: March 29, 2013
Time of Meeting: 10:00 a.m.

Dated: March 30, 2013

Alana Cambridge, representing
the Cambridge Family Trust,
MEMBER

Jim Holcomb, MEMBER

CONSENT RESOLUTIONS OF THE ANNUAL MEETING OF THE MEMBERS OF SALON SEN-SEY (THE "LLC")

We, the undersigned, being a majority of the Members of the above-captioned LLC, do hereby waive notice of the time, place and purpose of the Annual Meeting of the Members of the LLC and DO HEREBY CONSENT to the adoption of the following resolutions:

<u>Appointment of Chairman and Secretary of Meeting</u>

RESOLVED, that Alana Cambridge be appointed as Chairman of the Annual Meeting and that Jim Holcomb be appointed as Secretary of the Annual Meeting and charged with recording the Minutes.

<u>Approval of Managers</u>

RESOLVED, that the following persons or corporate entities are elected as Managing Members of the LLC for the forthcoming year:

Sherri Marks

Alana Cambridge

<u>Approval of Management Activities</u>

RESOLVED, that the Members approve, confirm and ratify the actions of the Managing Members for the previous year.

Dated: March 29, 2013

_____

Alana Cambridge representing the Cambridge Family
Trust, Member
representing 48% Membership Interests

_____

Jim Holcomb, Member
representing 4% Membership Interests

Sherri and Alana agreed that the point of this exercise was for Clint to hopefully forget about wanting to disrupt their annual meeting. Nobody would say anything, time would pass and Clint would go on and worry about and complain about something new.

And, indeed, as the year progressed, no one heard anything more.

Bobo and Morton

Bobo and Morton had survived in business for one whole year. And they were actually making money at it. Their parents, the Trenthams and McGills, hardly took notice. Out of sight, out of mind, was their attitude.

But Aunt Maddy was very proud of them. She met the two boys for lunch to congratulate them. She said they should celebrate with their corporation. Bobo and Morton agreed. They were always up for celebrating. But the how threw them for a loss. They wondered: "How do you celebrate with a corporation?"

Aunt Maddy said you had to think like a tycoon. They were puzzled. Think like their great- great-whatever grandfathers?

Aunt Maddy explained that a tycoon, like many members of The Club and many of the people they housesat for, would use a corporation not only for their protection but also for their benefit. A corporation could pay for things they wanted to do, and justify it as a business expense.

Morton shifted his spindly frame in the chair. He was calculating it all. "You mean if the corporation pays for something we want to do anyway and we like it we don't have to pay the corporation back—even though we liked it?"

Aunt Maddy indicated that was correct. Bobo and Morton looked at each other as if a huge light bulb lit up above each other's heads. "Whoa!" each of them gasped.

Bobo patted his barrel-chested girth. "You mean if we talk business here and I eat two meals that I really like I don't have to pay the company back—even though I was really hungry and liked the meal?"

Aunt Maddy explained that when it came to meals you could have the company pay for half of them. The IRS figured you had to eat anyway and only gave a 50% write off. Bobo and Morton nodded. That sounded fair.

But, as Aunt Maddy explained, the company could pay for them to travel to interesting places, as long as there was a business purpose to it. Bobo and Morton were warming up to the idea that even if you liked it the corporation could still pay for it.

"What if there is a business meeting at Disney World?" asked Bobo. "Does that count?"

Aunt Maddy smiled and pulled out a brochure. A kennel owner's trade show was going to be held in Orlando. Since the boys were handling more pets for their clients, there would be a business purpose to attend. If they happened to visit Disney World while they were there on business that was OK.

Bobo and Morton slapped out a loud, double -armed high five. "We're going to Disney World!"

Business Travel

Business travel can be an excellent deduction for business owners. If the primary purpose of the trip is business, and you engage in a bit of sightseeing along the way, well, enjoy it. That's how the Congressmen who write the tax laws do it when they are on their junkets.

The IRS breaks business travel down into two groups of expenses, those involved with getting there and getting back again (transportation expenses) and those involved with the necessities of life and doing business while you're there (on-the-road expenses).

Your transportation expenses break down into whatever it is that gets you where you're going, gets you around once you get there, and gets you home again. That includes planes, trains and automobiles, rental vehicles, trams and trolleys and airport shuttles. Your transportation costs when you're traveling for business, which includes traveling to seminars in your field and traveling for educational reasons, as well as traveling for business meetings, tradeshows and all the other reasons for business travel, are 100 percent deductible.

Your on-the-road expenses include everything necessary to sustain life and conduct business, from your lodging to your dry cleaning to renting meeting space, and it's all 100 percent tax deductible to the corporation except for meals, which are only deductible at 50 percent. (Remember, you have to eat anyway.)

Your primary reason for business travel has to be business, and you need to know what business you're going to conduct before you ever set the trip in motion. If your reason for taking a trip and having your corporation pay for it is to meet new business contacts, catch up with existing clients, work on a project, walk a new business site, follow up on referrals or take seminars and workshops in your field, you shouldn't have any problems with your deductions even if you do some sightseeing and some personal shopping while you're there. Where the line is drawn is dependent on timing—when the decision to do business is made. If you head to Disneyland with the kids, run into an interesting business opportunity while you're there and pursue it once you're home, this doesn't qualify in the IRS world as business travel. But if you line up meetings with your contact before you go, arrange to meet at Disneyland, conduct your meetings and do your work and follow up with an afternoon at the park, you're on a business trip.

If you take your spouse with you on business trips and you're both part of the business and both have bona fide reasons for making the trip, your expenses will stand as listed above. However, if you choose to travel with your spouse and he or she is not an employee of your corporate entity, your business travel is deductible but your spouse's is not. (But remember, your hotel room is a complete business write off. The fact that your spouse happens to also use it is OK.)

Similarly, whether you're traveling or just running corporate errands, you can take your spouse or dependents with you. You can deduct the costs of using your car for corporate trips even when you have passengers who are not part of the business.

Business or Pleasure?

Here are two points to consider when figuring out deductions for a business trip.

1. You made plans to meet clients or prospects or walk a property or take a seminar or do some other business-related activity before you made the trip.

    _____ Yes. This is actual business-related travel.

    _____ No. Personal travel is not deductible. Even if you conducted business while on the trip, if you didn't plan to ahead of time, deductions won't stand.

2. Was the trip for educational purposes within your field, to a seminar or conference, and did it last less than one week?

    _____ Yes. Deduct transportation and lodging costs as travel expenses. Deduct the cost of the seminar as education.

    _____ No. If the seminar was in a field outside your area of business, or if you spent more than half the time on activities other than business, this is not a business deduction.

Where are you going?

The USA. If you travel to a business meeting, trade show or convention in the USA, your expenses are deductible if you go straight there and come straight back when the show is over.

North America and the Caribbean. Going to a trade show in Mexico, Canada or the Caribbean allows for tax-free travel. But other expenses are only fully deductible if you are away no longer than one week and at least 75% of your time is spent on business. Otherwise you must keep a log and allocate your expenses between business and pleasure.

Beyond North America and the Caribbean. Travel further out is deductible if you can prove a valid business purpose for the trip.

Your actual traveling—the getting to and from or there and back again—are counted as business days and your expenses are deductible, unless you take non-direct routes for non-business activities. In that case, your business days are only the days it would have taken you to travel and do business and you can't include the non-business days.

The basic rule for figuring out if it's business or pleasure is the percentage of time for each day spent in each pursuit. If the majority of hours were spent working, it's a business day. Weekends, holidays and other necessary standby days are considered business days if they fall between business days. But if your business trip ends on a Friday and you take the weekend at the end of the trip in the business location, it's a personal and not a business day and your expenses are not deductible. That said, as we know, some airlines charge lower fares if a weekend stay is involved. So if your air, weekend hotel and meals are less than it would be flying home without the Saturday night you can deduct the extra stay. Of course, keep all your records on it.

Otherwise, if you include a non-business activity at either end of your business activity on a trip, you must allocate part of your expenses to personal. If you're out of the country for 10 days and two of those days are spent in personal pursuits, then 80 percent of your trip was for business and your expenses are deductible. None of your personal expenses are deductible.

As we have mentioned, for all of your business travel and business travel tax deductions, keep your receipts. Document everything and do it as soon as you can so you're not working from memory or notes somewhere down the line. Even if it's a nuisance (and it is) to stop each day and put together your receipts, you will have the paper trail that backs up your deductions.

You should try to keep a complete record of:

- where you traveled, by the name of the town.
- the hotels you stayed at and their locations.
- rental cars and other forms of ground transportation.
- airlines and other forms of transportation.

Know that you can deduct travel taken to look after real estate investments in other locations, to make repairs to properties you have outside your geographic location, visit other people in your field, visit with existing contacts and new referrals and to look for new work.

Education and Tax Considerations for Your Corporate Entity

Most professions offer some kind of continuing education. By state or industry rule the courses are required for professionals working in medicine, accounting, law, engineering and other fields. In addition, many industries have their own trade shows and conventions or conferences and seminars, where you can go and meet people who do what you do, attend panels with experts in your field, network and catch up on what's going on in your professional world.

If you travel to attend continuing education seminars or conferences in your field, the same rules for business travel apply. You also need to have a purpose in mind before you go. If you happen to be on vacation and there's a seminar in the area, you can probably deduct the cost of registration, but the rest of your travel expenses won't be deductible.

Internal Revenue Code Section 162 allows you to deduct 100 percent of your expenses for business-related seminars, including your registration, meals, lodging and transportation costs. The corporate entity takes the deduction and the costs are not considered part of your income (so you're not taxed on the benefits.)

Your corporation can also deduct the price of magazine subscriptions so long as the magazines are for your industry, and you can deduct the cost of membership in professional organizations in your field. If your profession requires periodic testing and licensing, your entity can pay those fees and deduct the costs as well.

If you're looking to learn more about your chosen field, the Internal Revenue Code Section 127 allows you up to $5250 in educational assistance each year for educational expenses, which is also not included in your gross income.

Get smarter and deduct it.

Rich Dad Tips

- As you enter your second year of business check to make sure your corporate veil is protected.

- Be sure to prepare (or have prepared) Annual Meeting minutes.

- Before you engage in business travel understand which deductions you can take.

Before we get into greater business activities, there are still a few year-end questions to answer...

Chapter Twelve

Year One

As you have finished your first year, there are always a few questions that arise. Our firm handles a significant number of corporate, LLC and LP entities, and what follows are some of the common questions we are asked:

End of Year Questions

Q. Why do I need a registered agent?

A. Every state (except New York, for some reason) requires that you have a person or company resident in the state you form in and qualify to do business in to accept service of process (i.e. a lawsuit). The purpose is so that someone suing you has a place in which to find you, rather than searching around the state for you. You wouldn't want to pay a process server to search the entire state of Alaska or Texas or California for the company you want to sue. So the name and address of the registered agent is available at each state's Secretary of State to streamline the process.

Q. If I form in Wyoming, and qualify to do business in California, do I need two registered agents?

A. Yes, you will need a registered agent in Wyoming and one in California.

Q.   Why can't I just use the Wyoming registered agent for both?

A.   Because the Wyoming registered agent is not resident in California. You need a resident in each state.

Q.   What if I don't pay the registered agent?

A.   The registered agent will resign and their name will be taken off the state list. If your entity does not have a registered agent, the person suing you can ask the court to permit notice of the lawsuit to be published in a newspaper. These notices are in very small print (you've seen them in the newspaper under Legal Notices). There's a very good chance you'll never know about the lawsuit, and thus not answer the complaint. When you don't answer in time, the plaintiff (the person suing) can apply to the court for a default judgment. Meaning you will have lost the case without ever getting your day in court. The better option is to pay your registered agent so you can receive timely notice of a lawsuit.

Q.   Do I need mail forwarding?

A.   It depends. If you are receiving bank statements and other mail at your registered agent's address, you will need to pay to have the mail forwarded to you. Our firm, Corporate Direct, offers this service from our Wyoming, Nevada and California offices for $360 per year. Other services may charge more or less. If you are only receiving the annual statements from the state we do not charge for forwarding those to you. Know that aggressive tax collection states like California will use the delivery of, for example, a Wyoming bank statement to your California address as a reason to tax you on everything involved. You are better off having such mail forwarded to you under separate cover.

Q.   Do I need an office package?

A.   In many cases you do not. Beware of promoters claiming that with, for example, a Nevada company, Nevada law requires a Nevada office and telephone for which you need to pay $3,000 a year. There is no such Nevada law. If you set up a Nevada company and qualify to do business in California, your California office is all you need. Engage in critical thinking in the face of all the claims made about the need for office packages and presence.

Q. Can I use my registered agent address as the address to register my vehicle or RV?

A. Most states will not let you use a commercial registered agent address for vehicle registration. Contact Corporate Direct for a Nevada solution to this issue.

Q. Why am I in default?

A. There can be several reasons. First, you must pay the annual fees in a timely manner to your state of formation and the state(s) you have qualified in to do business, as well as the annual registered agent fees. Second, know that some states have annual renewal dates and some have anniversary renewal dates. Meaning if your corporation was formed in August in Wyoming and then qualified to do business in California you'll pay your anniversary fee to Wyoming in August and your annual fee to California in January. So in the second year (or future years) if you paid the Wyoming fee in August but didn't pay the California fee in January you'll be in default in California.

Q. What does default mean?

A. It means that you are not properly doing business in the state. Many states have a daily penalty (which can really add up) for not being qualified. As well, many states prevent you from bringing or defending a lawsuit if you are in default.

Q. How can I cure a default?

A. By paying the fees you owe and, depending on the state, any penalties due you can reinstate your entity and cure the default. Know that if you are in default for too long (each state's rule is different) after several years your entity charter will be permanently revoked and you won't be able to bring it back.

Q. Are annual minutes necessary?

A. Yes. Each state requires that corporations hold an annual meeting. (Some states don't require annual meetings of LLCs or LPs but the better practice is to hold them. Especially since the IRS expects to see them no matter what your state law may say.) To prove you had the meeting you want a written record of it, which are the minutes. When the IRS comes knocking, or someone is trying to pierce the corporate veil, you want to have your corporate minute book filled with meeting minutes.

Q. Do I need a DBA for my company?

A. A DBA (which stands for 'Doing Business As') is needed in two main situations. First, if you, Joe Jones, are doing business as a sole proprietor (never recommended—unlimited liability) under the name Joe Jones Plumbing you will need to file a DBA form with the county (and usually publish notice in a local paper). This form is then given to your bank so they can deposit checks made out to Joe Jones Plumbing. The second scenario is when, for example, XYZ, Inc. does business under the name Lexxus Leisure. Again, notice is filed that XYZ, Inc. is doing business as Lexxus Leisure, the bank is notified and you can then deposit checks made out to Lexxus Leisure into the XYZ, Inc. bank account. However, if XYZ, Inc. is properly registered with the state and is doing business as XYZ, Inc. (and not Lexxus Leisure or any other name) then no DBA filing is necessary.

Q. Should I use a Series LLC?

A. The Series LLC is a new and untested structure, which is why I don't recommend them. Basically, the idea is that you form one entity and then put assets into two series or buckets (or whatever the promoter calls them).

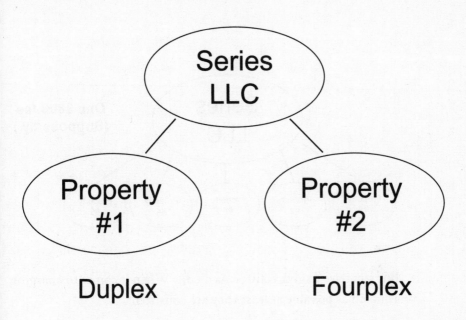

Supposedly, if you get sued over Property #1, a creditor can't reach Property #2. There are no cases to support this ethereal 'internal shield of liability.' Many states don't offer the series LLC, so we don't know if the 'shield' works in those states. As well, you can make one mistake on record keeping (like depositing a check into Bucket #1 that should have gone into Bucket #2) and blow all of your protection. That a bookkeeping mistake could lead to greater liability is not a good thing. Knowing these issues, the American Bar Association got their best LLC lawyers together and reviewed the Series LLC. The ABA declined to endorse them.

Finally, promoters told people to set up Series LLCs to avoid California's notorious $800 per year minimum franchise tax. "Set up one entity," they said, "protect five properties and pay $800 for the one Series LLC instead of $4,000 for five separate LLCs." They would illustrate it as follows:

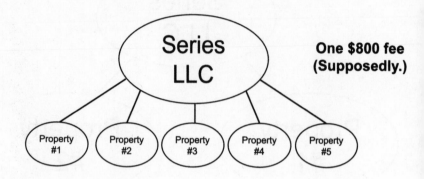

But you have to give California credit. When it comes to charging as much as possible at least they are consistent.

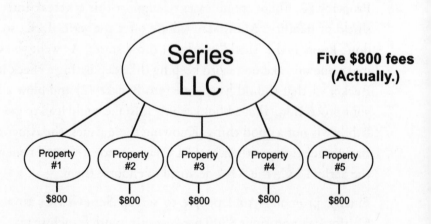

California will charge your Series LLC holding five properties in five separate buckets $800 per series, or $4,000, the same amount as if you had five separate LLCs. For greater certainty and protection you are better off with five separate LLCs anyway.

Q. How many properties should I put into one LLC?

A. That is a judgment call on your part. Know that a tenant or vendor suing in Attack #1, the inside attack, can get what is inside the LLC. Consider this illustration:

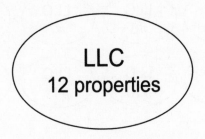

A tenant suing over one property could reach the equity in all 12 properties. Now consider this illustration:

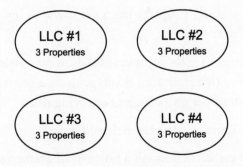

A tenant suing over a property in LLC #1 could get the equity in the three properties but not in the other 9 properties held outside of LLC #1.

Which is why some of my clients consider the following:

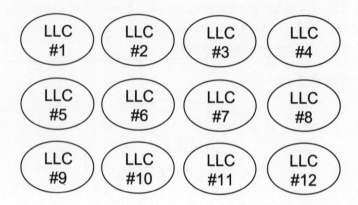

As this illustration indicates, a tenant suing over one property would not have any claim to the equity in the other 11 properties. Again, how you handle this is a judgment call on your part.

Q. When I transfer property from my name to my LLC which deed should I use?

A. I prefer to use a grant (or warranty) deed over a quit claim deed. You have better title insurance coverage using a grant deed. You should use one deed per property for conveying title.

Q. How do I protect my personal residence?

A. The first means is through a homestead exemption. Each state has a different rule on homesteads. (But the common rule is that you only get one homestead no matter where you live.) In some states, such as Texas, Florida and Kansas, there is an unlimited homestead, meaning a creditor can't get at your home. In other states, the homestead is a fixed dollar amount. In Nevada, the homestead is a generous $550,000 whereas in California it is only $75,000 in extra protection. (For each state's amount visit www.successdna.com and look under reports.)

The homestead, when properly filed with your county recorder, works as follows: If you have a $1 million home with a $450,000 first deed of trust against it, you have $550,000 in equity exposed. In Nevada, for example, you file the homestead exemption (which protects $550,000) and your property is fully encumbered. Creditors can't reach the equity. The $550,000 in equity is yours ahead of any creditor.

In California (which only protects $75,000) a homestead filing in the same example would leave $475,000 in equity exposed. ($1 million value, less $450,000 first, less $75,000 homestead equals $475,000 exposure.) To further encumber the property an LLC can be used. But know that a homestead can't be filed to protect a personal residence in an LLC. A homestead only works for your personal residence in your individual or family trust name. Also know that California has a bankruptcy case dictating that an LLC does not protect a personal residence in bankruptcy. That said, an LLC for a personal residence with equity well above the homestead limits may be your best strategy against creditors outside of bankruptcy.

Q.   What year end filings do I have to make regarding employee wages?

A.   As an employer, at the end of the calendar year you must prepare Federal Form W-2 Wage and Tax Statement for each and every wage-earning employee for your corporate entity—including yourself, if you're a shareholder-employee drawing a salary. A copy of the W-2 must be given to the employee, a copy kept in your neatly maintained records, and a copy sent to the Social Security Administration. This can be done online at the SSA Web site, or you can choose to have your tax professional prepare these forms.

Q.   What IRS forms need to be filed for employee wages?

A.   If your federal tax liability for payroll taxes is less than $1000 for the year, the IRS requires your corporation to file a 944 Employer's Annual Federal Tax Return instead of the 941 estimated quarterly taxes. Most likely you or your tax professional will be notified of this status by mail from the IRS itself.

Another document is the IRS form Combined Annual Wage Reporting (CAWR) which is generated by an IRS program that compares the wage information you've reported as the employer to the IRS and Social Security Administration information. If the amounts don't match, you may be required to provide a reason. If you don't respond in what the government considers a timely manner, additional taxes or penalties are assigned and the IRS will send you a bill.

Q. What about forms dealing with independent contractors?

A. If you've worked with independent contractors throughout the year, you'll need to file a Form 1099-misc form detailing compensation made to those non-employee workers. If, conversely, your corporation is set up so that you've worked as an independent contractor during the tax year, you'll need to keep track of the companies you worked for and make certain you receive 1099's from those companies as well as a W-2 from your own company.

Q. Are there any other forms to consider?

A. You bet. You are going to need a good bookkeeper/controller/CPA to figure out which ones apply to you. Some to consider include:

- Reporting forms for real property purchases or sales (Form 1099-S)

- Reporting forms for purchases of equipment (Form 8300)

- Reporting forms for depreciation of vehicles, business site, equipment (Form 4562)

- Reporting forms for medical insurance premium payments on employees and shareholder-employees

- State sales tax forms

Q. Should I use an online service to set up my entities?

A. Does the old saw "You get what you pay for" resonate with you? Have you ever paid for the cheaper version only to be greatly disappointed? And when it comes to your entire future and the specter of never ending unlimited personal liability does saving a few dollars to risk it all really makes sense?

No, you should never use an online service! You cannot believe the shoddy, incomplete and outright fraudulent work we see from some of these services. It is almost as if they are setting up entities which are intentionally designed to be pierced. (Yes, I do have an opinion on this topic.)

These online providers will 'set' you up by providing the articles but no bylaws or operating agreement or minutes. Or they will provide a large stack of papers which will be blank and require further action. You will think that you are protected and covered but you are not. Actually, you are in the same position as you were before you gave them your credit card to protect you. You are unprotected.

Many of these providers say that their documents are "accepted by courts in all 50 states." While this sounds really impressive it is in reality the absolute lowest threshold standard there is. (It is akin to Chevrolet advertising that their cars and trucks can drive in all 50 states. Of course they can!) Courts will accept anything—your 'document' can be written on a wrinkled and faded paper towel with a green crayon and it will be accepted by the court. Big whip there. Plus, the idea is to stay out of court not be accepted by it. So the online services' biggest claim of acceptability is really unacceptable to your goals and strategies.

One of the largest online providers claims that they set up entities at your specific direction, like that is a good thing. But watch out! If you are going to own real estate and you, not knowing any better, go online to form a C corporation for it they will mindlessly set it up. An attorney, on the other hand, will counsel you that a C corporation is the worst way to hold real estate and direct you to an LLC or LP. The several hundred dollars more you spend with an attorney will potentially save you hundreds of thousands of dollars in extra taxes.

Chapter Twelve

Yes, Virginia, you really do get what you pay for.

All right, we warned you. The government returns...

Chapter Thirteen

Eighteen Months

Alana and Sherri

Sherri knew there was trouble the moment Brenda, the OSHA inspector, walked in the door for a second visit.

Brenda and another male federal agent were officious and abrupt. They were there to search out repeat violations and they were not to be denied. They fanned out around the salon and began inspecting.

Brenda immediately checked the fire extinguisher which had been within certification the year before. She smirked and noted that it was now out of certification. Alana looked at the tag attached to the big red cylinder. Alana said the certification had expired only two days ago. "A repeat violation," was all Brenda would say.

Sherri followed the other agent to the electrical panel. As a result of the previous inspection, there was a sign next to the rectangular piece of metal that read: "Do not place items in front of the electrical panel."

Despite that warning, an employee—or someone—had set two shampoo bottles in front of the panel. "Another infraction," noted the agent, struggling to contain his glee. Sherri asked why two misplaced inert plastic containers were a safety hazard. As before, the agent would not answer why it was anything. He would only say that it was a repeat violation.

Brenda prepared a repeat violation report for the two violations. She noted on it that the fine for each repeat violation was $70,000. Sherri was incredulous. Alana began crying. They couldn't afford $140,000. Sherri got in Brenda's face. Was it the federal government's intent to throw the ten salon employees out of work for some imaginary problems? Was it in the government's best interest to put more people onto unemployment and collect less taxes?

Brenda replied that threatening a federal agent was a criminal offense. "What threat!" said Sherri. Was the use of logic a threat to them?

Brenda and the other agent stormed out of the salon.

Big Jim responded to Alana's tearful call and was there in five minutes. He knew from the previous year something was up.

The OSHA agents had lured the girls into a false sense of calm by waiving the penalty in the first year. This allowed them to come back at a later date to find repeat violations, which they could assess at $70,000 each.

Sherri said there was no way they could pay $140,000 for these fines. Big Jim knew how this had to be played. Politics and connections. He knew their local Congressman, who was a Republican, quite well. He also knew one of their U.S. Senators, who was a Democrat, pretty well. He put the problem into their bipartisan hands and let it be worked according to political influence. Within a month, the penalties were dropped.

Dealing with OSHA

Not every business owner has such connections. Not everyone can (nor should they have to) play politics just to do business. So you need to be very cautious when dealing with OSHA.

While this case may seem overly heavy handed, there are a few things to know. First, not every OSHA inspector acts in such a fashion. Some certainly take work place safety seriously but balance that with the needs of businesses which, after all, ultimately pay their salaries. Second, however, is the fact that some OSHA inspectors do have a chip, ideological or otherwise, on their shoulder and do seek to stick it to business owners. Cases such as the one here have been reported from around the country. OSHA has proudly stated that the number of repeat violation penalties has increased by over 200 percent in recent years. How many businesses have closed and jobs have been lost as a result?

How do you deal with the OSHA threat to your business? There are several steps:

1. Work on making your work space the safest in your industry. When you first open up, consider hiring an OSHA authorized trainer and safety consultant to do a review of your workplace. Have all of the exit signs and other signs and all fire extinguishers and every other safety facet covered. (Of course, the private marketplace, through the incentive of lower insurance premiums, self-regulates itself here. However, the government does not believe that.)

2. Do a review every few months to make sure you are in good shape. Speak with your safety consultant about conducting periodic reviews.

3. Think twice before settling with OSHA on an OTS violation. They may be trying to set you up for a later repeat violation penalty, which can be up to $70,000 per violation.

4. If faced with an initial violation talk to your safety consultant and attorney about fighting it through the OSHA hearing process.

5. Do not put in place any incentive programs designed to encourage work place safety. In government think such safety programs create a disincentive to report injuries and are thus now considered an OSHA violation. (When encouraging safety is penalized by the government agency in charge of promoting safety you have to start seriously thinking about the consent of the governed.)

6. If you have a bad experience with OSHA please consider telling everyone you know about it, including your elected officials. Please also consider taking out a quarter page ad in your local business journal to describe what happened. Until business owners are informed and collectively stand up to OSHA, these business and job-threatening raids will continue.

Bobo and Morton

Bobo and Morton needed TVs. Nice, high definition TVs. They were working a lot, taking care of their clients' properties and animals and other sundry and assorted matters. There was a lot to do.

At the end of the day, when they were tired, they each went home to the small studio apartments they each rented and they wanted to watch their own TVs. One TV wouldn't do. "No way!" declared Bobo. They each had their own apartment and they each wanted their own TV.

Together they pled their case to Horatio Manfred, their fastidious bow-tied bookkeeper. If the corporation could send them to Disney World, wasn't there a way for it to get them each a TV?

Horatio was amused by their request. The boys had been working hard and he liked that they were starting to see their corporation as a tool for covering what they needed, within reason. It was amusing that so many of his other clients (including certain Trentham and McGill family members) tried unreasonably to have their entity cover every single inappropriate expense—from jet skis to jets. And yet here the youngest Trentham and McGill kids just wanted their own TVs.

Horatio spoke to the boys about the money in the bank account. They were starting to get ahead a bit. "Was this the right way to spend it?" he asked. The boys were emphatic in their agreement. Horatio then asked how much they would need.

Morton indicated that $400 each would do it.

Horatio smiled and said there was a way.

Glockenspiel Ventura could give each of them a $400 Visa gift card as an award. Bobo was pleased. "I've always wanted to win an award," he said.

Horatio indicated that the company could buy the cards, which they could then use to buy their own TVs. The boys would have to pay income and payroll taxes on the $400. So Horatio underscored the fact that this wasn't free to them.

"It sure feels like free," Morton said with a grin. Bobo agreed, noting that Horatio would take care of all the taxes later. Meaning that for right now they were free to buy TVs, thanks to good ol' Glockenspiel Ventura.

The boys left their bookkeeper's office smiling. They were starting to like this corporation stuff.

Awards

When you're looking for ways to let your corporation work for you, awards can be a useful way to reward shareholder-employees and employees. Your corporation can take a deduction by making awards to employees going above and beyond. While Bobo and Morton had to pay taxes on the awards they received, in some cases the awards can be tax-free to the employee. For example, in a small corporation where husband and wife share corporate duties, the founder might receive an award for being the employee there the longest, while the other spouse might receive an award for creating a safe working environment at the corporate location. Know that the IRS requires that there be a written qualified award plan for this to work.

But done right, such awards are considered fringe benefits by the IRS. While some awards will be taxable and included as income for the employee others may be excluded from any taxes. Cash, its equivalent, gift certificates and other intangibles such as vacations, meals, lodging, stocks, bonds and other securities are always taxable. But tangible property (think golf clubs and TVs) may be excluded from taxation.

According to IRS Publication 15-B (A Guide to Fringe Benefits), generally a corporate entity can exclude the value of an achievement award from employee wages if the average cost of all employee awards does not exceed $400 for the year. The plan cannot discriminate in favor of highly compensated employees, those making more than $115,000 (at this writing).

There are some additional restrictions. Safety awards can't be awarded to the Company's managers or professional employees. And they can't be given to more than 10% of the employees who are receiving the awards. As well, length of service awards can't be awarded during the first five years of employment.

Be sure to work with your CPA to take advantage of this useful (and underutilized) corporate strategy. A worksheet to compute employee award taxation is found in IRS Publication 535.

Tom and Nancy

Tom and Nancy were starting to do well in their business. They had won several major engineering contracts and the larger firms were starting to take notice of their presence in the market.

Recently they had won a government contract for a school project. Eyebrows were raised because everyone assumed it would be awarded to Jones & Hunt Engineering Ltd. The Jones & Hunt firm always seemed to win the big bids. Eddie Jones' brother Bobby was a powerful state senator. The way things usually worked, Eddie was a lock for such state-funded government projects. The state senator's brother always seemed to have the inside track.

But Eddie had been too confident about getting the job, which was reflected in his higher bid. Green Engineers, P.C. had come in at a fair price and was awarded the bid.

This did not sit well with Eddie Jones. Power was perception and he couldn't allow any perceptions of doubt or weakness to persist. Working with his brother, the state senator, and other cronies Eddie concocted another government barrier to entry.

Two months later state agents gathered to raid the home office of Green Engineers, P.C. Coincidentally, TV stations were tipped off and present to record the confrontation.

Using their gun stocks, the agents loudly banged on the front door of the Green's home office on Elm Street. With the TV cameras rolling it was so much more impressive to use gun stocks than simply ringing the doorbell.

What happened next was horrible, and caught on video.

Tom Green opened the front door and agents flooded into the home. Dooger, the Great Dane, was instinctively alarmed and protective. The big dog went after one of the agents. Two other agents pulled their guns and shot Dooger. With a loud howl, the Great Dane collapsed and died instantly.

The outrage was immediate, but would only fully spread later.

Tom was in shock. Nancy was in tears. They couldn't believe the government would kill their dog. The agents could care less. Stepping over the dead Great Dane in their black boots, they carted out boxes and file cabinets from the Green's house in front of the TV cameras.

Tom was incredulous as agents flooded through their home office, and their home.

Tom demanded to know why they were being subjected to this indignity. "Who is the officer in charge?" he yelled. No one would respond.

Nancy was weeping uncontrollably. "What had they done?" she sobbed. Finally, the lead female agent took her aside. The agent said the state had passed a new certification requirement for engineers. If you were going to work on green energy projects you had to be certified.

Nancy had never heard of this requirement. And since they didn't do that kind of work anyway, why did it matter? The agent replied that you couldn't hold yourself out as a green engineer without being certified. Nancy still didn't understand. Why were they being raided? The agent calmly said it was because they did business under the name Green Engineers.

Nancy was in disbelief. Green was their last name. They did business under their last name. The agent replied that under the new law it didn't matter. They were clearly holding themselves out as green engineers without being certified.

Tom came over to ask why they didn't just place a phone call. Why didn't they provide them with some sort of notice before raiding them?

The agent just shrugged. She said that wasn't how the government worked anymore.

Tom was further enraged and again demanded to know why they had killed his dog. Dooger was trained to protect their house. He was killed for following his instincts. The agent said sometimes bad things happened in a raid.

With the shocking death of Dooger, the TV stations did not air any video of the raid. They were afraid of what the state senator and his cronies would do if they were embarrassed by the truth. And so the free media made a political calculation to stay silent.

The case against Tom and Nancy proceeded at light speed. The district attorney and judge were closely aligned with Eddie and Bobby Jones.

The law used against the Greens was a very clear strict liability statute. If they used the word "green" with engineering and they weren't certified it didn't matter if they intended to break the law or not. They were guilty. The law provided for a one year prison term. On the advice of his attorney, and to get it all over with, Tom agreed to plead guilty and accept a lesser sentence. As part of the deal Nancy was not penalized.

When the settlement was finalized, Tom was sentenced to two months in prison.

The Criminalization of Business Activity

Both federal and state governments have significantly expanded the number of rules and regulations which now constitute criminal activity. Whereas it used to be that knowledge of a crime was required, our government has taken short cuts to prove a crime, with the result being that more and more business owners are being ensnared in the criminal justice system.

As well, as America seemingly devolves into narrow self-interests and as companies actively engage in crony capitalism to the exclusion of their less well funded competitors, government becomes a crass tool for the politically connected. The money flows to politicians who use the levers of government to deny and harass the disconnected for the benefit of their campaign contributing patrons.

Our transition from a free-wheeling, open economy to one dominated by focused special interests is being noticed around the world.

America's standing on the World Corruption Index has steadily declined to 24th out of 178 nations. In the top three spots are New Zealand,

Denmark and Finland. Also ahead of the United States are countries such as Barbados, the Bahamas, Qatar and Chile. The group advancing the index is Transparency International. They define corruption as "the abuse of entrusted power for private gain." Are you pleased by all the Wall Street bailouts?

By including this information we are not trying to discourage you from starting and/or running a business. Quite the contrary, the country needs entrepreneurs like you to pursue great opportunities and employ others along the way. So please do not be deterred. But please also be realistic. Government investigations and raids are on the rise. Some are brought against bad people who deserve to go to prison. However, a certain percentage of these government actions are brought against innocent actors, such as Tom and Nancy, who had no intent to violate any law. But as the government now writes the laws, intent is not a factor.

The point, then, of this section is to give you the tools and information you will need in the event of a problem.

The following are six tips for dealing with such issues:

1. Know the Standard

As mentioned, many crimes are now of the strict liability variety, where no intent is required. It didn't used to be this way.

The common law test for criminal liability comes from the Roman Empire's use of the Latin phrase "actus non facit reum nisi mens sit rea" which means "the act does not make the person guilty unless the mind is also guilty." The Romans had a good sense of things. Why should you be held liable for something if you never intended for it to happen? And so it was handed down that there must be both an "actus reus," a criminal act, along with some level of "mens rea," or a guilty mind. But now there are modern day exceptions to this ancient and prudent policy. Now there are the strict liability crimes, where no "mens rea" is needed. With strict liability, if you commit the act you are guilty of the crime. Whether you had no clue it was a crime or had no idea your actions could even lead to a problem does not matter. With strict liability if the act is committed you are at fault. A judge can summarize the situation in three words: "Guilty. Next case." But in our convoluted and complicated system of laws is this fair and just?

A famous recent strict liability case involved a facilities engineer at a Washington D.C. military retirement home. *("A Sewage Blunder Earns Engineer a Criminal Record," Wall Street Journal, December 12, 2011.)* To stop the noxious flooding from backed up toilets where military retirees were residing, the engineer diverted the blocked sewage system into an outside storm drain pipe, which everyone believed was tied into the city's sewer system. Instead, the pipe ran to a nearby creek. As such, a strict liability environmental law was violated. The engineer had no intent to pollute. He assumed the government knew where its own pipes went. But the wheels of our criminal justice system do not always roll smoothly or logically. The engineer received one year's probation and was placed under court ordered supervision. For dealing with backed up toilets to help out military retirees the engineer now has a criminal record.

As well, there is a new legal violation known as "the Responsible Corporate Officers Doctrine." This doctrine allows misdemeanor prosecutions without any proof of intent. If the defendant corporate officer presides over a division of the corporation where a violation by someone else occurred they can be held responsible—even if they had no notice of the act. The Department of Justice is using this doctrine with increasing frequency. So you have no notice of what is occurring, you have no intent for it to occur, and the government sends you to jail for its occurrence. Again, is this fair or just?

As our state and federal governments enact ever more regulations with strict liability standards it becomes nearly impossible for the average business owner to keep up with them. Belonging to a trade group that monitors legislations affecting your industry makes sense. But even then, you may not catch everything. Which is why the remaining points are important to know.

2. Hire the Right Lawyer

You may deal with the best tax or real estate attorney in town. In almost all cases, they will not be the right lawyer for you when the government comes calling.

At the first sign of a government investigation—whether you are to be a witness or a target—you need to retain competent counsel. The right attorney will be one who has dealt with the investigating agency and the matter being investigated. Typically, they are referred to as 'white collar' criminal attorneys. They know how to interact with government agencies which is vital since the relationships, rules and consequences are completely different from the norm.

3. Respond

Ignoring the government is not a good idea. They are not going away. Any government inquiry must be met with an immediate response from competent counsel. Your attorney should contact the lead agent or head prosecutor to find out if the company is a target or a witness. If a target, you need to know why. What do they plan to charge you with and what evidence do they have for indicting you? If the company or an employee is just needed as a witness you are in a safer spot but you still need counsel. You will want your attorney to make sure you are cooperating with all of the government's requests for information.

4. No Destruction

Speaking of information, don't destroy any of it. Even routine, pre-planned document destruction should be halted until the matter blows over. It may be difficult and time consuming for the government to prove the underlying case. By contrast, it is very easy for the government to prove obstruction of justice nowadays. ("Was the shredder on? Strict liability.

What size orange jump suit do you wear?") Don't hand them the easy case by destroying documents. Besides, it makes you look guilty.

5. Subpoenas and Search Warrants

If you receive a subpoena requesting the production of documents you are typically a witness in a government investigation. Even so, contact your white collar criminal attorney to assist with the production.

If you receive a search warrant at your place of business from a team of armed agents, take a deep breath and contact your attorney immediately. You are the target of a government investigation. You will be told to stand aside while the agents take whatever documents they want. Hopefully, your attorney gets there in time to monitor the search. Hopefully, they will be allowed to make copies of the documents seized.

Neither the owners nor the employees can be forced to give interviews during the search. That doesn't stop agents from trying to interview people, and if it's voluntary you can't prevent it. A better strategy is to send everyone home at the start of the search. Tell them to call in the morning. Get them off the premises. Any necessary personnel should be told about interview rule but also told to otherwise cooperate with the agents.

6. Next Steps

If you are a witness, work with your attorney to prepare for any document production and interviews. If you are a target a good attorney is going to make a big difference. You are going to want to promptly deal with the government and aggressively work on resolving the matter.

A good lawyer may be able to convince the government there is not enough evidence or that the evidence is flawed. Sometimes a 'deferred prosecution agreement' can be negotiated whereby fines are paid, reforms are implemented and there is full cooperation with the investigation. Later meeting the requirements can result in a dismissal of the charges.

Sometimes the government has brought pressure to bear so that you will be a witness against a bigger fish up the line. A good attorney may be able to work out a favorable deal with prosecutors.

Know that, like earthquakes and lawsuits, a government investigation can arrive out of the blue. Remember the steps we have discussed above to protect your interests.

Rich Dad Tips

- Know that government at all levels is increasingly involved in business activities.

- Join a trade group that effectively monitors new government rules and regulations affecting your business.

- And with all the risks you face, don't forget to give yourself an award once in a while.

And now let's review a few more upsets that can occur along the way...

Chapter Fourteen

Year Two

As we have discussed throughout, your corporate veil is important. It protects your personal assets and your company's assets. As you complete your second year in business, take a minute to review some of the maintenance actions that keep your corporate veil strong.

- Are you keeping complete corporate records of all decisions?

- Are you and your directors and shareholders remembering to present the world with corporate notice and signing all documents with corporate title?

- Are all annual filings up to date?

- Are corporate formalities in place, including a registered agent filed with the state?

- Is the corporation sufficiently capitalized, with its own bank account(s)?

- Are you making certain you keep personal and corporate assets separate?

- Will you be filing a separate tax return for your corporate entity?

Again, as Robert Kiyosaki said, basic asset protection is not enough anymore. You must take the necessary steps throughout your entity's history to ensure that your corporate veil is strong, secure and, above all, protective.

Alana and Sherri

Clint was at the lodge when Wilson, his attorney buddy, asked the question, "Whatever happened to the annual meeting about the salon that you wanted advice on?"

Clint sipped his beer and tried to remember. He hadn't thought about it for quite a while. He didn't think there had ever been notice of a meeting. Was that bad?

Wilson indicated that they were supposed to hold a meeting once a year. And now they were going on two years without a meeting. That wasn't good. But on the other hand, Wilson noted that the salon seemed to be doing well. Wilson asked, "Are they making any money?"

Clint did not want to admit there was more money in the household due to the salon. All he experienced was Sherri spending more time at work and at networking events and not enough time at home. He was not happy about things.

Clint asked Wilson if the girls should be holding an annual meeting. Wilson said yes. That was all Clint needed to hear.

Clint erratically drove to the salon and loudly confronted the girls as they were closing up. Sherri and Alana were both embarrassed by his tone and inebriated demeanor in front of several customers leaving for the night. They sat him down in the supply/break room and told him to keep still until they finished closing,

After calming their customers and escorting them out they returned to see Clint looking through their file cabinets.

Alana angrily brushed him aside. She told him he had no business going through their files.

Clint demanded to see the annual meeting notes. Or, he sneered, did they not have them?

Sherri tried to calm her husband down. But he was lit up and would not listen to anyone telling him to calm down.

Alana reached into the open file cabinet and pulled out several documents. They were the Waiver of Notice of Annual Meeting and the Written Consent of Meeting forms.

Alana said they had held last year's and this year's meetings without him. They didn't want him there and the law allowed them to conduct it that way.

Clint was furious. He and Sherri had 50% of the salon. They couldn't do it without him.

Alana, with obvious relish, told Clint he had no idea what he was talking about. She and Will had 48% and Big Jim had 4% of the salon. With 52% they could legally hold the meetings without him.

Clint glared at Sherri, who was scared and near tears. How could she go behind his back like this?

Alana interjected. They did it on advice of counsel. So he wouldn't be mindlessly disruptive, as he was now.

Clint screamed at Sherri. She was listening to that weasel attorney Jay over her own husband. He yelled she had violated their marriage vows.

Sherri was sobbing now. All she wanted was to benefit her family.

Clint saw no benefit in all of this. He shouted that he wanted a divorce. He moved towards his wife as if he would hit her and Alana interceded. She demanded he leave.

As soon as Clint left, still swearing and yelling, Alana was on the phone to Big Jim. He needed to collect his granddaughter, little Ellie, from the babysitter. Sherri and Ellie would be living with Alana for a time.

Tom and Nancy

When Tom was released from his two month prison sentence, there were film crews from around the world to record it and thousands of well-wishers there to greet him.

A great deal had occurred since Tom was sentenced. A TV station intern who recorded the raid was incensed that her station wouldn't air the video of the government killing Dooger. She snuck out a copy and released it on YouTube. Everyone in town (except Betty and the bank manager) loved Dooger. They were shocked at the graphic and unnecessary death of the Great Dane. Friends told friends. The video went viral and the raid became global news. Groups from PETA to the Tea Party were outraged that the government would kill a dog trained to protect the owner's house.

As well, the story behind the raid began to emerge. The community and eventually the country became offended at the crass manipulation of government for private benefit. Creating a green certification to target a competitor named Green became a symbol of government corruption. State Senator Bobby Jones, the judge and the D.A. were recalled and thrown out of office.

People stopped requesting bids from Jones & Hunt Engineering Ltd. And business grew for the newly named Hardcastle Engineers, P.C. (Hardcastle was Nancy's maiden name). But at what emotional cost?

Two days after his release, Tom received an ominous letter from the IRS. Payroll taxes, withholding taxes plus penalties and interest were due immediately. If payments were not made, criminal penalties were a possibility.

After all they had been going through, Tom and Nancy were shocked by this latest salvo. Tom suggested they call Betty and find out what was the problem. Nancy thought otherwise. Betty had not been very responsive lately. She noted that perhaps Betty was the problem.

They promptly made an appointment with Katherine, their lawyer. They scanned and emailed the IRS letter to her so she would be ready for their meeting the next day. In an hour Katherine had them scan and email an authorization for her to speak to the IRS on their behalf.

On his call with Katherine, Tom wanted to know if this IRS problem was tied to his other run in with the government. Was it a conspiracy to harass him?

Katherine replied that there was no evidence of the IRS playing politics since the end of the Nixon Administration. She felt it was more of a coincidence than a conspiracy. Since the IRS audited everyone nowadays she did not see any signs of favoritism in their actions. With the IRS, everyone was an equal opportunity target.

When they sat down in her office the next day Katherine was ready. She had called the IRS contact to learn about the problem. Katherine had seen it before. It related to the $5,000 payment they received their first week in business.

Tom and Nancy were confused. That was over two years ago. Why would it surface now?

Katherine informed them that it took the IRS that long to match things up.

Match what up?

Katherine explained that the IRS eventually got around to matching the Form 941s, the quarterly federal payroll tax payment forms, with the W-2s, the form which reports wages paid for the prior year.

When Katherine spoke to the IRS representatives they indicated that there was trouble on both forms. First of all, they had taken a $5,000 payment in their first quarter of business and had not filed a Form 941. Not only did they not file the form but they didn't withhold any monies on the income.

Nancy argued that the $5,000 was not a salary but was used to pay necessary expenses. They were behind on the mortgage and other bills that had to be paid right away. Katherine explained that those were all personal expenses, which were paid for with after tax dollars. Meaning that you had to pay withholding and payroll taxes before you got to pay off your pressing bills.

Katherine continued by explaining when they didn't pay the taxes for the 1st Quarter the money that they did pay in the 2nd Quarter was applied to pay off the 1st Quarter. The IRS always applies moneys to the first unpaid obligation. Of course, this meant that payments intended for the 2nd Quarter payment weren't paid (they had gone to the 1st Quarter.) As such, penalties and interest were due for the late 2nd Quarter payment.

Katherine further explained how this all could snowball into large IRS fines. Essentially, since the beginning they were always late. The 3rd Quarter payment paid off the 2nd Quarter but now the 3rd Quarter payments were late, and so on and so on. The penalties and interest for always being one quarter late really added up.

The lawyer then laid out the second problem. She could only surmise since she hadn't yet spoken to Betty, but she had seen it before and guessed at what happened.

Betty must have noticed at the end of year one that a salary payment, the $5,000 first week payment, was made out to Tom and Nancy. Because it was salary she included it in the W-2 statement of wages. The problem was that she didn't amend the Form 941 to include the withholding that should have been made on the salary payment. As such, the W-2 and the 941's did not match up.

When that happened alarms went off at the IRS. The fact that it took them a year or more to match things up did not matter. They owed penalties and interest from the date of the infraction, not the date it was discovered.

Katherine explained that the IRS held the individuals involved personally responsible. It didn't matter if it was the bookkeeper's mistake. The owners were to blame. Katherine suggested that it might make sense to pay the penalties and interest off now, before additional penalties, interest and sanctions were added to the amount. She noted that the IRS charged a penalty of 2% for tax deposits made one to five days late. It rose to 15% for payments not received within ten days of an IRS demand for payment.

The total amount owed was $15,000. All for one missed filing and payment. Tom and Nancy grudgingly agreed to pay and be done with it.

Audits

As you run your own corporation you may sometimes feel like you are running it for the federal government as well.

You must overcome this nagging feeling by knowing that: Your business is being run for the benefit of the federal government. Of course, you are running it for your benefit, and if done right you will benefit handsomely. But, like it or not, the government is a beneficiary of your business success. And not only that, but if you don't pay what the IRS super computer determines is fair you are going to be checked on for the accuracy of Uncle Sam's cut.

That's just the way it is.

As a business, especially an enterprise involving self-employment, the IRS audit rate is four times greater than that of wage earners. Face it, with the withholding of personal income taxes and limited write offs, there isn't that much for the IRS to get from a wage earner that they haven't already attached. A business, however, with its deductions and ability to control the receipt of income and payment of salaries is fertile ground for the IRS. (But again, please don't let any of this deter you from owning and operating a business. You can get through it, as we'll discuss ahead.)

When it comes to businesses, the IRS audits sole proprietors at a five times greater rate than corporations or LLCs. (This is to your advantage because you are not going to operate as a sole proprietor anyway.)

Why the greater IRS scrutiny on sole proprietorships? Well, look at it from the IRS point of view. If you are serious about your business you will want the asset protection of an entity. If you aren't concerned about unlimited personal liability and operate as a sole proprietorship, maybe you aren't that serious about your business. (Who wouldn't want to be protected?) Hence, maybe your business isn't really a serious business and, if so, maybe it should be audited. Sole proprietors, who report their business income on Schedule C of their Form 1040 individual tax returns and in many cases do not have professional tax help, are prime targets for this reason. Collecting from sole proprietors is easy pickings for the IRS.

So operating as a corporation or LLC will reduce your audit risk. But it won't reduce it altogether. Your corporation, LLC or LP is still filing a tax return that is reviewed by the IRS super computer. This powerful, all knowing computer is constantly checking the ratios of your business income to its expenses, and comparing it to other operators in your industry. For example, if you are a florist and your cost of flowers is 52% when everyone else in the field is paying 38%, you may be flagged for review.

The IRS computer also tracks which industries indicate a high rate of noncompliance. It can identify herd movements, which may be car dealers one year and funeral parlor operators the next. If your trade group is inviting offshore tax shelter promoters to speak at your annual convention (which, for some reason, dentists seem to do all the time) count on being audited in a few years' time as your herd moves into risky territories. As well, the longer you are in business the greater the chance you will be audited. That is just a fact of business life.

And since you are going to run your corporation for a good, long time it is important to know ahead of it what is involved with an audit.

Audit Behavior

An IRS audit not only reviews your tax return but also reviews you and your business. You are not dealing with a computer at this stage but a real live person who is making subjective observations about you and your honesty.

As such, how you behave is important.

But first, it is important to know that you have some rights in all of this. To keep the IRS in check, Congress passed a Taxpayer Bill of Rights. (It is discussed in IRS Publication 1 found at irs.gov.) The four main Rights are:

1. You can have a representative meet the auditor on your behalf.
2. You can participate in setting the time and place of the audit.
3. You can tape or video record your meetings with the IRS.
4. You can speak with the auditor's manager if you feel like you are being treated unfairly.

Know your rights, and know that there are three types of audits. With a correspondence audit the IRS has you mail in requested documents. With an office audit they have you bring the documents to the local IRS office and go through them with a tax examiner.

Then there is a field audit. A field audit is much more involved than an office or correspondence audit. These are generally performed on corporations, LLCs or sole proprietorships with annual revenues of $100,000 or more. The IRS revenue agents (or field auditors) conducting these field audits are much better trained than the office auditors. They are also good at delivering results. The average adjustment (meaning extra taxes, penalties and interest) collected for the IRS from field audits now averages over $15,000 per case.

Given the numbers, how you behave becomes important.

The first field audit tip is to not meet at your office. One of your rights is to meet the field auditor away from your business. If their presence would interfere with your business (and how could it not) you can meet at the IRS office or, if you have a CPA, at their accounting offices.

Also, by not meeting at your office, the field auditor is denied the opportunity to observe your business and form the impression that it is doing better than you've reported. As well, the auditor is not able to talk to your employees and make further impressions.

Finally, by meeting elsewhere, the auditor's request for further documents is delayed. ("Sorry, they're back at the office.") The auditor may drop the request or, if they are still sought, you can edit out materials not relevant to the audit.

What if you have a home office? Absent a court order you don't have to let an auditor into your house. If you've claimed a home office deduction, photographs and drawings of your home office space will generally suffice.

A second suggestion is to have your accountant meet with the field auditor. An experienced CPA is used to dealing with such types. They know the language and the boundaries. They are less likely to be intimidated. You, on the other hand, may very quickly devolve into a nervous wreck.

But, if you must go, please behave accordingly. Aside from offering a coffee or a soda don't offer anything to the auditor. Generosity borders bribery in this arena. Also know that the auditor is not your friend, and don't try to make them into one. It won't work and it's not appropriate. Conversely, they are not Satan's agent from hell intent on destroying your life. (Keep this straight, that is your ex, not the IRS.) You must tell yourself that the field auditor is just doing their job. Knowing that, your response is to be cordial and concise.

Please watch what you say. When certain people get nervous they will rattle on about anything and everything. The IRS knows this and welcomes it. And so the fact that you saw the Hagia Sophia will not lead to a pleasant chit chat of how wonderful it is to see a beautiful and massive church built in 537 AD. Instead, it will lead to a suspicion of how you could afford a trip to Istanbul and Turkey.

Your best response to an auditor's direct question is "yes" or "no." If you don't know the answer, say so. Tell them that you'll get back to them or that you'll check with your accountant.

If you feel like you are in over your head, like you are sinking to the bottom, ask for a break. You can always request a bathroom or lunch break. But as well, remembering the Taxpayer Bill of Rights, you have the right to bring in a tax representative at any time. If you need to reschedule so that you can have professional assistance, that is your right. Be firm with the auditor on this point if they press you to continue.

If you run into a field auditor who is nasty or hostile you also have rights. Most auditors are very professional. The one I dealt with could not have been more courteous. (Yes, I have been audited, and I always had my CPA at my side.) But some, like a very small number of cops, for whatever reason have a chip on their shoulder, and they like to dish it out. If you face such hostility ask them to stop. (Remember that one of your other rights is to record the meeting.) If the hostility continues, ask to speak with their manager. If that doesn't work, walk out. You are entitled to calm and courtesy and you do not have to put up with anything less. Send your CPA to the next meeting, which is also your right to do.

Audit Time Lines

How long does the IRS have to audit a tax return? The general rule is that three years after the date the return was filed is the cut off. Filing starts the clock ticking, which is a good thing. Of course, if you didn't file a return in any one year there is no cut off. The IRS can audit you at any time for a long time. Similarly, if you file a fraudulent tax return there is no audit time limit.

There is one other exception to the 36 month audit cut off rule. The deadline is extended by three years to a total of six years if you understate your income by 25% or more.

If you are to be audited you will receive notice via first class mail 12 to 18 months after filing your tax return. (Beware of email scammers pretending to be the IRS to get at your personal information. The IRS never sends out emails.) After 19 months without IRS notice consider yourself free from audit on the returns you filed 19 months ago, subject to the exceptions for fraud and under reporting previously mentioned.

If you do receive an audit notice the IRS seeks to finish the audit within 28 months from the date you filed the return in question. The 28 month time frame is an internal IRS guideline that allows for appeals and such so that the case can be finalized within the 36 month Statute of Limitations.

These timelines are important for you. Auditors are under time pressures to close out your file. The older the case the more pressure the auditor feels. As well, their job performance is partly based on wrapping up cases. Given those conditions, use them to your advantage when negotiating a settlement. Know that while the IRS claims that auditors are not allowed to negotiate, a certain give and take over many issues is common. Having an experienced CPA at your side will be advantageous for this drill.

What Is An Auditor Looking For?

Well, put yourself in their shoes. What would you look for? That's right. You've got it.

Unreported income.

If you don't report it they can't tax it. But if you are paid by check they can find out by your bank deposits to both business and personal accounts. If you don't voluntarily turn over the records they can get them from the bank.

If you are a cash business, watch out. The IRS is institutionally suspicious of all cash businesses. Think of laundromats, bars, restaurants and minimarts. They all deal in cash, and are frequently audited.

But it can be pretty hard for them to prove that you received cash. So the IRS has to get creative and even more suspicious. On the creative side, for example, certain laundromat owners were reporting very little income. How could the IRS prove the machines were being used? Some smart auditor figured out to check the water bills. The more water usage, the more loads of laundry and the more unreported quarters. Now the water bill trail is standard procedure.

On the suspicion side they will look at your lifestyle. When a low reported income is matched with vacation homes, sports cars, jewelry and boats you had better have received a large inheritance or won the lottery. Otherwise, you can expect an aggressive audit and perhaps a criminal investigation.

After unreported income issues the auditors are next after improper business expenses. Have you ever taken something as a business expense that perhaps was really a personal expense? That's ok. You are not alone.

But know that in an IRS audit you must prove the deduction was for a profit-making purpose. Meaning the IRS doesn't have to do anything but raise the issue. You have the burden of proof, so you'd better have good records. Certain fertile fields for IRS scrutiny include:

- Travel and entertainment
- Auto expenses
- Personal living costs
- Vacation costs

As you can see, having good records will greatly assist you. Working with a good bookkeeper or CPA will be a huge advantage for you in an audit. With proper assistance, you may not be audited to begin with, which is a good thing. At last check, you have a business to run.

Bobo and Morton

Glockenspiel Ventura had grown in the last two years. Bobo and Morton now had two employees working with them. They performed all sorts of services for families in an expanding radius. They had a fully licensed kennel where they kept animals overnight and longer. They performed inventory services for homeowners who needed to identify what they owned to insurance companies. They had developed an iPhone app program to assist with the inventory work. They subcontracted a window washing service and oversaw the work when a family was away. Whatever request a homeowner had for a unique or different service the boys tried to meet it.

All was going well until they were served with a lawsuit.

The Pickelson family was suing Glockenspiel Ventura and Bobo and Morton personally for the theft of three very valuable paintings by Percy Gray, a master impressionist painter of California landscapes in the early twentieth century.

Immediately, everybody in the area was talking. It turned out not many people really liked Kelly and Kelli Pickelson. They were newly rich and liked to flaunt their new wealth. Bobo's newest client called them 'show oafs.' Another client laughed that the missing paintings were not Monets or Matisses but just Percy Grays. Why all the fuss?

Aunt Maddy confided to the boys that one of the Trenthams had blackballed them from The Club. She speculated the lawsuit was in retaliation for that.

But a lawsuit had been filed and it had to be dealt with. The Trenthams and the McGills wanted the boys to promptly go meet with Parker T. Ruxton. The boys refused. They didn't like the family's stuffy, condescending and overpriced lawyer. Besides, the insurance company had been notified and they were assigning their own attorney to handle the case.

Two days later, Bobo and Morton, along with their bookkeeper Horatio Manfred met with Raj Patel, the attorney for the insurance company. Raj had spoken to the attorney representing the Pickelson family. Reading between the lines it seemed as if the Pickelsons were indeed pursuing Bobo and Morton personally so that they could reach the Trentham and McGill family fortunes.

Bobo and Morton wanted to know how they could do that. Parker T. Ruxton had set them up as a C corporation. Why would they be personally responsible?

Raj showed them two documents. One was their contract. It listed Glockenspiel Ventura but did not indicate that it was a corporation. It didn't say Inc. or Corporation at the end of it where you sign. So the Pickelson family could infer they were working with Bobo and Morton individually, as general partners. In which case, they would be personally liable.

Bobo was angry. They had their contract reviewed by Aunt Maddy's attorney. But then Morton remembered they had told the attorney not to change anything at the end of the contract. The attorney had followed their directions.

Raj then showed the boys their business card. Nowhere did it indicate that Glockenspiel Ventura was a protective business entity. Again, the words Inc. or Corp. or Corporation were not on the card, leaving the impression that Bobo and Morton were general partners. Again, such an impression would allow the Pickelsons to sue them personally.

Horatio Manfred had been smiling throughout the examination and discussion of the two documents. Raj finally asked the bald bow-tied bookkeeper what was so amusing.

Horatio pulled out two documents of his own. The first was an invoice to the Pickelson family. At the top it read:

Statement
Glockenspiel Ventura, Inc.

At the bottom it read:

Please make payment to:
Glockenspiel Ventura, Inc.
c/o Horatio Manfred Bookkeeping, LLC

Raj smiled when he saw the invoice. His smile grew when he reviewed Manfred's second document. It was a copy of a check written by Kelli Pickelson. It was made out to Glockenspiel Ventura, Inc.

This was good, Raj noted. It would be difficult for the Pickelson family to maintain they were doing business with Bobo and Morton individually when Mrs. Pickelson had made a check out to their corporation for services rendered.

Obviously, Raj stated, changes would have to be made to their contracts, cards and other literature. The corporate designation of Inc., Corp. or Corporation had to be included in such documents to provide corporate notice. He reiterated that they should always let the world know that they were doing business with an entity and not an individual. But with a nod to Horatio he said the check made out to their corporation would certainly help carry the load.

Bobo then brought up a new item. He and Morton had performed their inventory service for the Pickelson family. The three Percy Gray paintings were not a part of their iPhone inventory.

Horatio interrupted Bobo's discussion. He was immediately taken by their inventory service. Horatio had billed for it but had never seen it work. Bobo was happy to show him. With their iPhones they took a picture of the item. It was stored in a file. The file was connected to a database of property values. When it was all done they provided the insurance company with a complete file of pictures and values for each household. The insurance companies loved the service and had started asking them to sell it or license it or whatever. Bobo and Morton hadn't really decided how to proceed. Horatio smiled at the opportunity.

Raj brought the discussion back to the case. Did Bobo say that the Percy Gray paintings were not part of the inventory? That was correct, according to Morton. They had never recorded such paintings. They had since learned that Percy Gray was a leader in the early California landscape movement and that his paintings were appreciating quite nicely. But how could they steal them if they'd never seen them?

Raj played devil's advocate. Wouldn't it be smarter to steal them and then not include them on the inventory list? Bobo slammed his pudgy hand on the table and swore that they didn't steal anything. Raj calmed him down. He explained that to develop the case they had to look at all angles, both good and bad. He said that the fact that the paintings did not show up on their inventory would be argued to their advantage.

Raj further explained that the insurance company was covering their defense costs. There could possibly be a settlement in the future to make the case go away. But for now, he would answer the complaint and be in touch with them as the case developed.

Two weeks later, the lives of the Trentham and McGill families were turned upside down forever.

Two stunning developments occurred within two days of each other.

First, Frank Fodom, the genius investment guru at The Thracian Club was indicted for running a Ponzi Scheme. Many Club members, including the Trenthams and McGills, had invested heavily with him. All their money was missing.

Second, a group of brokers at one of Wall Street's top investment banks had sought to maximize their commissions by inflating property values in a complex securities offering. The Trenthams and McGills had both invested heavily in this offering at the suggestion of their trusted commission-based advisors. The offering was now turning out to be worthless.

And so, in a matter of days, the family fortunes of the Trenthams and the McGills were lost. And many other families that had confidently invested with The Club guru and with the top Wall Street investment bank were also suddenly way, way back on their heels. For the Trenthams and McGills many felt—but never spoke of—the irony of the whole situation: Several generations of hard work, manufacture and industry were completely lost in several years of a commission-fueled frenzy of financial chicanery. Many lives would never be the same.

The shocking reversals severely affected the business of Glockenspiel Ventura. Instead of house-sitting for families going to the Caribbean or Aspen, families were now selling their vacation homes and sitting idly in their own homes, wondering how they would pay the bills.

The very public loss of wealth suffered by the Trentham and McGill families had an effect on the case brought against Bobo and Morton by the Pickelson family. It was dropped.

The attorney for the Pickelson family said there was nothing to get. The boys believed that Aunt Maddy had been right. The case was brought in retaliation for Tom Trentham blackballing the Pickelson family from joining The Club. And now, after the Ponzi and other schemes wiped out the wealth of The Club, the Pickelsons could have walked in and bought the whole facility for pennies on the dollar.

Raj was not easily thrown off the track. He believed that the boys had never seen the Percy Gray paintings when they took their inventory. He got the sense that the Pickelsons were up to something. And he worked for an insurance company that liked to pursue such people. It was his company's belief that the fewer sophisticated people playing the angles was better for all insurance companies. Raj had an insurance investigator pursue all sales of Percy Gray paintings. After six weeks he received notice that a sale of three Percy Grays had been made in Buenos Aires eight months earlier. Incredibly, they had been able to trace four transfers of money through intermediaries back to the Pickelson family.

Raj provided all the information in a gift wrapped box to the local district attorney. It was all he needed to convict Kelly and Kelli Pickelson for insurance fraud.

But for Bobo and Morton a bigger issue was at hand. Their families, including Aunt Maddy, were destitute.

Alana and Sherri

Clint was once again speaking to Wilson down at the lodge about his legal issues. Once he had asked for a divorce, Big Jim and the rest of the family shut him out. Sherrie and little Ellie were now living with Alana, and not even Will would talk to him anymore.

Clint asked Wilson to represent him in the divorce, figuring he'd do it for free, or at least at a reduced rate. Wilson said he had no experience in that area, but that he could give him the names of some expensive junk yard dog attorneys. Clint didn't want expensive. In that case, Wilson said, he had the name of a cheap paralegal.

Clint thought that with the salon doing so well that he would make out just fine. He'd get a new house and a new life with a new wife.

But Clint soon came to learn that divorce never involves a joyous exit, especially with a paralegal who can file the paperwork but not fight the fights.

The issue had to do with the Buy Sell Agreement Big Jim had forced Clint to sign. It called for him to receive book value of his interest. Through their Living Trust he and Sherri owned 48% of Salon Sen-Sey LLC. Clint thought his 24% share of the business would be worth a lot of money.

That is until Clint learned that book value was the lowest measure for valuing an interest there was. Instead of valuing its ongoing concern value, with all the money coming in the door, it just measured the book value of the equipment, a much lower amount.

Clint complained to Wilson at the lodge about what was happening. He was getting screwed by the Buy Sell Agreement. Wilson said not to blame him. He had told Clint not to sign it.

Clint said Big Jim forced him to sign it. Wilson had heard this before and again told Clint that he needed a good attorney to press that point. Buy Sell Agreements were modified all the time when pressure or duress was used at the outset to get a party to sign. A good attorney could get him a good result. But, Wilson said again, a paralegal was not an attorney, and couldn't fight for him in court.

When Clint once again said he couldn't afford an attorney, Wilson said he couldn't afford not to have one. And as Clint went on and on about the unfairness of it all, even Wilson tuned him out.

A key element in a Buy Sell Agreement, as Clint learned, is how you value the interests. Book value is the lowest valuation, and will result in a very low, perhaps artificially low, pay out. On the other hand, the going concern value, or a value based on what a private party would pay for the cash flow and the opportunity to expand the business, will result in a higher pay out.

It is also important to know that the attorney who prepares the Buy Sell Agreement most often represents the Company. That means they do not represent you. You need to get your own attorney for advice and counsel. You need to have someone on your side to make sure you are not pressured into signing an agreement that will haunt you later. Buy Sell agreements are covered in greater detail in our companion volume, *Start Your Own Corporation.*

As it turned out, the divorce and child custody and property settlement agreements went better than expected for Sherri. She could thank Jay for that. He and his firm were there every step of the way for her.

Early on Jay had explained that because he had represented the Company he could not represent Sherri personally in her divorce proceedings. However, there was another lady in the firm named Melissa who was an excellent divorce attorney. He would have Melissa work with Sherri. If Clint ever complained about a conflict they would deal with the issue. He knew plenty of good divorce attorneys outside the firm as well.

As luck would have it, Clint was too cheap and short sighted to get a real attorney. The paralegal did not pursue, much less raise, the issue of a potential conflict of interest with Jay's firm representing both the company and Sherri personally. Of course, the paralegal was not (and really could not) be paid to render such advice. And if the conflict issue was not raised then it was waived. Meaning it was Sherri and Melissa, the experienced divorce attorney, versus Clint and his honest but thoroughly overmatched paralegal. The resulting arrangement left Sherri with a full 48% interest in the salon, the house and custody of Ellie. Sherri refinanced the house into her name and pulled some money out to pay off Clint.

Clint moved to a city 350 miles away. He did not visit Ellie as often as he could.

Once the proceedings were all final Jay invited Sherri down to his office. He said there were two items to be taken care of to finish it up. First, the ownership of the 48% needed to be transferred into Sherri's name. Jay had prepared the paperwork. Sherri signed in all the correct spaces and asked Jay what the second matter involved.

Jay said he had wanted to ask her something since the first time she came in. But with the marriage and the divorce and all he couldn't until now.

"What is it?" she asked.

Jay smiled and said, "Would you join me for dinner?"

Sherri agreed to their first date.

LLC Managers and Corporate Directors and Officers Review

As they hold considerable power in your business, it's important for you to review every now and then your corporate directors and officers and/ or LLC managers. Of course, if it is just you recognize that there are still formalities to be followed for 'just you.' You want to keep that protective corporate veil in place. As such, you want the following done on an annual basis:

- LLC

  Member(s) elect Manager(s)

- Corporation

  Shareholder(s) elect Board of Director(s)

  Board of Director(s) elect Officer(s)

In many states you must fill at least three corporate officer positions: President, Secretary and Treasurer. In Wyoming, Nevada and certain other states one person can serve in all three positions. You then have the option of filling other positions such as chief operating officer, chief financial officer, vice presidents and the like if the Board of Directors so decides.

A review is in order for a variety of reasons. First, you only want people listed as an officer, director or manager if they are still involved. Someone who has drifted off but is still listed as an officer may have the power to obligate the Company. You really don't want any nasty surprises.

Especially considering that directors, officers and managers who have not been formally removed can:

- Sign contracts that obligate the company

- Purchase assets

- Sign leases

- Incur debts

- Have access to the Company bank account

Because of this power, directors and officers as well as LLC managers are under a fiduciary duty to act at all times in the best interests of the entity and its owners. Does that mean everyone will? Of course not. Protect your Company and your corporate veil by reviewing your Company officers, directors and managers. Remove those who are inactive, non-responsive or lost.

A review will also determine those who are worthy of protection.

Directors and officers may be indemnified in either the articles of incorporation or the bylaws of a corporation. (The same is true for LLCs but for ease of discussion we will focus on just corporations for now.) Indemnification protects officers and directors against personal lawsuits brought by shareholders or third parties. If personally sued for actions a director or officer took on behalf of the corporation, indemnification allows the officer or director to seek reimbursement from the corporation for any claims or legal defense costs. The corporation can also insure against such risks (see Business Insurance, Chapter 9). Remember that indemnification does not protect against malfeasance or acts committed that involved personal gain, willful misconduct or illegal behavior (i.e. bad personal acts). Also remember that poor business judgment and bad decisions made by officers and directors may not be breaches of fiduciary duty but can still result in lawsuits, liens and debts.

Directors owe the corporation a duty of care and a duty of loyalty, but you owe it to your corporation to make certain you have checked out your board of directors before giving them power. Before a director is appointed to the board, it's a good idea to do a background check and to have each director sign a consent to act as director and a conflict-of-interest check which includes information such as:

- Whether the director has filed for bankruptcy personally or as an officer or director of a company that filed for bankruptcy within the last five years.

- Whether the director has been convicted of a criminal offense.

- Whether the director is currently subject to any orders, judgments or decrees of a court, or limited by judicial order to the types of business, securities or banking activities that director can be engaged in.

- Whether the director has been found to have violated federal or state securities or commodities laws or regulations.

- Whether the director has ever been determined incapable of managing his or her own affairs because of mental infirmity.

These are important issues. Knowing who your officers and directors are is further covered in Chapter 16 of *Start Your Own Corporation*. The fiduciary duties involved are more fully discussed in an ebook primer entitled *Rules of the Company Road* that can be obtained from various online booksellers.

Please don't let years go by without reviewing who has the title, power and authority in your Company. Afterthoughts can become train wrecks.

Rich Dad Tips

- Are your filings up to date? You should check on this every year.
- Always involve your CPA if you are being audited.
- Remember at all times the importance of corporate notice.

As we head into Year Three there are a few more important things to consider...

Chapter Fifteen

Year Three

Tom and Nancy

In the year since Tom had been released from prison a number of things had occurred.

First, Tom became a sought after speaker on government corruption and excess. His real life story and prison sentence, along with all the media attention he had received, gave him a platform. He took advantage of it. Tom had been in Toastmasters for many years and knew how to give a good speech. Now he had the context and content to deliver a great one.

People of all political persuasions were offended that the government would kill a dog that was instinctively protecting an owner's home. Dooger became a symbol and reminder of what a certain segment of Americans believed was an increasingly authoritarian government. Tom used the memory of Dooger in all of his speeches.

Secondly, and again due to what they had been through, their business soared. Everyone sought out Tom and Nancy and the newly renamed Hardcastle Engineers, P.C. for their engineering work.

Their home office was now too small for all the work coming in. Tom and Nancy rented a bigger office in a downtown professional building. They also brought in two more engineers, one with 15 years' experience and one just out of grad school.

To get a good senior engineer the Greens had to be willing to give. The arrangement with Nelson Barry, the more senior engineer, was that if within a year he produced at a high level and brought in his own work he could buy into the business and own a 5% interest in Hardcastle Engineers, P.C. Most professionals wanted an ownership stake. To get a good professional, the Greens knew that equity had to be on the table.

And now with a year up and Nelson producing good numbers for the firm it was time to work out the details of the transaction. Tom and Nancy used Katherine, their attorney, to handle the matter. The first thing to do was make sure that Nelson Barry could become a shareholder. (Remember in our initial organization stages we learned that in most states to be an owner of a professional corporation one had to be licensed in the profession the business engaged in. When you brought aboard new shareholders the same was true.)

Since Nelson was a properly licensed engineer, he was qualified to become a new shareholder of Hardcastle Engineers P.C. With that checked out, a buy sell agreement had to be prepared. It stipulated that if Nelson was ever terminated, quit, lost his license or left for any reason he would have to sell the stock back to Tom and Nancy for what he paid for it.

Nelson's attorney didn't like this provision. It meant that Nelson could not participate in any appreciation of the stock. Katherine agreed that the attorney's complaint was accurate. According to the Buy Sell Agreement, if Nelson paid $15,000 for his 5% interest he would get back the same $15,000 in return when he sold it back to the Company. The key, Katherine noted, was that Nelson would now receive 5% of the flow through profits while he worked for Hardcastle Engineers. Nelson was buying a stream of income. Take it or leave it.

Nelson saw a significant future at Hardcastle. He liked the idea of a salary and bonuses and, on top of that, 5% of the distributable profits. Nelson took the deal.

Katherine then prepared several documents. First, since Betty was no longer doing the bookkeeping, and because the original stock certificates had been lost, a lost certificate statement had to be prepared with minutes issuing replacement certificates to Tom and Nancy. Then the corporation had to hold a meeting to issue the stock to Nelson. Katherine prepared all the corporate minutes for the meeting.

After the documents were signed, Nelson Barry owned 5% of Hardcastle Engineers, P.C. and the business continued to thrive.

Stock Ledger

We are focusing on the stock ledger in the third year for two reasons. First, people frequently lose their certificates and the lost certificate procedure is an easy way to handle this common problem. As well, there was so much information at the start to deal with that we thought that the stock ledger could be dealt with later, especially since it is an issue that always comes up later.

You need to make sure that you keep your stock ledger—the record of what shares in your corporation or what membership interests in your LLC—in order. Why? Let's consider what can happen. Suppose you issue five stock certificates to the original founders as follows:

Name:	Shares:
David Anderson	23,750
Chuck Dickenson	23,750
Bill Faulkner	23,750
Scott Ghormley	23,750
Helen Marcus	5,000

The corporate secretary at the time doesn't record the issuances in the stock ledger. Helen Marcus, a web designer who received shares for her web work, leaves the area and is forgotten. Years go by. The company becomes very successful. Further years later Helen shows up with her stock certificate wondering when she can receive some dividends.

The owners have completely forgotten about her. But she has a claim to 5% of their company. Had they written down her certificate they could have dealt with the problem as they were becoming successful (and more valuable). They could have bought her shares back. If they had a Buy Sell Agreement in place, depending on the terms, that could be very easy to do. (Are you appreciating the value of a Buy Sell Agreement?) Even without a Buy Sell they could have come up with a dollar amount that was enticing enough to clear out the problem. If Helen wouldn't sell they could dilute her interest. Since David, Bill, Chuck and Scott had been working in the business the whole time they could grant themselves shares and stock options and such so that instead of owning 5% of the Company Helen's 5,000 shares only equaled a .001% interest in the Company. All these types of strategies are available. But you've got to know how many shares are issued. Which means you've got to keep your stock ledger in order from the start.

Shares of stock in a corporation or membership interests in an LLC are evidence of ownership and control of the company. They come in the form of certificates and are generally issued in exchange for cash, services or property. Certificates can also be issued in exchange for intellectual property—designs, formulas, copyrights, trademarks, patents and the like—or for real property or tangible assets.

The issuance of certificates are authorized by a corporate resolution (either a consent resolution entered into the corporate book, or as part of the minutes of a meeting).

Issuing certificates (be they for corporate stock or LLC membership interests) is an important part of the process of capitalizing your corporation for two reasons. First, being undercapitalized is grounds for piercing the corporate veil in some states and getting at the shareholder's personal assets. You want to put enough money in the Company and issue certificates for that injection of capital. Secondly, the failure to issue stock in and of itself is grounds for piercing the corporate veil in some states. So you want to do it for your immediate protection. (Please know that most discount incorporation services do not prepare certificates of ownership, leaving you wide open for a veil piercing.)

As we have illustrated, keeping records of certificates issued in a ledger is equally important. Not only do you need to know for your own purposes, but you need to know under the law. Corporate stock and LLC membership interests are securities, meaning they are governed by the sometimes very restrictive state and federal securities laws. Issuing certificates with abandon can lead to serious legal problems. Think of the Mel Brooks movie *The Producers* where 500% of the shares to the musical "Springtime for Hitler" were sold. The musical was going to be so bad that no one would notice the five times over issuance of shares. And guess what happened?... In real life, the securities regulators don't have a healthy sense of humor about such activities. (For more information on the securities laws see Chapter 14 of *Start Your Own Corporation*.)

When stock is issued, it needs to be recorded in a stock ledger. The information in the ledger should include:

- Stock certificate number

- Number of shares

- Shareholder to whom shares were issued

- Address of shareholder to whom shares were issued

- Date of issue

- Amount paid for the shares

- A notation covering the history of the transfer of stock (i.e. why it was transferred)

Some states require two ledgers to be kept—one that records the original issuance of the share and a second that records the number of shares each shareholder owns. That second ledger can be used to determine the numbers of shares owned by each shareholder.

Other states require a copy of the stock ledger be kept by the corporation's registered agent. Check with your professional team to make certain you're following the rules for your state. As we discussed, improperly kept stock ledgers can lead to your corporate veil being pierced. Enough said.

Record Retention

Just as it is key to keep a current stock ledger, it is critical to know which records you must retain over the years.

The issue is this: Massive amounts of information you want to get rid of vs. massive amounts of information the government wants you to keep.

To deal with this, businesses frequently implement a Document Retention Policy. And as you are in your third year of business you will be aware of how much information has piled up and, even if it is in an electronic format, how much it costs you to keep it.

The purpose of a Document Retention Policy is to determine how you will preserve and destroy information. This streamlining will help you save time when searching out necessary information and will also help if documents are requested should litigation (be it a government or business dispute) come into play.

Typically, a Document Retention Policy is developed by the Company's senior management, with input from all the employees in the business. The employees, being on the front lines and dealing with accumulating masses of data, should always be consulted. As well, the company attorney, who should know the legal retention time periods for your specific business, and your IT guy (or Information Technology professional) will also be involved.

The issues to consider include:

- What documents are involved?
- Where are these documents?
- How are they stored?
- Who has control over them?
- How long should the documents be kept?
- Who will decide which document are kept or destroyed?
- How will the documents be destroyed?
- Who is in charge of enforcing the policy?

A significant issue will be determining which laws apply to your business.

At the federal level you have an alphabet soup of agencies and rules, including the IRS, SEC, OSHA, FDA, FLSA, FTC, HIPAA and ERISA.

At the state level you will need to be aware of the requirements of agencies that regulate your business as well as statute of limitations time periods (a period of years in which a claim must be brought). If you do business outside the United States you should also consider the requirements of any international laws.

Now, if you find an inconsistency (i.e. federal law dictates a 5 year hold vs. a state requirement of 4 years) go with the longer hold period. Know that the feds really don't care what the state law says and vice versa. Holding for the longest required period is just prudent.

So let's review some of the holding periods. (We will discuss the permanent and relative designations at the end.) Please know that this is not the full and complete list that applies to your specific business. Also know that time periods and other requirements do change. As you may now gather, we are encouraging you to work with your attorney and other team members to suss out your own situation. But for now:

1. Corporate Records

    • Articles of Incorporation (or Organization) - Permanent

    • Bylaws (or Operating Agreement)   - Permanent

    • Meeting Minutes   - Permanent

    • Other board and committee materials   - Permanent

    • Press Releases   - Permanent

    • Publically filed documents   - Permanent

    • External company audit reports   - Permanent

    • Internal company audit reports   - 3 years

2. Correspondence/Emails   - Relative

3. Banking and Accounting

    • Bank statements, reconciliations, checks   - 3 years
      and deposit slips   (unless relating to
                                                 a major purchase)

    • Accounts payable ledgers and schedules   - 7 years

    • Inventories and products, supplies and   - 7 years
      materials invoices

4. IRS tax documents
   - Federal (and state) tax returns — Permanent
   - Depreciation records and agreements — Permanent
   - Tax return supporting information — 7 years

5. Personnel Records
   - Application for employment — 1 year if not hired

     — 3 years after employment if hired

   - Promotions, warnings, file notes — 5 years after employment

   - Accident reports — 6 years

   - Family and Medical Leave Act (FMLA) date of leave and payroll information — 3 years

   - Fair Labor Standards Act (FLSA) — 3 years

   - Payroll records — 4 years

   - Billing and deduction records — 2 years

   - I-9 Employment Verification Forms — Life of employment and (usually) 3 years after termination

6. Insurance Records
   - Claim documents — 3 years from settlement or resolution

   - Liability Insurance — 3 years after life of policy

   - Property Insurance — Life of property insured

Can you sense your closet/storage unit/warehouse filling up?

When we note that a record must be held permanently we are referring to the common meaning of a really, really long time. But what if your business goes under? What does permanent mean in that context? There is no permanent answer for that one. I can only suggest you talk to your attorney. Have them send you a letter saying it is OK, for example, to destroy certain documents five years after your business goes under. If there is a later problem you at least have the defense that the destruction was done upon the advice of counsel.

What do we mean by the term relative? That there are various situations and each time period relates to each situation. Suppose your state has a 6 year statute of limitations for bringing suit on a contract matter. For any emails or correspondence relating to a specific contract you may want to hold onto them for 7 years or longer. Some states allow for claims to be brought for 6 years after the date of discovery of a problem, which may mean you will want to keep certain records permanently just to be safe.

The specific correspondence and emails should be culled and kept in a separate file, be it hard copy or electronic. You want to segregate these out so you can get to the wholesale purging and destruction of all the tides of information you get every day.

As part of your Document Retention Policy you will set forth an automatic email destruction date. For example, your policy could state that after four years all emails not pulled aside for relative retention reasons will be destroyed. You really don't need to keep all the thousands and thousands of emails from four years ago related to solicitations, clarifications, confirmations, directions and meetings for beer. It is costing you to keep it. So get rid of it.

The Policy should be understood and followed by all employees, and employees who don't follow it should be disciplined. Yes, it is that important. The Policy should be periodically audited for compliance and reviewed for legal and technology updates.

Your Document Retention Policy should also deal with "The Litigation Hold." When litigation is 'reasonably foreseeable' you have to put the brakes on any document destruction. As a party to a lawsuit you have a duty to preserve evidence. The Policy should set forth who is in charge of declaring a Litigation Hold and what to do when one is in place.

The question then becomes when is litigation reasonably foreseeable? Well, service of a lawsuit certainly qualifies. At that point you've been sued. But a demand letter or a legitimate verbal threat of litigation is also considered a reasonably foreseeable event. As is any initial investigation by any governmental or law enforcement agency. An incident or accident involving a property or personal injury also qualifies. In such situations, or in similar matters, it is best to consult with your attorney.

Because the duty to preserve evidence kicks in when litigation is reasonably foreseeable, courts really don't like to see any document destruction after that point. If documents are improperly destroyed a court can order a number of penalties. Sanctions, or monetary penalties, can be assessed if there is evidence of a bad faith intent to destroy in order to suppress the truth and prejudice the other party. As well, a court can strike out certain pleadings or defenses, limit the introduction of certain evidence, issue contempt orders or dismiss the entire action. So you don't want to be destroying evidence.

The key buried in all these documents is to strike a balance. You can't—and don't have to—keep everything. As well, you must keep certain things. Develop a policy, follow the hard and fast rules, and all will be fine.

Alana and Sherri

Alana and Sherri were proud to have just opened their second location. Salon Sen-Sey now had a gleaming new facility on the growing south side of town. Their advertising effectiveness just doubled. Paying for the same TV spot they could now advertise two locations.

There was one area where doubling caused problems: Social Media.

The new Salon Sen-Sey stylists wanted to set up their own page on Facebook. Alana and Sherri agreed to this since their original Facebook page had brought in a fair amount of business to their first location. The problem was content.

The new stylists had moved to Salon Sen-Sey from two other competitors in the area. Their leaving was not a happy departure for all involved. These hard feelings spilled over onto the new Facebook page.

The words 'ugly and 'bitch' were soon combined in all sorts of posts about former employers, former coworkers and current relationships. The owner of one competing salon had his attorney send a letter threatening to sue Salon Sen-Sey and its stylists for libel—a claim based on printing a written statement that unjustly injured a person's reputation. In a salon setting, wrote the attorney, it was highly derogatory and very damaging to refer to someone as 'ugly.'

That is when Jay got involved. He and Sherri had been dating for a year now and all was going well. Sherri greatly appreciated him going to bat for their business, and for the fact that lately they never seemed to receive a bill for his legal services.

Jay wrote a letter to the other attorney explaining that the words 'ugly bitch' had now come to mean 'I don't like you.' The emotional charge of the words twenty years ago had become dissipated with their unfortunate overuse, and thus no libel could attach. If everyone was being termed an 'ugly bitch' then no one person's individual reputation could suffer.

Jay knew the attorney on the other side of the case quite well. They shared a good laugh over his letter. The whole matter was amicably resolved.

But the lesson was learned. As business owners, you must monitor your Social Media.

Social Media

Facebook, Twitter, LinkedIn and all the other social media sites on the internet offer both promise and perils for businesses.

In terms of promise, the use of social media can increase your visibility and lead to new customers. For perils consider public relations nightmares and potential liability for libel and defamation.

If your company uses social media and allows its employees to participate, a Social Media Policy for your business may be appropriate.

What issues should be considered? Let's review some:

1. To whom does the Policy apply?

Are some employees authorized on behalf of the Company to use social media while others are not? If one group is representing the Company and another group is merely using Social Media for personal purposes you may need two separate policies. On the authorized side the policy should deal with how you want the Company to be portrayed online. Draft your do's and don'ts with this in mind. Regarding employee's personal use, the Policy should address how you the employer expect your employees to communicate online, which hopefully includes the words 'professionally' and 'with restraint.'

2. Are Ethical or Professional Rules Applicable?

If your industry has ethical or professional rules for regular speech those rules certainly apply to online speech. Think of the attorney—client privilege for lawyers. Attorneys must keep their confidences in cyber space just as they do in the real world. Your Social Media Policy should address these boundaries.

3. Are Communications Confidential?

Your Social Media Policy should also stress that confidential and proprietary information must stay confidential. Because many posts and tweets are quick and informal, a lack of forethought is commonplace. (At least you would like to believe that they didn't think it through when they posted some incredibly stupid tweet.) Employees should be encouraged to carefully consider how their communications could be interpreted before they hit 'Send.'

4. Personal Responsibility or Money Damages?

Employees must be made aware that they are personally responsible for all social media content they post. Once it is posted it is difficult to retract. There are no online 'mulligans.' When you hit 'send' there are very few do-overs. As such, prudence and caution should be encouraged, especially given the liability for monetary damages that exists. Privacy right violations, disclosures of confidential client information, libelous, defamatory and other infringing posts can all end up costing the post person.

5. Negative, Inaccurate or Accusatory Comments. On the Web?

Has humanity always been this bitter? Or does the web, with its guise of anonymity, allow us to reach new depths of blameless blasphemy? Whatever the case, unfavorable comments about your Company will probably come in. Employees should not immediately respond to them but, as set out in the Policy, rather notify management about them. The Policy may also set forth how the Company will respond in such situations.

6. Will you Require Disclaimers?

As an employer you can't infringe upon your employee's rights of free speech. The National Labor Relations Board has found that many employer policies were overly broad when they attempted to limit discussions of wages, employment investigations, terminations and management, even when the comments were disparaging. (These rules will apply even if you are not a union workplace.) Still, these comments and others on any facet of the business should be attributable to the employee. A disclaimer stating, "The views expressed are mine alone and do not necessarily reflect the views of *Company Name here*" should be used.

7. Will you monitor the posts?

The Policy should clearly state what monitoring of an employee's social media posts the Company will conduct. When using social media for business purposes, the Company should be privy to what sites are being used by employees and what user names or 'handles' the employees are using. As well, it should be clearly started that employees have no expectation of privacy for their internet postings.

8. Will you train your employees on the Social Media Policy?

Once you have prepared your Social Media Policy what will you do with it? Put it on the shelf next to the other unused policy manuals? A suggestion would be to train your employees on it. Make sure they understand their obligations when using social media.

Bobo and Morton

Glockenspiel Ventura was growing. Bobo and Morton now had even more employees. Horatio Manfred, the bald, bow-tied bookkeeper, made sure all was running smoothly.

But Horatio saw one area for improvement. The boys were still in their early 20's. They didn't yet understand that even though they were younger than some of the employees, they had to be older, or at least more perceptive, in terms of leadership. Bobo and Morton had to learn to become the leaders of Glockenspiel Ventura.

So Horatio signed the boys up for a leadership training seminar.

Bobo and Morton were a bit taken aback by this. "How do you learn to become a leader?" asked Bobo, "I thought you either were or not. And we're not."

Horatio explained that you could learn to do anything in this country. Even to be leaders, which, he added, this country needed.

"Which shows it doesn't work," said Morton.

Horatio overcame their objections. The two had been cast by their families as little brothers without merit or promise. And that was still how they saw themselves. Horatio knew they had to get through that and overcome it in order for Glockenspiel Ventura to reach the next level.

Horatio chose the seminar wisely. It was in Anaheim, California, in a hotel next to Disneyland.

The boys brightened at this. Road trip, business expense, Disneyland, California Adventure. They could spend two days in a seminar.

Leadership Issues

As your company enters its third year of business (or perhaps even before) you have to ask yourself: Am I a leader of this business?

By this we do not mean are you controlling or dominating your business. That is not leadership. Ordering someone to take out the trash is not leading. Creating a team where everyone works together, and the trash somehow gets taken out as part of that effort, is what you will succeed with.

So what are some of the points Bobo and Morton, and you, will learn at a leadership class? Here is a sampling of relevant topics:

Integrity

You know what is right. You don't have to be told that. So do what is right at all times—even when no one is looking. It is not that hard to do. In fact, once it becomes part of you, it is really easy. You never have to think about ethical challenges and shadings, who you told what to and how you are going to explain this or that issue. Follow the guiding star of integrity and all that baggage falls away.

Clients want to be told the truth, even if the news is bad. Operate from a position of integrity and your problems are minimized and manageable.

Accordingly, honor, truth and reliability will become you. Your employees will notice, and they will be free to follow. And they will. And what do you know, without thinking about it, you are leading.

Enthusiasm

As Winston Churchill, the great British leader during the depths of World War II, said: "Nothing is won without enthusiasm." That is as true as it gets.

Enthusiasm is contagious. Have you ever noticed how many more people become fans when the local team is winning? Why is that? Because it is a rush, it is exciting, it brings us together.

Why not have that in your business? You don't need to hire cheerleaders. But you do have to be upbeat. Dragging yourself into the office complaining about this or that brings everyone down. Try being more positive—even if things are challenging. Flash a smile, share a laugh, celebrate the small victories, and the big ones will follow.

Goals

I know some people who are put off by the whole idea of goals. They think it is a phony, touchy-feely concept for the lame who will never reach them. And I compare this attitude to the hard-charging, focused entrepreneurs who set goals and reach them to great ends.

You need goals. Don't let anyone tell you otherwise.

With goals, you know where you are and what you need to do to win. Set goals, and go for them. Give your business an objective standard focus and achievement.

Add in enthusiasm and good things will come.

Mentors and Team

Studies have shown that the smartest people are the ones who realize that they do not know it all. Maybe it is evolutionary. The cocksure caveman may have been the one more likely to walk off a cliff. (Just as today.)

Studies also show that the best leaders know that they don't have all the answers. They are willing to learn from the experiences of others, which is why they seek out and use mentors on a regular basis. They are willing to use their team of experts for specialized advice and counsel. Contrary to the image of the lone ranger entrepreneur/hero taking on all odds with only his trusty laptop, leaders realize that they must collaborate with others, synthesize information, and move forward together. Let your team help, and they will help you avoid that cliff.

Belief

The creator of one of the world's most popular and deeply resonating brands was Walt Disney. Is it any wonder that Bobo and Morton are so attracted? The images of family and childhood and all that is good are deeply baked into the Disney brand. That did not happen by accident. Leaders understand the transformational power of belief systems. As

Walt Disney said: 'When you believe in a thing, believe in it all the way, implicitly and unquestionably."

The five topics above are examples of what is taught in the leadership arena. While this is not a book on leadership strategies, it is a book on what you must do to properly run your corporation. As your business grows, you—as the owner—must think about yourself not as just an owner but also as a leader. To grow your business, to take it forward, you will need a team. And a team needs a leader. It may be someone you bring in to do it or it may be you. In either case, you need to know what qualities and support a leader needs.

Consider reading books on leadership. Consider taking a leadership training seminar. Because after several years into all this, you need to get ready for even better things to come.

Rich Dad Tips

- Keep track of your stock ledger. You don't want any nasty surprises, or to have your veil pierced.

- Develop a Record Retention Policy for all your incoming documents as soon as is practicable.

- If you are going to engage in Social Media strategies, understand the risks and pitfalls.

And now, in Year Five, some interesting conclusions...

Chapter Sixteen

Year Five

Alana and Sherri

Sherri felt it was time to slow down. Properly operating the salon business took a lot of time. She and Alana had built it up to three locations around town, and all were doing well. And the two sisters were doing better than they had ever anticipated.

Now that she and Jay were married and had just brought forth twin boys, Sherri liked the idea of more time at home with her children. The twins, Justin and Eric, along with her daughter Ellie, were her chosen focus now.

Alana and Will had brought forth two children as well. Alana was all in favor of spending more time with the family. Running three locations and managing all of the personalities one found in their business—from dark Goths to loud divas—was quite a chore. While raising kids was also work it was the work Alana now wanted to do.

In the last year they had received several nibbles about selling the business. The girls had not taken them seriously, feeling they were from competitors who wanted to get a sense of what they would sell for—so that the competitor could in turn sell their own salons. But Jay took it as a sign that a real offer could be on the horizon.

As Alana, Sherri, Jay and Will talked further about selling the business, Jay made several key points. First, all their records had to be in order. Jay had read *Buying and Selling a Business* and had participated in several sale-of-business transactions. He knew that when a potential buyer showed up all the key components of the business—financials, corporate minute book, contracts and leases, intellectual property rights and the like—had to be ready. If the documents weren't ready, and you have to put them together over a period of weeks or months, your best sale opportunity could be lost. You had to be prepared and ready when the right buyer showed up.

Jay's second point had to do with their trademark. They had gone through quite a challenge with the name of their business. Now that they had the federal trademark for Salon Sen-Sey they needed to keep it active. Jay explained that a key form had to be submitted to the US Patent and Trademark Office between the fifth and sixth year of use. If you failed to file it you would lose your trademark. Jay noted, and the others agreed, that a potential buyer would certainly want to purchase the name of their salon chain along with the other assets. Jay arranged for this important form to be filed with the USPTO.

Exit and Legacy Strategies

Your corporate legacy begins with your exit strategy or your succession planning. The two terms are not the same but are often used as if they're interchangeable. They are not.

An exit strategy is about you as an owner of a business either leaving the business to your children or family members, liquidating the business or selling to someone within or outside the business. As it sounds, exit means leaving.

Succession planning is different than an exit. Succession planning means planning for what happens after you leave. Succession planning is all about your corporate legacy—what happens to your corporation when you are no longer present.

Let's focus on exit strategies. Having an exit strategy doesn't necessarily mean preparing for the worst. There are as many reasons to leave a business as there are reasons to form one in the first place. For some it's the lure of unstructured time. For others, it's the challenge of starting up another business and doing it all over again.

Some of the choices you have in exiting include:

1. Liquidate. You can go out of business if need be. You can sell off all your assets to pay creditors or, if you have more creditors than assets, file bankruptcy. By shutting down you may or may not come out ahead, but you may also be freed from a tough situation. Once your head clears you may be able to get into a better business situation. If you liquidate you may end up dissolving the company. For more on dissolution please see *Start Your Own Corporation*.

2. Gift or Transfer. You can transition ownership of the business to your children (or other relatives). This is a good option if these relatives are interested in the business you'd like them to inherit, if they have training or can get training in the field, and if you're comfortable with their vision of the company. If you've built something you care about, you generally want it to go to someone who shares your vision and who will care about it, too.

3. Sell. You can sell your business to an interested party looking for an existing venture to take over, or to an employee, or to a competitor who's been waiting for such a chance. This is another time when having kept your records in good order will stand you in good stead. The better your records, the easier to find a buyer and make the sale.

If you decide to sell, be sure to work with your professional team. They'll be able to guide you through the transfer, sale and taxation issues.

Selling to a third party requires approval of the Board of Directors and corporate shareholders (or Manager and Members of an LLC). You may also choose to sell to another shareholder by mutual agreement or by using an existing buy-sell agreement.

Recall the buy-sell agreement Sherri and Alana had. In the event that an owner leaves due to death, divorce, disability or withdrawal or due to irresolvable differences with the other shareholders, a buy-sell agreement can be used by the remaining owners of a small, closely held business to cover the buyout of shares. (Generally with a large, publicly traded company, where the shares can be traded freely, a buy-sell agreement isn't used.) For smaller enterprises, a buy-sell agreement between shareholders can save a lot of time and attorney's fees by setting forth a clear path for resolution. It allows corporations to force a shareholder to sell shares either back to the corporation, or to other shareholders. The buy sell agreement should provide a method for valuing the Company's shares or membership interests. Common methods call for an appraisal by a business valuation firm or an agreed upon price set each year to be used in the event of a future sale.

If selling the business is the path you anticipate following, it's a good idea to run your business on a daily basis as if you intend to sell at any minute. A flawlessly protected corporate structure that has followed all formalities and shows more successes than failures and profits than losses is clearly more attractive to a buyer than the alternative.

When planning an exit strategy, take into account your own motivations and expectations. For most business owners, the decision to move on can be activated by:

- Having made enough money to live a comfortable life;

- Having grown the company to a certain size or level of success;

- The desire to move on to another challenge (the serial entrepreneur); or

- To have built a business to pass on to future generations.

As you work to bring about your exit strategy, consider ideal outcomes. Will you find a buyer who shares your vision of the business and its employees, someone who is aligned with your beliefs, values and dreams for the business? You may want to include certain conditions in the sales agreement to start your employees out on the right foot with the new owner or to make sure certain community and/or charitable support continues. If the buyer wants your business enough they will agree to such conditions.

When exiting you must consider your obligations to any other shareholders/members in the Company, if any. Typically, you must have their vote to sell the assets of the Company, or wind up or liquidate the Company. Be sure to keep them informed of what you are doing. You owe that to them.

If your business is an entity with employees and relationships with vendors within the community you live and operate in, your business and its existence within the community may become a part of your corporate legacy. Depending on the size of the company you've built, closing up shop as an exit strategy can have an impact on the community including:

- Economic hardship for employees who have lost their jobs.

- Economic strain on the community that has lost a significant employer and income stream.

- If your business is located in a small community, withdrawing can cause other related businesses, vendors, suppliers and distributors to withdraw as well, depriving the community of more business.

- If your company provided a service and no other business steps up, the community loses the service your business provided, creating a hardship for the community.

By choosing your exit strategy well in advance of the time you intend to implement it, you give yourself—and your corporation—time to understand the ramifications of your chosen exit on the employees who have shown loyalty to your company and the community that has supported it. While your first duty is to you and your shareholders, it never hurts (even if it is not required under corporate law) to consider the other affected players in it all.

If you've put time and thought into your exit strategy, worked with your professional team and mitigated the impact on employees and surrounding community, it's easier to leave a community with a positive corporate legacy intact.

When you're preparing to activate your exit strategy, keep in mind that timing is important. Just as the community around your business can be affected by your decision, your employees are also impacted. Revealing your exit strategy too far in advance can make employees nervous, or cause them to leave, thus reducing the value of your business. Revealing your exit strategy too close to implementation can make employees angry, and make it harder on the new owner. It sounds difficult and it is. So good luck with this. As they say, timing is everything.

Leaving Your Business to Your Heirs

One frequent exit strategy is to leave the business to your family. Whether you're leaving it to your children or other family members, there may be some pleasure in the idea of continuity, that this ongoing and growing concern you've created will stay in the family and benefit future generations.

But if it's your wish that they continue the business it's a really good idea to see if they want to continue it. Many a business owner looking to exit has been surprised when they learn that the kids didn't share the dream. Now, under current law you cannot force family members into your dreams. (And if you're asking why not, you need to take a step back.)

If the kids and other heirs don't want the business please know that the business will not thrive and you will end up disappointed. You are better off letting go, simplifying your life and selling the business to a third party.

When selling always be mindful of the corporate veil. Even if you've been following corporate protocol every step of the way, once the decision to sell is made you should go through your records and make sure everything is in order. No savvy entrepreneur is going to step up and purchase a business with a weak corporate veil, a business that hasn't been observing corporate formalities.

Your professional team will come into play as well. You'll need to work with your accountant and your lawyer. And you may need to add some new team members—a business broker and a business valuation professional. Both will help you establish an asking price for the business. In this whole process you will need to:

- Formalize and organize all documents and records.

- Document all transactions for the business.

- Review any leases the business has for vehicles, equipment or real estate.

- Evaluate company assets.

- Bring all financial records up to date.

- Review all contracts with suppliers, vendors or distributors.

- Review all customer or client contracts.

- Review and document all company policies.

There is a great deal of work getting a business ready for sale. The sooner you start the better.

Tom and Nancy

In the last several years Tom had become a well-known and sought after speaker on the dangers of crony capitalism and government interference. He was a clear and excellent speaker and he could effectively communicate issues that voters—liberal, conservative and in between—were commonly concerned about. As well, many citizens strongly believed that the government had no right to kill your dog when they were raiding your house, and bonded with Tom over the loss of Dooger.

Eventually, some political types approached him about running for Congress. Tom said he would have to speak with his wife Nancy and get back to them.

The couple considered the offer. Tom was passionate about the misuse of government to benefit campaign contributors. When influence went to the highest bidder the wrong decisions were made for everyone else. The whole system was corrupt and now rotting. Nancy reminded him that he could actually become even more disillusioned by running for office. Tom acknowledged that the system he would try to change would try even harder to change him. It was a real worry.

Nancy then spoke about their business. With Tom running for Congress Hardcastle Engineering would be shorthanded. It would be more difficult to operate the business without his full attention to it.

Tom noted that with his name out there on the campaign trail even more business could come in. Once again, it would be tougher to handle even more work if he was campaigning and perhaps elected.

But Tom had an idea on how to handle it all. Michael King, the President of TriState Engineering, had made an off-hand comment a year ago at a regional American Society of Civil Engineers' meeting. King had said if the Greens ever wanted to pursue something new they should call him. TriState Engineering could be interested in an arrangement.

And so a year later Tom and Nancy made a call.

In a week, Tom and Nancy were two states away, 300 miles from home, sitting with Michael King in the TriState Engineering offices. King explained that their firm had been in business for over 80 years, was stable and was looking to develop more business in the Green's market area. For TriState, the state engineering licenses that Tom and Nancy possessed would be an important part of the transaction.

Tom explained that he would soon be announcing his run for Congress. King smiled, knowing that an election run could bring even more business to TriState.

King explained that TriState would like to structure a merger with Hardcastle Engineers. In this transaction, TriState and Hardcastle would merge, and become one entity. TriState would be the surviving corporation and move forward. The Green's state engineering licenses would be changed to show an affiliation with TriState. Once the merger was complete, Hardcastle Engineers P.C. would be formally dissolved with the Secretary of State's office.

Nancy inquired how the merger would work as to the stock of each company. King's attorney went to the whiteboard and drew the following chart:

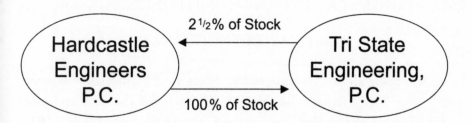

The attorney explained that for the purposes of illustration the percentages were based on the gross revenues of each firm, and would be adjusted later after a due diligence review was completed. But for now, since TriState had $100 million in revenue and Hardcastle had $2.5 million, the example was as follows. Hardcastle would transfer 100% of its stock to TriState in exchange for TriState issuing Hardcastle 2.5% of TriState's stock. Hardcastle would transfer the stock to Tom and Nancy, as well as to Nelson Barry, their other shareholder, and thus the three would own 2.5% of TriState.

Tom and Nancy liked the idea of owning a small piece of TriState. The larger engineering firm had all the support personnel and infrastructure to handle the business of business. Nancy would not have to worry about bookkeepers and IRS filings any more.

The attorney explained that there would have to be corporate meetings and minutes and agreements and all. He prepared sample documents that the Greens could review with their attorneys. The basic, initial document read as follows:

CONSENT RESOLUTIONS OF THE DIRECTORS OF

HARDCASTLE ENGINEERS, P.C.

We, being all or a quorum of the directors of Hardcastle Engineers, P.C. (the "Corporation") hereby WAIVE notice of the time and place of a Meeting of the Directors of the Corporation and DO HEREBY CONSENT to the adoption of the following resolutions:

WHEREAS all of the outstanding common stock of the Corporation is owned by

The Green Family Trust	9,500 shares
Nelson Barry	500 shares

WHEREAS the Board finds in the best interest of the Corporation to restructure by merging Hardcastle Engineers, P.C. with TriState Engineering, Inc., continuing as the surviving corporation under the name of TriState Engineering, Inc. and Hardcastle Engineers, P.C. being dissolved and ceasing to exist;

NOW, THEREFORE IT IS:

RESOLVED that the Board does hereby adopt, approve and authorize the Corporation to execute, deliver and perform its obligations under the Plan and Agreement of Merger (the "Plan"), attached hereto and incorporated herein by reference, and any related Articles of Merger, between the Corporation and TriState Engineering, Inc.

RESOLVED FURTHER, that the Corporation call a Special Meeting of the Shareholders to approve the above-noted Plan of Merger as soon as practicable and in accordance with state law and the Corporation's Bylaws.

RESOLVED FURTHER that TriState Engineering, Inc. as the surviving corporation, shall file applications for authority to do business in all states and other jurisdictions as to which such authority is made necessary by its newly-acquired operations or property.

RESOLVED FURTHER that the officers of the Corporation be and hereby are, together or singly, authorized and directed to execute and deliver resolutions on behalf of the Corporation, approving and ratifying the various acts and transactions described in these resolutions.

RESOLVED FURTHER, that the officers of the Corporation be and hereby are, together or singly, authorized and directed on behalf of the Corporation to execute and deliver such documents and to take such other and further actions as may be necessary or appropriate to carry out the full intent and purpose of the foregoing resolutions.

Dated: _____

_____ _____ _____
Tom Green   Nancy Hardcastle Green   Nelson Barry

After thoroughly reviewing the transaction with Katherine, their attorney, Tom and Nancy, along with Nelson Barry, agreed to the merger. The attorney for TriState complimented them at the time at how well their corporate records had been kept. It made the merger go much smoother to have such complete corporate records.

Once the merger was complete, Tom, Nancy and Nelson were now shareholders in TriState Engineering, and also well paid engineer employees.

Tom was given a leave of absence from TriState to run for Congress. It was a grueling race, filled with mudslinging and the kind of unauthorized, outside negative ads on each side that had the average citizen wondering if voting was beneath them. But when the results were tallied Tom Green was elected to Congress. Nancy continued to work at TriState and spent many weekends in the Capitol. She moved to Washington, D.C. after their first child was born. From Righteous Rock, to the raid, to the race, it had been quite a ride.

Alana and Sherri

Jay sat in his law office conference room with his wife Sherri and his sister-in-law and brother-in-law, Alana and Will. Across from them sat Mr. Fine, the owner of Salon Concepts, a large salon operator from the southern part of the state, and Mr. Fine's attorney.

Salon Concepts wanted to buy Salon Sen-Sey, LLC in order to enter the northern part of the state. The attorney for Salon Concepts was very interested in the status of the trademark. Had they done all the filings? Were there any challenges to the name?

Before Jay answered those questions he had a question of his own. Would Salon Concepts be using the name throughout the State? The other attorney hedged his answer.

Jay zeroed in on the issue: Salon Concepts used different salon names for their twelve salons in the south. Were they intending to use the name Salon Sen-Sey for all the locations?

Mr. Fine, the owner, was not as reserved as his attorney. Yes, he responded. They would consider rebranding under the Salon Sen-Sey name for the entire state.

Jay nudged Sherri under the table and smiled. The price just went up. Salon Concepts was not only buying the three locations but their trademarked and federally protected name as well.

Mr. Fine wanted to talk about Alana and Sherri's continued involvement. He wanted them to work in the salons up north for another year to provide continuity. They all talked about more or less work, with Alana and Sherri arguing for some flexibility due to their young children at home. Also part of the discussion was the fact that Mr. Fine wanted a three-year non-compete from the sisters. Once their year of work was up he didn't want either of them opening a competing salon for at least three years.

Jay noted that in some states non-competes were void as against public policy. Courts didn't like putting productive people on the sidelines. Instead, they wanted entrepreneurs out there starting new businesses, employing people and generating more tax revenue.

Mr. Fine's attorney acknowledged all that but said in their state non-competes were allowed. Jay agreed that twelve month non-competes were not a problem but that a thirty six month agreement usually came with an extra payment of money.

Mr. Fine agreed to the extra payment. It was worth it for him to have the sisters work for him a year and then not compete with him for another three years. In four years he would own the market.

The next big issue was how to structure the sale. Would Salon Concepts buy the assets of Salon Sen-Sey or would they buy the shares? It was an important issue.

Jay had drawn a chart for the sisters before the meeting to explain the consequences. An equity (or stock) sale looked like this:

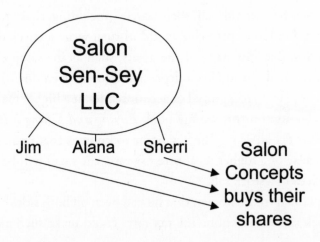

In this way Salon Concepts was the new owner of Salon Sen-Sey LLC. Because the sisters and Big Jim had held their membership interests for over one year the sale (as of this writing) was subject to capital gains rates of only 15%.

The problem for Salon Concepts under an equity (or stock) sale was that they now owned Salon Sen-Sey, LLC, the company, including whatever liabilities the company had. If one year after the sale a disgruntled former employee of Salon Sen-Sey sued for harassment, Salon Sen-Sey, the business entity now owned by Salon Concepts, was still responsible. Not many attorneys liked the unknowns of a stock sale.

Jay had also charted out how an asset sale would work:

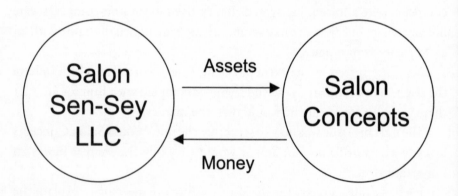

Salon Sen-Sey would sell their assets (including their trademark) directly to Salon Concepts, who would in turn write a check directly to Salon Sen-Sey. Because many of the assets, such as the salon equipment and furniture, had already been depreciated (or written down) the write offs would have to be recaptured or accounted for at a higher tax rate. (For more information on this see my book *Buying and Selling a Business* or speak to your tax advisor.) The key point to know is that in an asset sale, in part because of a higher recapture tax rate, the taxes will be higher to the seller than in a stock sale.

Jay explained to the women that he had been on both sides of the asset sale or stock sale transaction. The tax rates could make such a difference that he had seen sellers offer to receive less in total purchase price for a stock sale so they could get benefit from the lower tax rates.

As it turned out, Mr. Fine wanted nothing to do with any skeletons that could be lurking in the Salon Sen-Sey's closet. For too long he had managed the varied and different personalities (to put it kindly) that one found in a salon. He well knew that any one of the delicate flowers who worked in the industry could years later file a bizarre claim against Salon Sen-Sey. He wanted no such future surprises.

And so an asset sale was arranged. The attorney for Salon Concepts favorably commented on how well the corporate veil for Salon Sen-Sey, LLC had been maintained. He noted the transaction was much easier for it. Salon Concepts bought the assets (including the valuable trademark) from Salon Sen-Sey. Salon Sen-Sey in turn distributed the money to Sherri, Alana and Big Jim. It was an excellent payday. Of course, Clint received none of it.

At Jay's suggestion, they kept Salon Sen-Sey, LLC current with the Secretary of State for six years. In this way, if a lawsuit was ever filed the claim would come against Salon Sen-Sey, an empty entity with no money in a bank account and no future prospects. Importantly, the claim would not be brought against Sherri or Alana, as successor trustees to the Company. Jay explained that is was always best to leave an empty company open for a number of years to protect against later claims.

With the sale of the business complete the girls settled down. It had been quite a ride, with some ups and downs and new beginnings. Big Jim was proud of them, as were Jay and Will.

Sherri and Alana's foray into entrepreneurship had been rewarding on many levels.

Bobo and Morton

In the three years since the economic collapse that had seen the fortunes of most of their families disappear, Bobo and Morton had managed to survive. The house-sitting business was down to almost non-existent. But people took care of their animals in any market. And in a downturn owners came to appreciate even more the unquestioning loyalty and devotion of a pet. Compared to that of, say, a banker.

With the help of Horatio Manfred, their bow-tied bookkeeper, Glockenspiel Ventura had brought on a veterinarian on a revenue-sharing arrangement. Their kennel was now a full-service facility, and doing quite well. People seemed to like working with Bobo and Morton. They were unpretentious and true to their word.

It was with the iPhone inventory scanner that they were doing really well. Horatio had taken a keen interest in their product. He saw all sorts of opportunity with it. After speaking with Aunt Maddy and other advisors, the boys issued Horatio five percent of the shares of Glockenspiel Ventura, Inc. They gave him an incentive to earn another five percent.

With that, Horatio went to town. He immediately started working with a patent attorney to patent and protect every possible improvement the boys had come up with. They obtained a trademark for the service. And they began licensing the unique hand-held inventory scanner to networks of insurance firms. The big insurance companies loved having a picture and an independent appraisal for each household item. It saved them a great deal of time (and reduced the threat of owner fraud) when dealing with a house fire or a theft. Some insurance companies were now requiring agents to use the iPhone inventory scanner in order to even submit a household inventory policy.

And the license fees were flowing into Glockenspiel Ventura, Inc.

Eventually a large company came knocking on their office door. The hand-held scanner service fit nicely into their product mix. They had the money, needed to acquire more revenue, and wanted to buy the business.

And so a meeting was set up to discuss a sale of the business.

Bobo, Morton, Horatio, Aunt Maddy and their business attorney sat in a very large conference room listening to the Company's proposal.

The Company, predictably, did not want to buy the kennel business. They were only interested in the hand-held inventory device. They were willing to pay a very large amount for the scanner assets from Glockenspiel Ventura, Inc. And in this way, it was explained, Glockenspiel Ventura could continue uninterrupted with its veterinary and kennel activities.

Horatio spoke up. He asked the Company to consider a stock purchase. When the Company's attorney promptly said "No," Horatio asked for them to hear him out. He drew a chart on the whiteboard as follows:

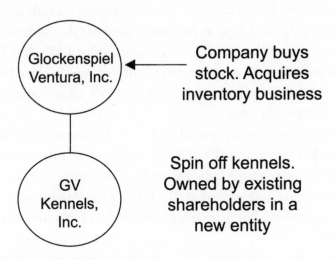

Using this illustration, Horatio explained that the kennel business would be spun out into a separate entity owned by the existing shareholders, who would continue to own and run their kennel business. Once that transaction was completed, the Company would then buy the stock of Glockenspiel Ventura, Inc. directly from the existing shareholders, giving the Company control of the hand-held scanner business.

The Company's attorney said he would prefer an asset sale. With all due respect, he said he had no idea what skeletons lurked in Glockenspiel Ventura. If he bought the stock his Company would be responsible for any later liabilities.

Horatio had a plan for that. But first he asked the Company to consider Bobo and Morton's tax situation. Their shares had been issued between September 28, 2010 and December 31, 2011. Under the Small Business Jobs Act of 2010, if the stock in their C corporation was held for more than five years there was no capital gains tax to be paid when the stock was sold. This special, one-time provision only applied to C corporations, not LLCs or S corporations.

The Company attorney smiled. He remembered hearing about that wrinkle in the tax law. He figured some well-connected entrepreneurs had pushed it through but he had never heard of anyone actually using it.

Horatio recounted how at formation the boys should have probably been set up with a flow through S corporation or LLC. But Parker T. Ruxton had foisted the oddly named C corporation on them because he couldn't use it otherwise. It was a stroke of luck that would save them millions of dollars in taxes.

The Company attorney noted that Parker T. Ruxton hadn't had much luck himself lately. He had just been convicted of taking undisclosed and unauthorized commissions for sending his clients to Frank Fodom, the Ponzi scheme mastermind at The Club. Aunt Maddy winced at the name Frank Fodom. For his connivances, Parker T. Ruxton would never practice law again.

The Company attorney said he clearly understood why Bobo and Morton would want to sell their shares and not the assets. The tax savings would be enormous. Perhaps the purchase price could be reduced a bit to get them their tax savings.

Bobo laughed loudly and said they hadn't even started talking about price yet. Aunt Maddy smiled at her nephew's posturing.

The Company attorney returned to Horatio's plan for dealing with any liabilities inside Glockenspiel Ventura, Inc. They did not like dealing with unknowns. Horatio responded that they would put a million dollars into an escrow account. If any claims arose within two years, the million dollars could be applied. If there were no claims, the money would be returned to the shareholders.

The Company attorney said that a three million dollar escrow and a five-year time frame would be more appropriate. The Company attorney then asked if they had shareholder approval for such an arrangement. Horatio said they had 90% of the votes already lined up. Aunt Maddy wondered to herself why they didn't have 100%. But the conversation moved on. As to the escrow arrangement, Horatio said that the details could be worked out.

And so a deal was reached. The Glockenspiel Ventura records were in perfect order (thanks to Horatio) and the transaction came together very quickly. Bobo and Morton kept their kennel business. They sold their stock in Glockenspiel Ventura, paid no capital gains tax thanks to an odd wrinkle in the law and received a huge payday.

Horatio also came out just fine. Because he had acquired stock after 2011, he had to pay a capital gains tax on the sale of his shares. But once the taxes were all paid Horatio was happy to tell Bobo and Morton that he was set for life. Horatio said he greatly appreciated their friendship and faith in him.

A week after the closing Bobo and Morton arranged for a celebration. They invited Aunt Maddy, their mentor, and Mrs. Muller, their first client, to a very nice restaurant. Everyone was in as good a mood as could be expected. The financial collapse still reverberated throughout the community. Another family friend had just been indicted in the Frank Fodom scandal. The month before there had been another suicide.

Mrs. Muller, on the other hand, was in great financial shape. She had previously told the boys that she only invested in what she understood, which were mobile home parks and municipal bonds. She had said that the Ponzi scheme and complex Wall Street offerings had made no sense to her. The sales people couldn't even properly explain them. So she had stayed away. And her lifestyle had not changed.

Aunt Maddy had not been so fortunate. Her husband had placed the family fortune with Frank Fodom. The supposedly consistent 11% returns looked so good. Of course, they were good as lies but not as facts. It was increasingly likely that they would see no return of their money that went into the Ponzi scheme.

But Aunt Maddy, as always, kept her chin up. She did not complain or bemoan her fate. Things would work out.

And at this dinner she told Bobo and Morton how proud she was of them. They had turned things around, just as she knew they would.

Bobo winked at Mrs. Muller, who was in on the surprise. He reached into his blue Burberry blazer and pulled out a check. Bobo handed it to Aunt Maddy.

She was confused and then shocked and then burst into tears. She was overcome with emotion.

Bobo gave her a hug and so did Morton. Bobo explained that right at the start, in gratitude for her help, they had issued her shares equaling 10% of Glockenspiel Ventura, Inc. Like them, her shares were not subject to capital gains tax. Like them, she was entitled to a very, very nice payday.

To which Morton added that if the Company didn't assert any claims after five years she'd receive another payday from the money sitting in escrow. And better yet, Bobo joked, she still owned 10% of an awesome kennel company.

Aunt Maddy eventually regained her composure. She thanked the boys with all her heart. The four of them toasted to one of the happiest days of their lives.

And as dinner progressed, Bobo and Morton picked Mrs. Muller's brain for her insights into investing in mobile home parks.

It was all turning out well.

Conclusion

Well, there you have it. Our three teams followed the rules, protected their corporate veil and stuck with it. In five years' time they did quite well.

So can you.

Be sure to appreciate the need to preserve your corporate veil. Holding meetings, making all of your filings on time and following the other formalities will make a huge difference. As Robert Kiyosaki said at the start, basic asset protection isn't enough anymore. In these times you must also constantly maintain to completely protect. You need a good entity defense—that well maintained corporate veil—to survive the offense (and sometimes offensive) attacks of litigants and their attorneys.

As you grow your business you need to beware of, and know how to handle, the pressures applied by all levels of government. Know that it exists and resolve to rise above it. Other business owners and investors do so every day. The country needs you to do so as well.

Use your entity to your advantage. The laws allow for your corporation, LLC or LP to benefit you. Work with a good CPA to maximize these strategies.

Above all, enjoy it. Your business activities can certainly be a source of compensation and reward. They can also be a wellspring of satisfaction and personal growth. Enjoy every minute of it.

Best wishes in all your endeavors.

Appendix

For free downloads of forms and documents visit:
http://www.corporatedirect.com/run-your-own-corporation/

Index

About the Author

Garrett Sutton, Esq., is the bestselling author of *Start Your Own Corporation, Run Your Own Corporation, The ABC's of Getting Out of Debt, Writing Winning Business Plans, Buying and Selling a Business* and *The Loopholes of Real Estate* in Robert Kiyosaki's Rich Dad's Advisors series. Garrett has over thirty years' experience in assisting individuals and businesses to determine their appropriate corporate structure, limit their liability, protect their assets and advance their financial, personal and credit success goals.

Garrett and his law firm, Sutton Law Center, have offices in Reno, Nevada, Jackson Hole, Wyoming and Rocklin, California. The firm represents many corporations, limited liability companies, limited partnerships and individuals in their real estate and business-related law matters, including incorporations, contracts, and ongoing business-related legal advice. The firm continues to accept new clients.

Garrett is also the owner of Corporate Direct, which since 1988 has provided affordable asset protection and corporate formation services. He is the author of *How to Use Limited Liability Companies and Limited Partnerships*, which further educates readers on the proper use of entities. Along with credit expert Gerri Detweiler, Garrett also assists entrepreneurs build business credit. Please see CorporateDirect.com for more information.

Garrett attended Colorado College and the University of California at Berkeley, where he received a B.S. in Business Administration in 1975. He graduated with a J.D. in 1978 from Hastings College of Law, the University of California's law school in San Francisco. He practiced law in San Francisco and Washington, D.C. before moving to Reno and the proximity of Lake Tahoe.

Garrett is a member of the State Bar of Nevada, the State Bar of California, and the American Bar Association. He has written numerous professional articles and has served on the Publication Committee of the State Bar of Nevada. He has appeared in the *Wall Street Journal, The New York Times* and other publications.

Garrett enjoys speaking with entrepreneurs and real estate investors on the advantages of forming business entities. He is a frequent lecturer for small business groups as well as the Rich Dad's Advisors series.

Garrett serves on the boards of the American Baseball Foundation, located in Birmingham, Alabama, and the Sierra Kids Foundation and Nevada Museum of Art, both based in Reno.

For more information on Garrett Sutton and Sutton Law Center, please visit his Web sites at www.sutlaw.com, www.corporatedirect.com, and www.successdna.com.

Rich Dad said, "Business and investing are team spor

Robert Kiyos
Author of the international best
Rich Dad Poor Dad and the Rich Dad S

"Corporations and LLCs require **ongoing maintenance** for limited liab
protection. You must be vigilant. This book is your **road map and guid**

Garrett Sutton, F
Corporate attorney, asset protection expert and a

The Rich Dad Advisors series of books has sold over 2 million
copies worldwide as the how-to content for *Rich Dad Poor Dad*

Run Your Own Corporation is the companion book to the bestselling *Start Your (
Corporation*. It follows three teams of entrepreneurs through the ups and down
their first five years in business. The stories are engaging and filled with illustra
lessons for all readers. Throughout, *Run Your Own Corporation* provides
necessary information to follow all the rules and regulations so that business ow.
and investors are properly protected from the claims of others.

Run Your Own Corporation will teach you to:

- Protect your corporate veil from the threat of personal liability
- Handle all the payroll and accounting requirements
- Deal with government audits and raids
- Understand the rules involving employees and independent contractors
- Use business deductions for your benefit

"*Run Your Own Corporation* is a must for any entrepre
who wants to protect their business and see it grow
sustainable way!"
– *Pacific Book Re*

Garrett's book impacts all eight sections of Rich Dad's B-I Triangle®.
The B-I Triangle is introduced in Robert Kiyosaki's book *Rich
Dad's Guide to Investing*.

Look for other Rich Dad Advisors' books to complete the B-I Triangle

$20.95 US | $22.95 CAN

$20.95
ISBN 978-1-937832-10-0
52095>

Visit
BZKPress.com

Product
TEAM   Legal   LEADERSHIP
Systems
Communications
Cash Flow
MISSION